THE AVENGERS

WRITER
BRIAN MICHAEL BENDIS

PENCILER
JOHN ROMITA JR.

INKER
KLAUS JANSON
WITH **TOM PALMER & SCOTT HANNA**

COLORIST
DEAN WHITE
WITH **PAUL MOUNTS, RAIN BEREDO,
LAURA MARTIN, MORRY HOLLOWELL
& MATT MILLA**

COVER ART
**JOHN ROMITA JR., KLAUS JANSON,
DEAN WHITE & MORRY HOLLOWELL**

ISSUE #12.1

PENCILER
BRYAN HITCH

INKER
PAUL NEARY

COLORIST
PAUL MOUNTS

COVER ART
BRYAN HITCH, PAUL NEARY & PAUL MOUNTS

LETTERER
VC'S CORY PETIT

ASSOCIATE EDITO⬛
LAUREN SANKOV⬛

⬛RT

Collection Editor: JENNIFER GRÜNWALD • Editorial Assistants: JAMES EMMETT & JOE HOC⬛ ⬛CKLEY, Publisher & President - Print, Animation & Digital
Divisions; JOE QUESADA, Chief Creative Officer; JIM SO⬛ ⬛LSON RIBEIRO
Editor, Special Projects: MARK D. BEAZLEY • Senior Editor, Special Projects: JEFF YOUNGQUIST Senior Vice President of Sales: DAVID GABRIEL
SVP of Brand Planning & Communications: MICHAEL PASCIULLO • Book Design: JEFF POWELL

Editor in Chief: AXEL ALONSO • Chief Creative Officer: JOE QUESADA • Publisher: DAN BUCKLEY • Executive Producer: ALAN FINE

AVENGERS BY BRIAN MICHAEL BENDIS VOL. 2. Contains material originally published in magazine form as AVENGERS #7-12 and #12.1. First printing 2011. Hardcover ISBN# 978-0-7851-4504-2. Softcover
ISBN# 978-0-7851-4505-9. Published by MARVEL WORLDWIDE, INC., a subsidiary of MARVEL ENTERTAINMENT, LLC. OFFICE OF PUBLICATION: 135 West 50th Street, New York, NY 10020. Copyright © 2010
and 2011 Marvel Characters, Inc. All rights reserved. Hardcover: $24.99 per copy in the U.S. and $27.99 in Canada (GST #R127032852). Softcover: $19.99 per copy in the U.S. and $21.99 in Canada (GST
#R127032852). Canadian Agreement #40668537. All characters featured in this issue and the distinctive names and likenesses thereof, and all related indicia are trademarks of Marvel Characters, Inc. No
similarity between any of the names, characters, persons, and/or institutions in this magazine with those of any living or dead person or institution is intended, and any such similarity which may exist is purely
coincidental. **Printed in the U.S.A.** ALAN FINE, EVP - O⬛ ⬛UCKLEY, Publisher & President - Print, Animation & Digital
Divisions; JOE QUESADA, Chief Creative Officer; JIM SO⬛ ⬛nt; TOM BREVOORT, SVP of Publishing; C.B. CEBULSKI,
SVP of Creator & Content Development; DAVID GABRIEL⬛ ⬛unications; JIM O'KEEFE, VP of Operations & Logistics;
DAN CARR, Executive Director of Publishing Technology; ⬛rations Manager; ALEX MORALES, Publishing Operations
Manager; STAN LEE, Chairman Emeritus. For information ⬛grated Sales and Marketing, at jdokes@marvel.com. For
Marvel subscription inquiries, please call 800-217-9158. ⬛softcover), by R.R. DONNELLEY, INC., SALEM, VA, USA.

10 9 8 7 6 5 4 3 2 1

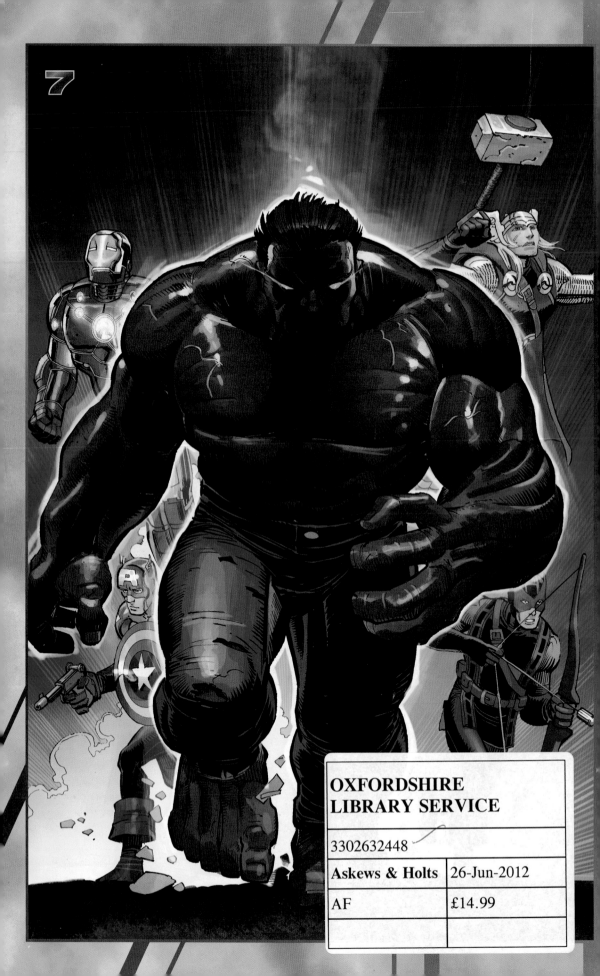

And there came a day, a day unlike any other, when Earth's Mightiest Heroes found themselves united against a common threat! On that day, the Avengers were born, to fight the foes no single super hero could withstand!

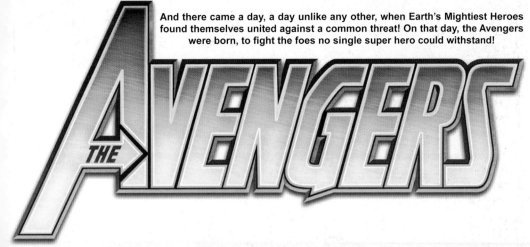

THE AVENGERS! WOLVERINE, IRON MAN, SPIDER-MAN, THOR, CAPTAIN AMERICA, SPIDER-WOMAN, THE PROTECTOR AND HAWKEYE ARE HAND-PICKED BY STEVE ROGERS TO LEAD THE PREMIERE AVENGERS TEAM!

AFTER AN AMAZING POWER-PLAY FOR CONTROL OF THE CRIMINAL EMPIRES OF THE MARVEL UNIVERSE, PARKER ROBBINS, A.K.A. THE HOOD, WAS DEPOWERED AND IMPRISONED BY THE AVENGERS.

LONGTIME HULK NEMESIS GENERAL THUNDERBOLT ROSS WAS IRRADIATED AND TRANSFORMED INTO THE RED HULK. NO ONE KNOWS WHO HE REALLY IS OR WHAT HE PLANS TO DO NEXT.

FORMER AVENGER WONDER MAN HAS TAKEN A SURPRISINGLY ANTI-AVENGERS STANCE AND HAS GONE SO FAR AS TO ATTACK THEM.

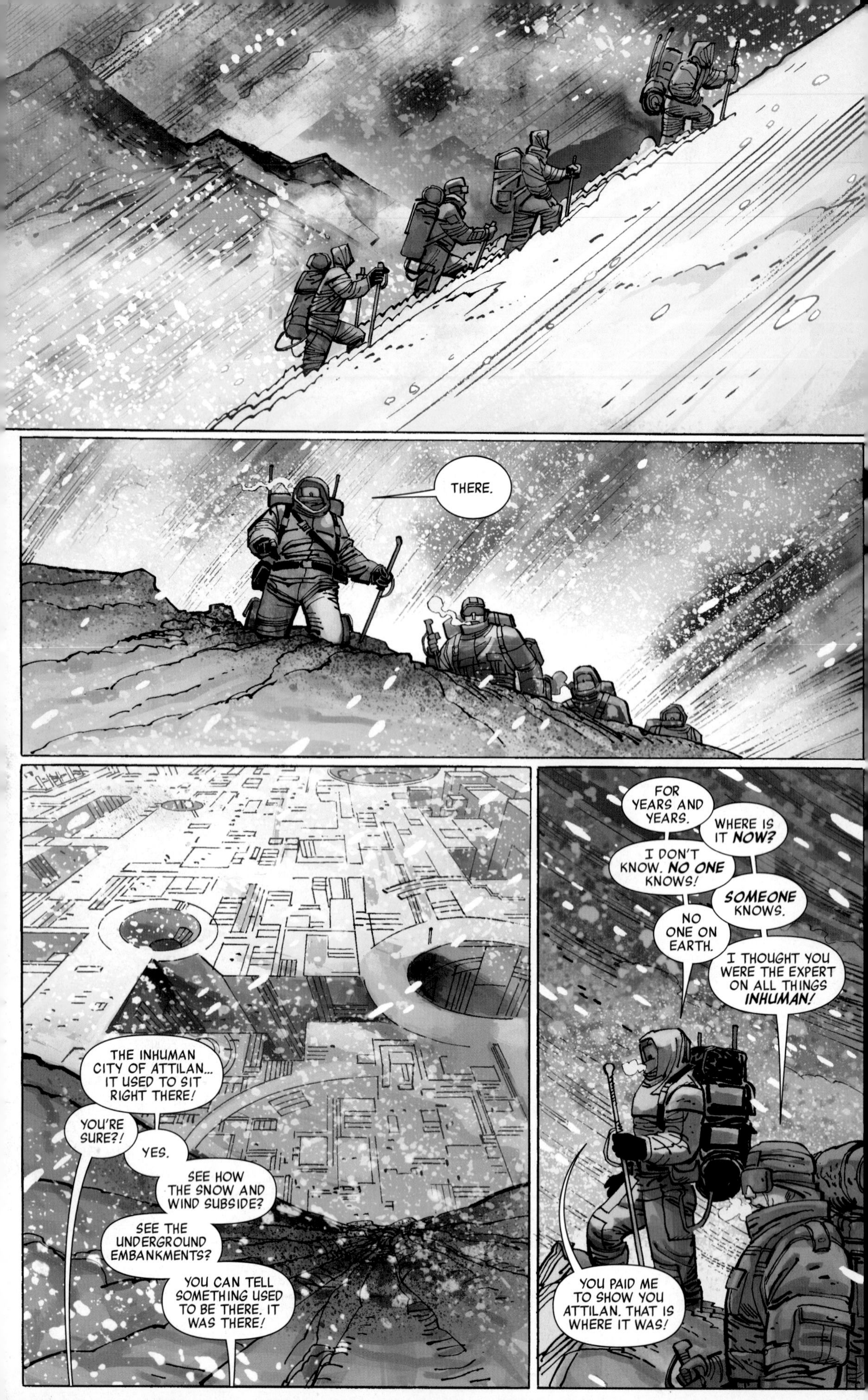
THERE.
THE INHUMAN CITY OF ATTILAN... IT USED TO SIT RIGHT THERE!
YOU'RE SURE?!
YES.
SEE HOW THE SNOW AND WIND SUBSIDE?
SEE THE UNDERGROUND EMBANKMENTS?
YOU CAN TELL SOMETHING USED TO BE THERE. IT WAS THERE!
FOR YEARS AND YEARS.
WHERE IS IT NOW?
I DON'T KNOW. NO ONE KNOWS!
SOMEONE KNOWS.
NO ONE ON EARTH.
I THOUGHT YOU WERE THE EXPERT ON ALL THINGS INHUMAN!
YOU PAID ME TO SHOW YOU ATTILAN. THAT IS WHERE IT WAS!

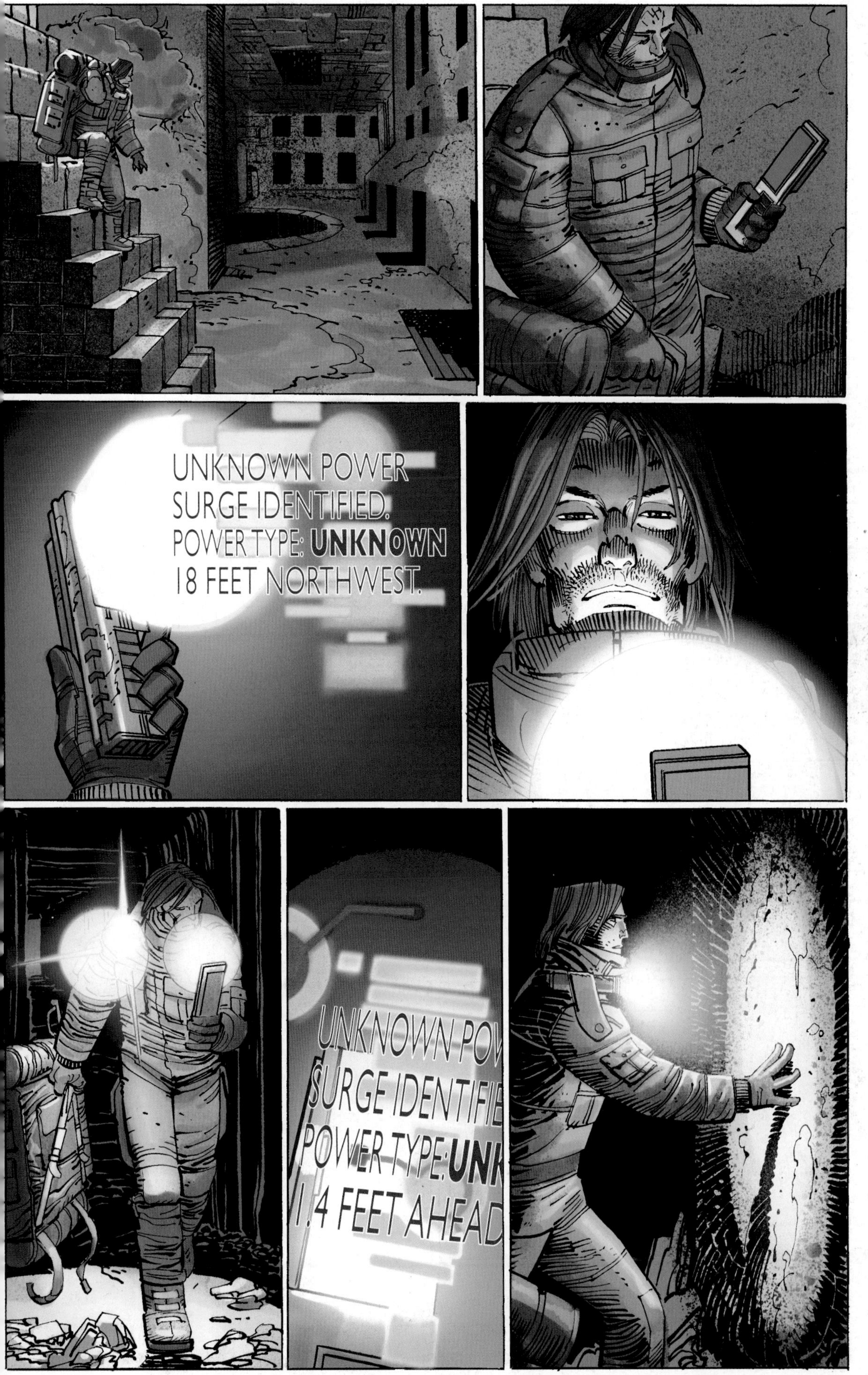
UNKNOWN POWER
SURGE IDENTIFIED.
POWER TYPE: UNKNOWN
18 FEET NORTHWEST.
UNKNOWN POW
SURGE IDENTIFIE
POWER TYPE:UNK
1.4 FEET AHEAD

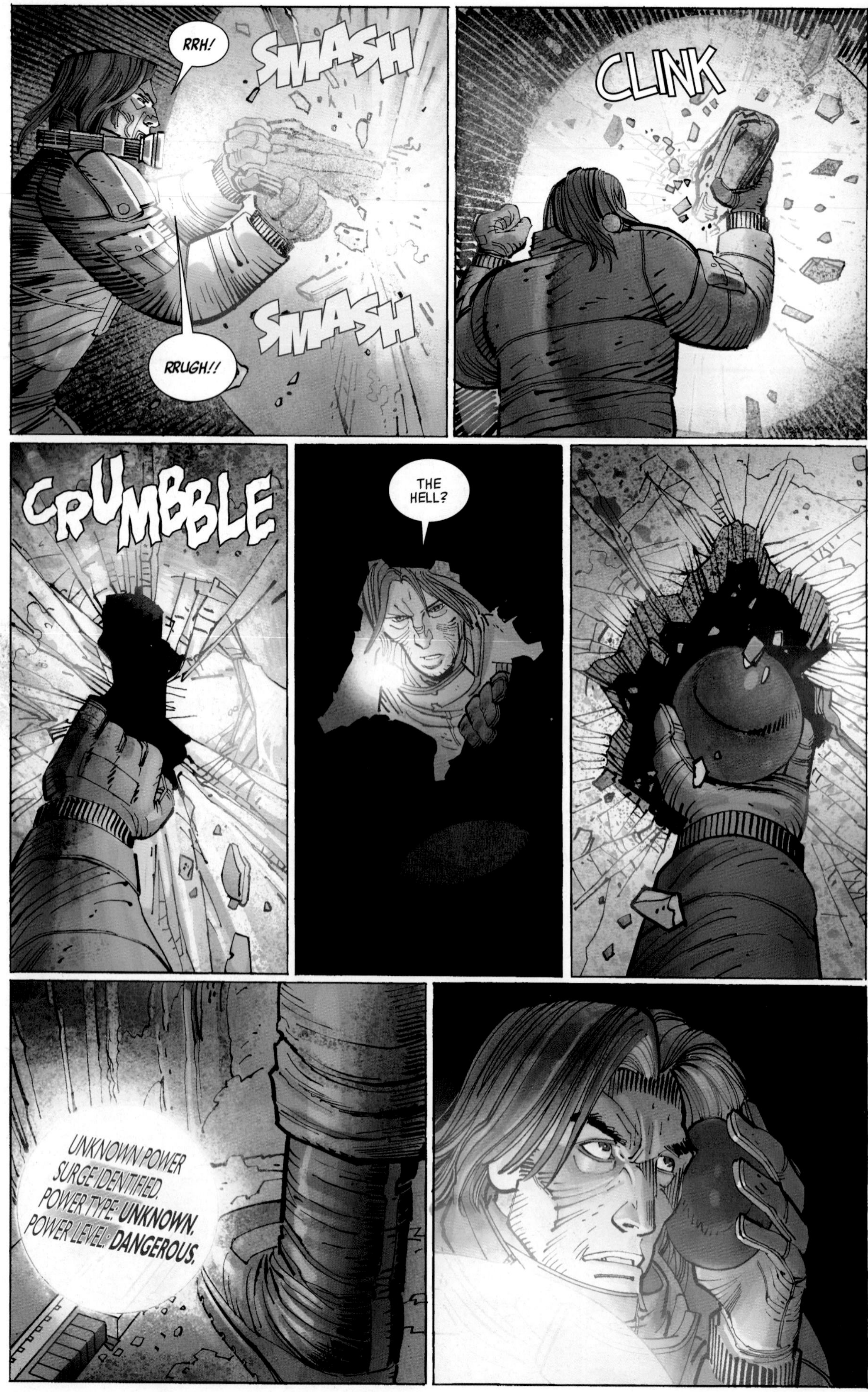
RRH!
SMASH
SMASH
RRUGH!!
CLINK
CRUMBBLE
THE HELL?
UNKNOWN POWER SURGE IDENTIFIED.
POWER TYPE: UNKNOWN.
POWER LEVEL: DANGEROUS.

NO SEAMS.
@#$@$!
COME ON...
ALL THIS WAY...
RRAAGH!
TANG
COME ON!
COME ON!
ALL THIS WAY!!
FIP
SPING
SPING
SPING
COME ON!!!

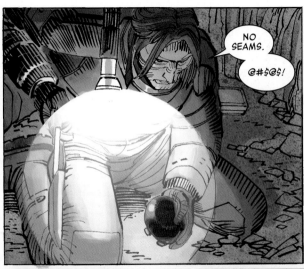

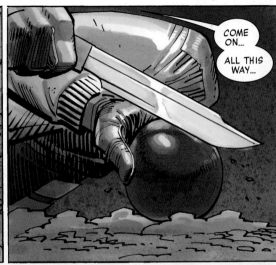

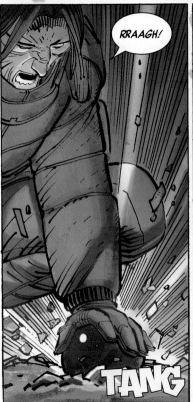

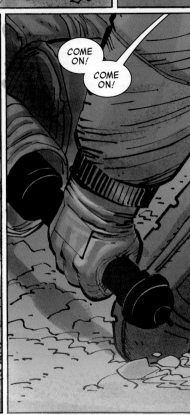

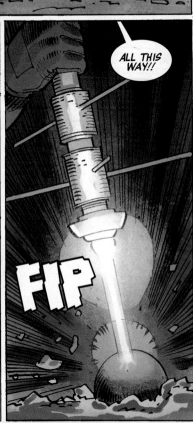

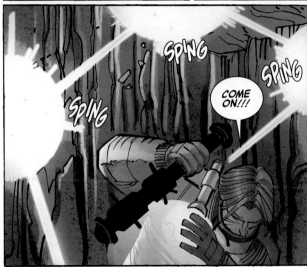

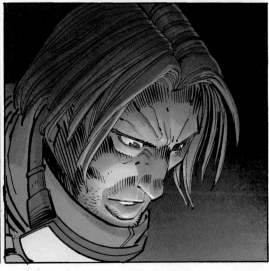

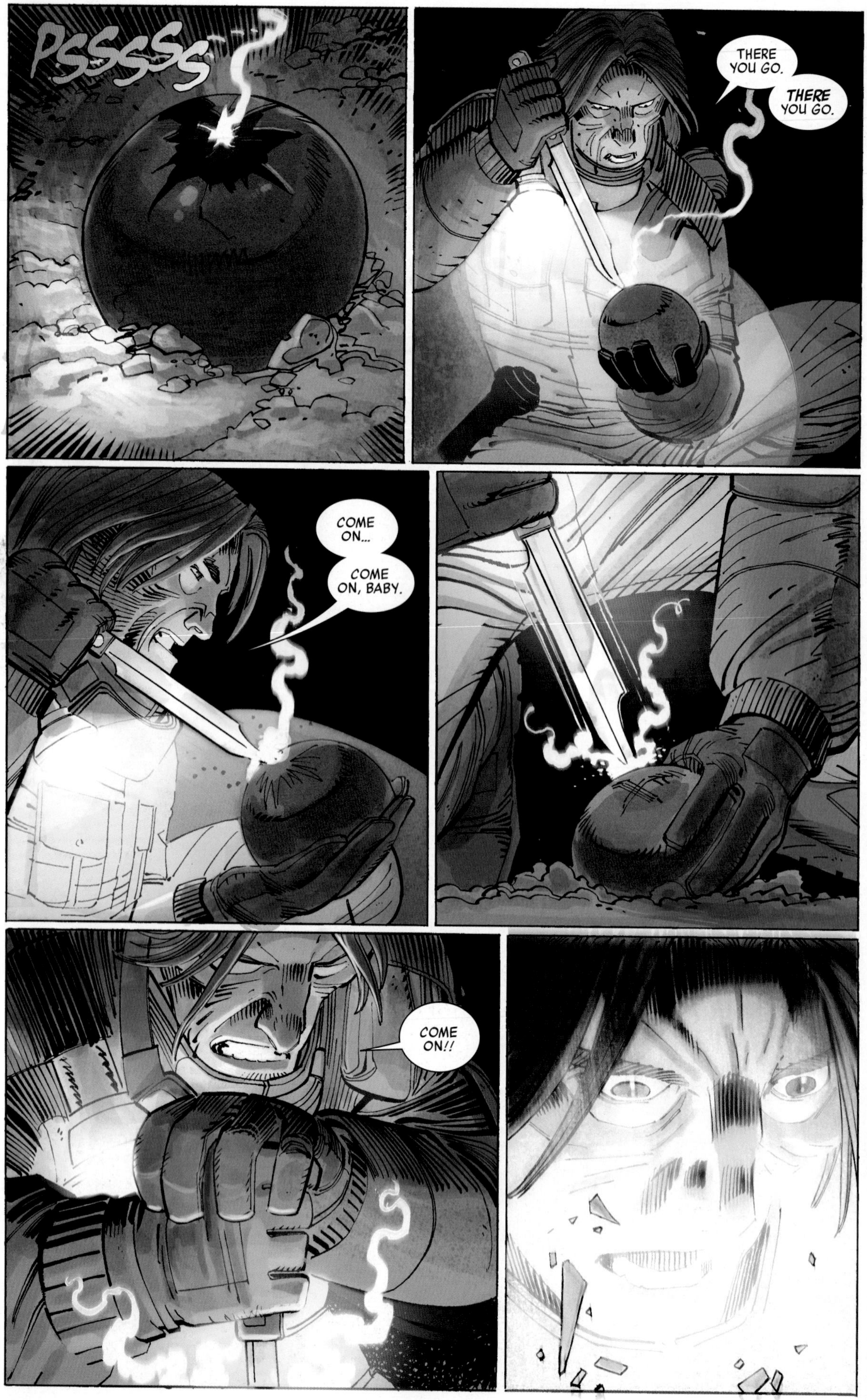
PSSSSS
THERE YOU GO.
THERE YOU GO.
COME ON...
COME ON, BABY.
COME ON!!

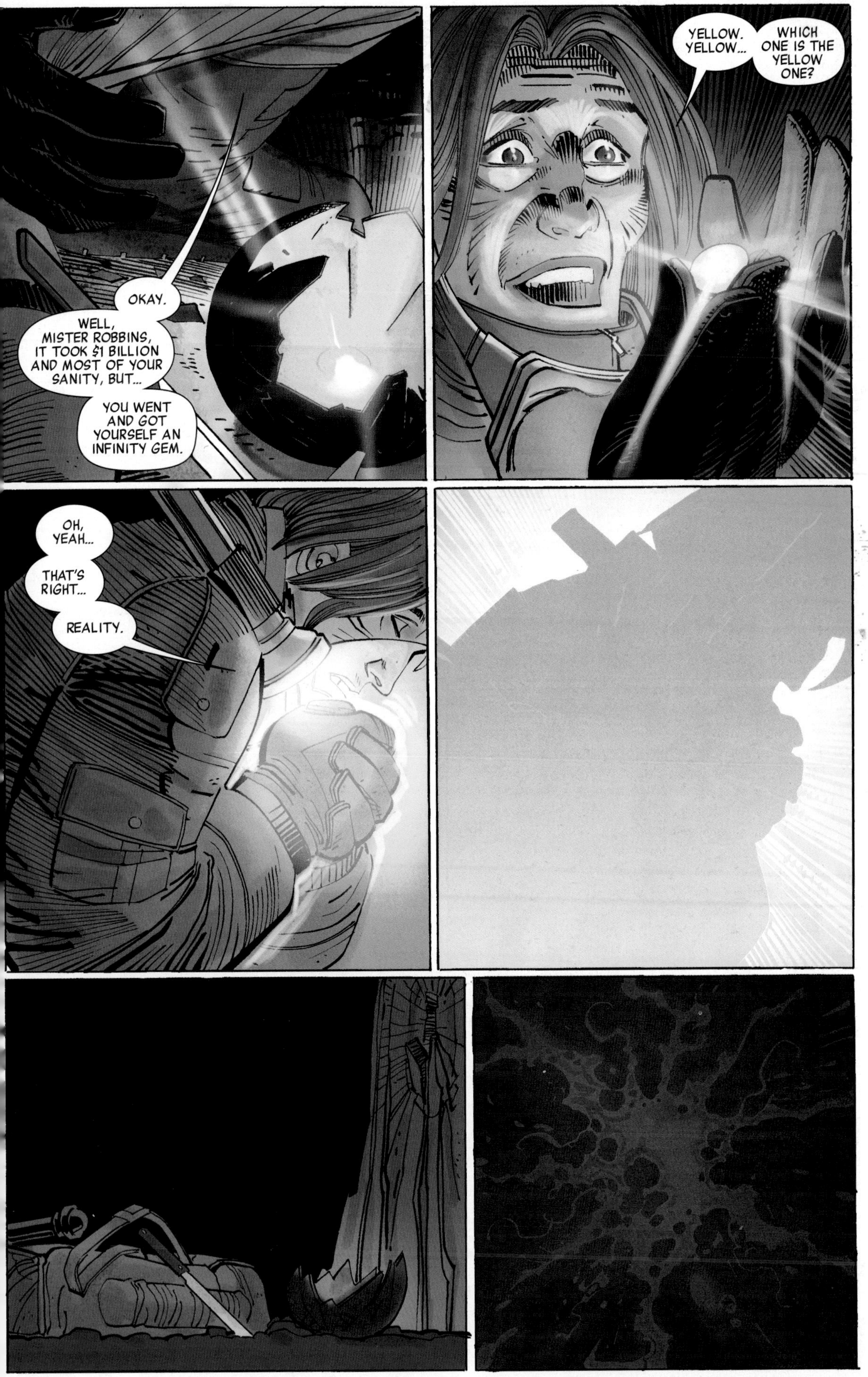
OKAY.
WELL, MISTER ROBBINS, IT TOOK $1 BILLION AND MOST OF YOUR SANITY, BUT...
YOU WENT AND GOT YOURSELF AN INFINITY GEM.
YELLOW. YELLOW...
WHICH ONE IS THE YELLOW ONE?
OH, YEAH...
THAT'S RIGHT...
REALITY.

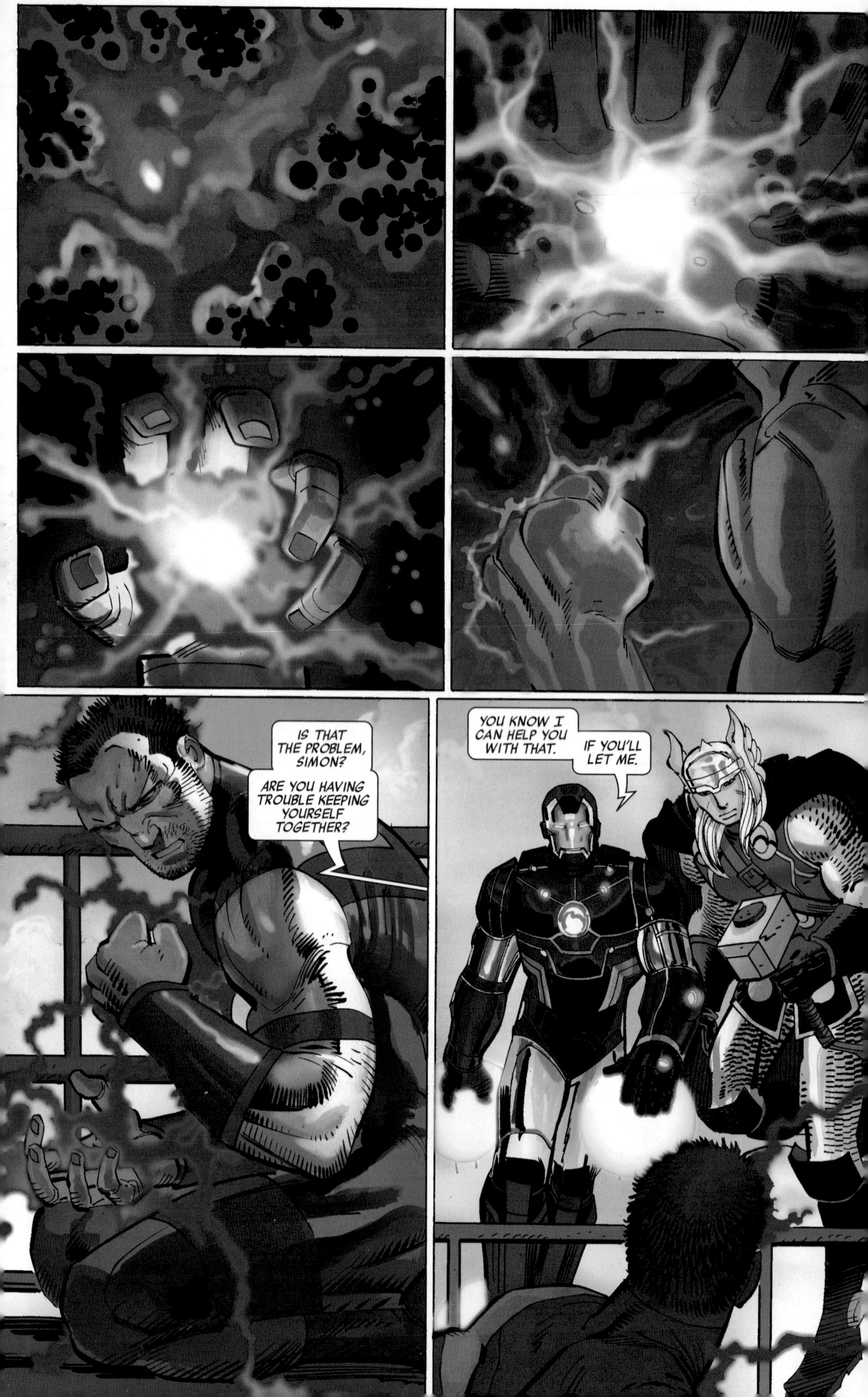
IS THAT THE PROBLEM, SIMON?
ARE YOU HAVING TROUBLE KEEPING YOURSELF TOGETHER?
YOU KNOW I CAN HELP YOU WITH THAT.
IF YOU'LL LET ME.

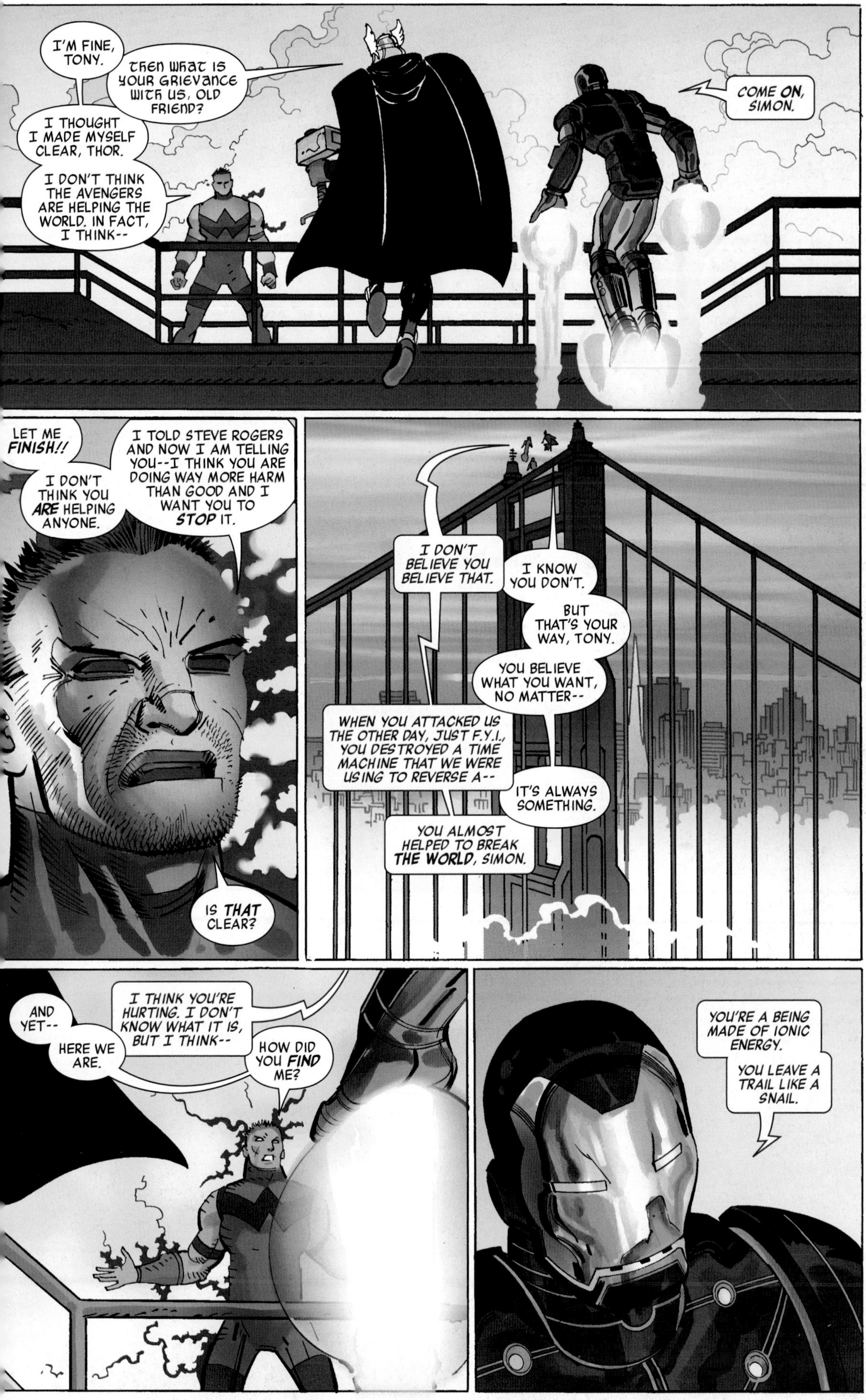
I'M FINE, TONY.
THEN WHAT IS YOUR GRIEVANCE WITH US, OLD FRIEND?
COME ON, SIMON.
I THOUGHT I MADE MYSELF CLEAR, THOR.
I DON'T THINK THE AVENGERS ARE HELPING THE WORLD. IN FACT, I THINK--
LET ME FINISH!!
I DON'T THINK YOU ARE HELPING ANYONE.
I TOLD STEVE ROGERS AND NOW I AM TELLING YOU--I THINK YOU ARE DOING WAY MORE HARM THAN GOOD AND I WANT YOU TO STOP IT.
IS THAT CLEAR?
I DON'T BELIEVE YOU BELIEVE THAT.
I KNOW YOU DON'T.
BUT THAT'S YOUR WAY, TONY.
YOU BELIEVE WHAT YOU WANT, NO MATTER--
WHEN YOU ATTACKED US THE OTHER DAY, JUST F.Y.I., YOU DESTROYED A TIME MACHINE THAT WE WERE USING TO REVERSE A--
IT'S ALWAYS SOMETHING.
YOU ALMOST HELPED TO BREAK THE WORLD, SIMON.
AND YET--
HERE WE ARE.
I THINK YOU'RE HURTING. I DON'T KNOW WHAT IT IS, BUT I THINK--
HOW DID YOU FIND ME?
YOU'RE A BEING MADE OF IONIC ENERGY.
YOU LEAVE A TRAIL LIKE A SNAIL.

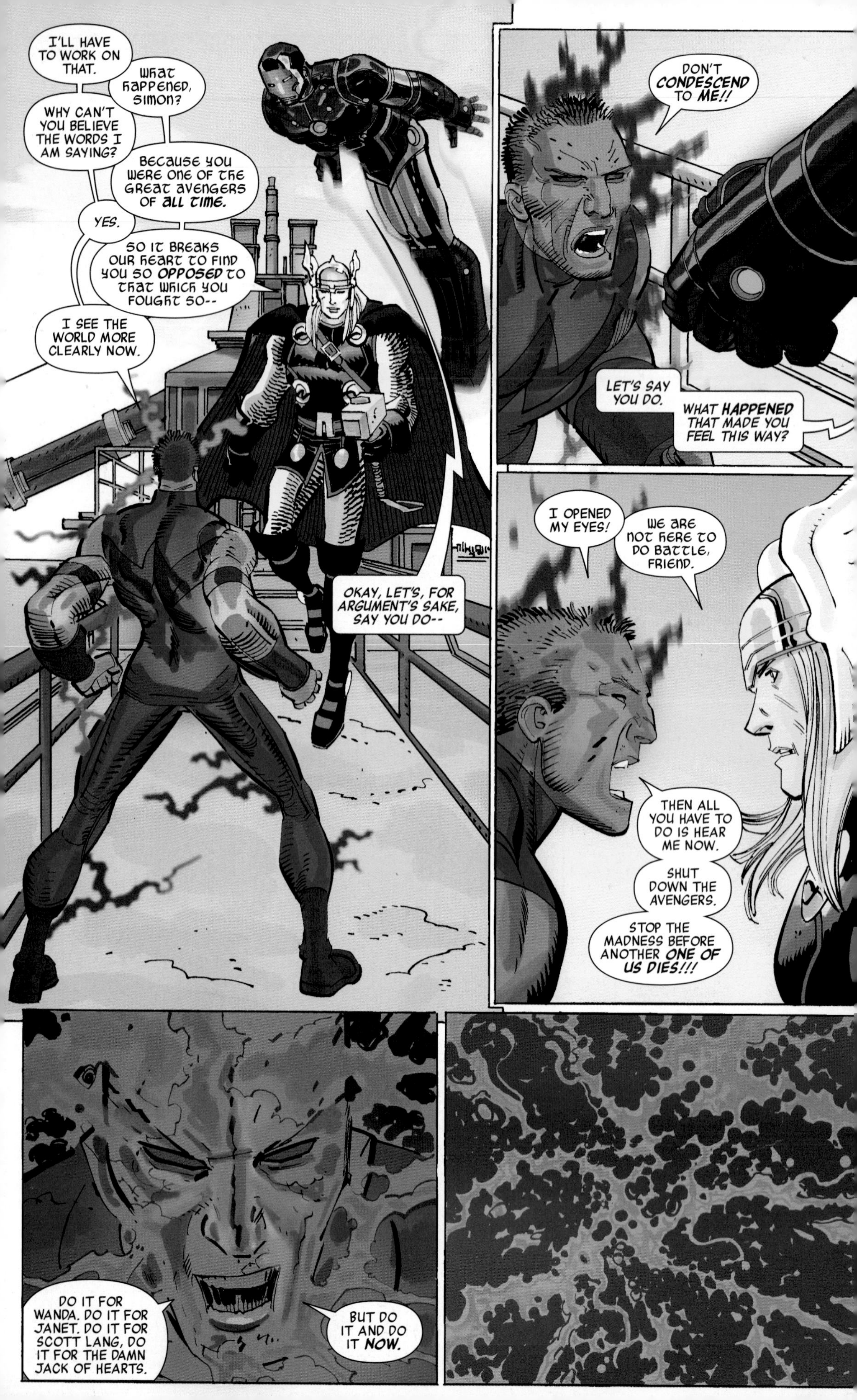
I'LL HAVE TO WORK ON THAT.
WHAT HAPPENED, SIMON?
WHY CAN'T YOU BELIEVE THE WORDS I AM SAYING?
BECAUSE YOU WERE ONE OF THE GREAT AVENGERS OF ALL TIME.
YES.
SO IT BREAKS OUR HEART TO FIND YOU SO OPPOSED TO THAT WHICH YOU FOUGHT SO--
I SEE THE WORLD MORE CLEARLY NOW.
OKAY, LET'S, FOR ARGUMENT'S SAKE, SAY YOU DO--
DON'T CONDESCEND TO ME!!
LET'S SAY YOU DO.
WHAT HAPPENED THAT MADE YOU FEEL THIS WAY?
I OPENED MY EYES!
WE ARE NOT HERE TO DO BATTLE, FRIEND.
THEN ALL YOU HAVE TO DO IS HEAR ME NOW.
SHUT DOWN THE AVENGERS.
STOP THE MADNESS BEFORE ANOTHER ONE OF US DIES!!!
DO IT FOR WANDA. DO IT FOR JANET. DO IT FOR SCOTT LANG, DO IT FOR THE DAMN JACK OF HEARTS.
BUT DO IT AND DO IT NOW.

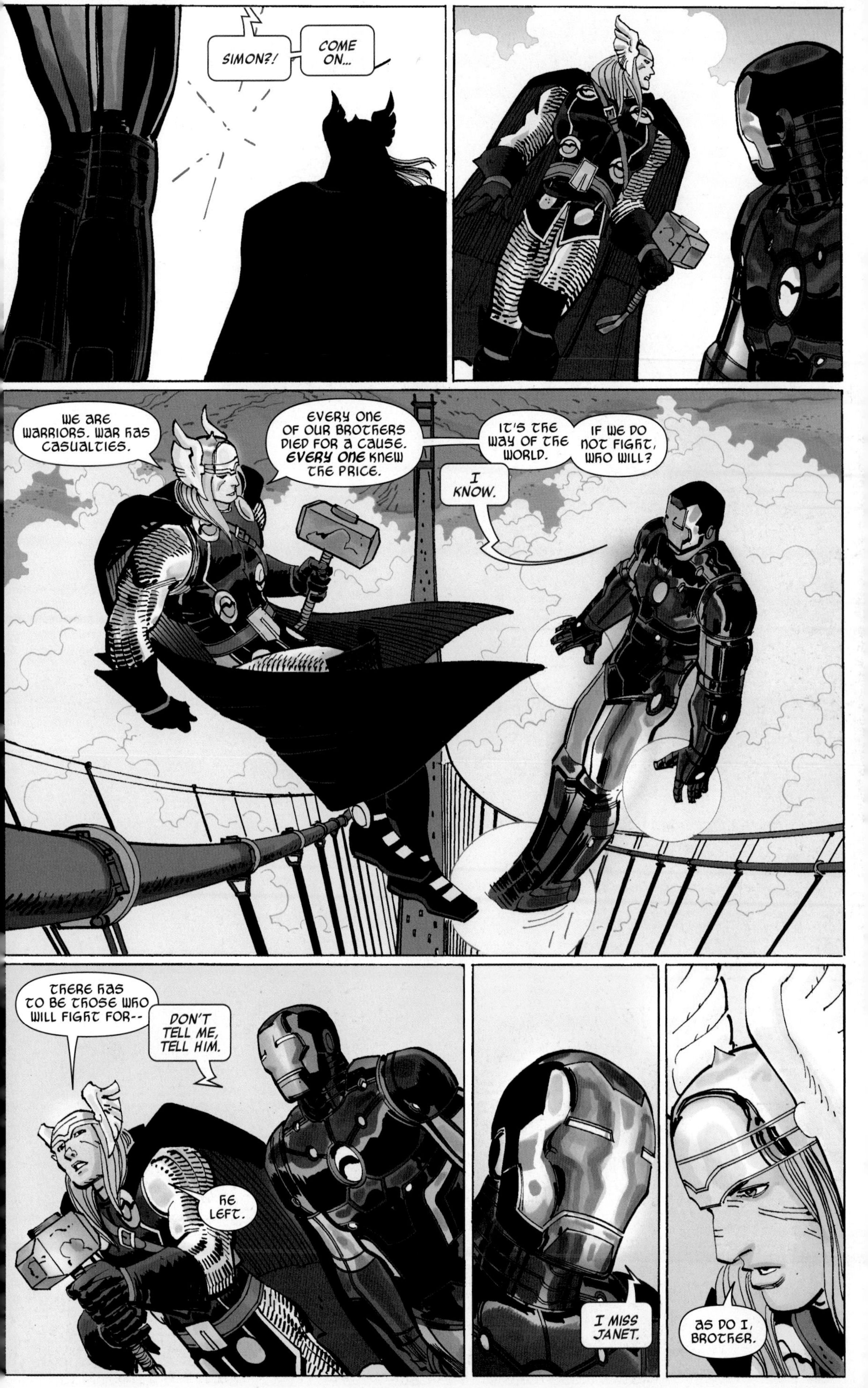
SIMON?!
COME ON...
WE ARE WARRIORS. WAR HAS CASUALTIES.
EVERY ONE OF OUR BROTHERS DIED FOR A CAUSE. EVERY ONE KNEW THE PRICE.
IT'S THE WAY OF THE WORLD.
IF WE DO NOT FIGHT, WHO WILL?
I KNOW.
THERE HAS TO BE THOSE WHO WILL FIGHT FOR--
DON'T TELL ME, TELL HIM.
HE LEFT.
I MISS JANET.
AS DO I, BROTHER.

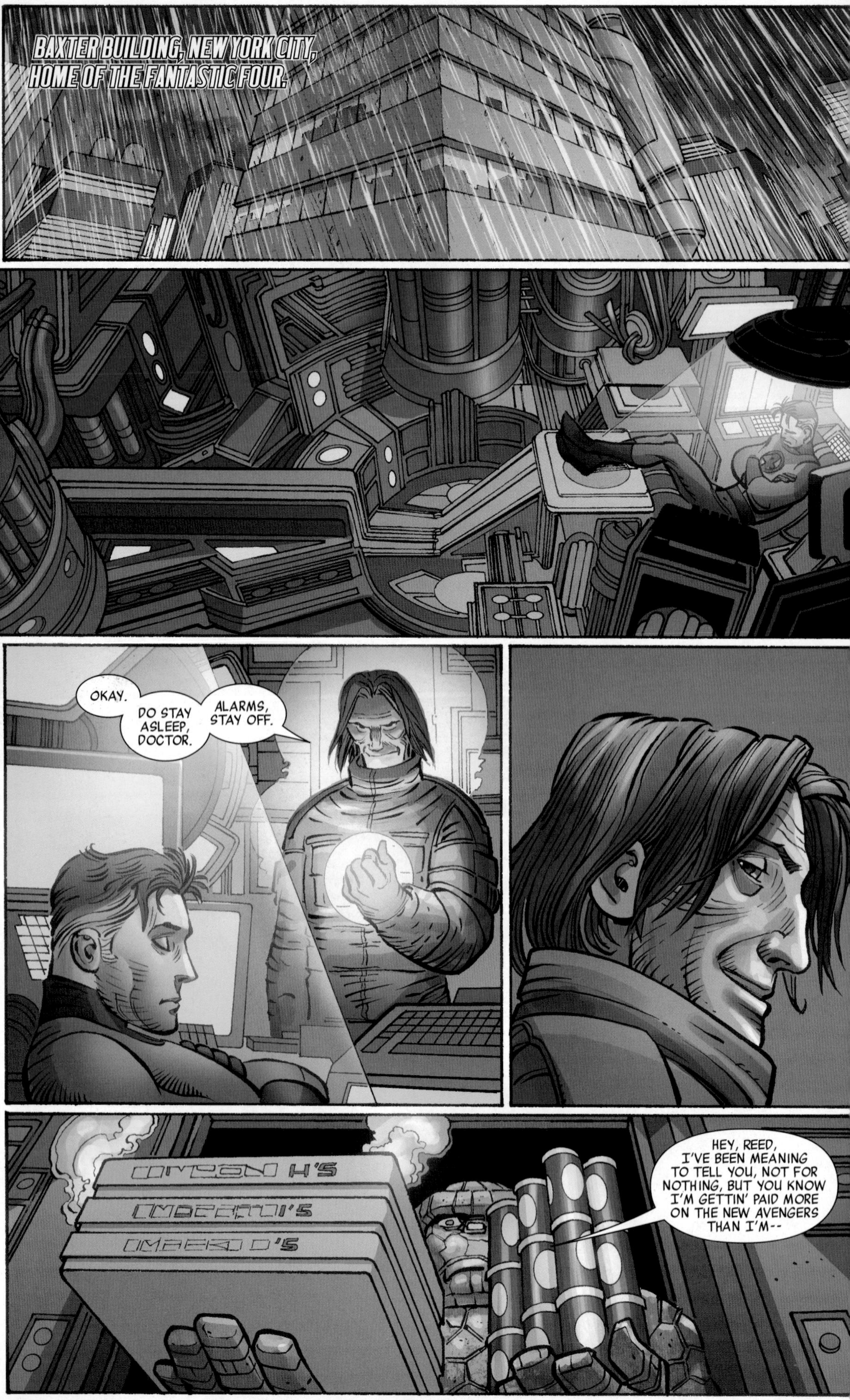
BAXTER BUILDING, NEW YORK CITY, HOME OF THE FANTASTIC FOUR.
OKAY.
DO STAY ASLEEP, DOCTOR.
ALARMS, STAY OFF.
HEY, REED, I'VE BEEN MEANING TO TELL YOU, NOT FOR NOTHING, BUT YOU KNOW I'M GETTIN' PAID MORE ON THE NEW AVENGERS THAN I'M--

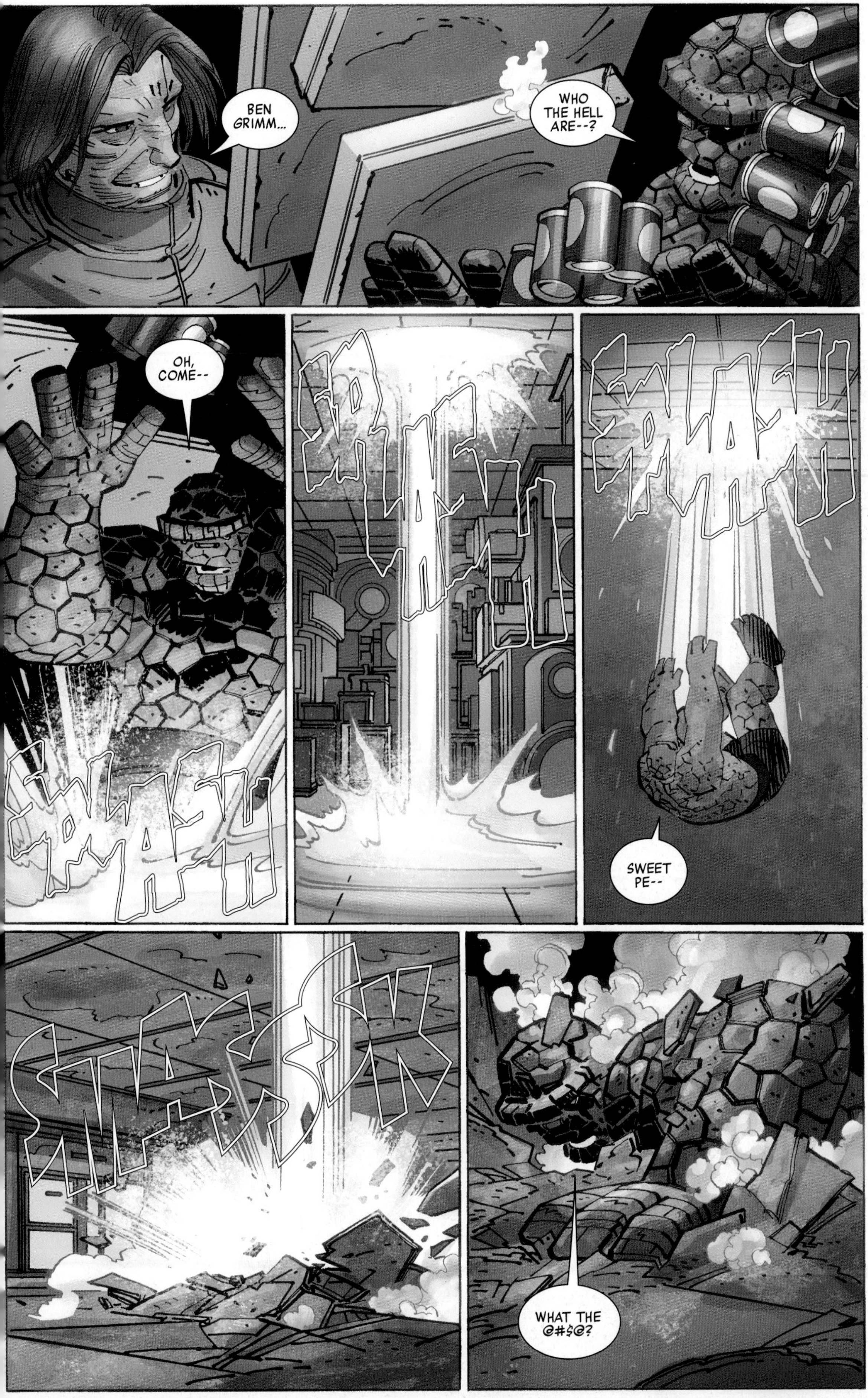
BEN GRIMM...
WHO THE HELL ARE--?
OH, COME--
SWEET PE--
WHAT THE @#$@?

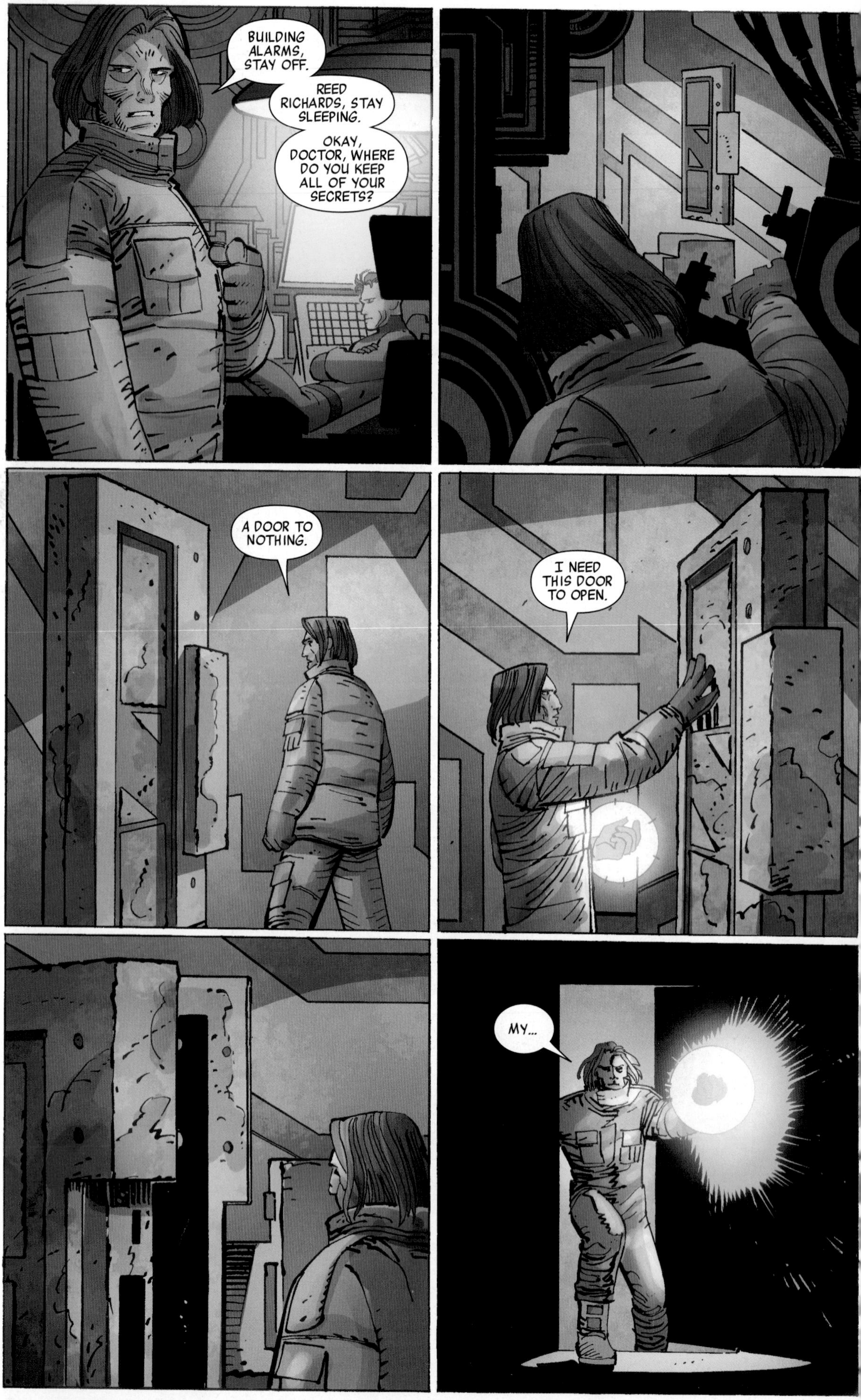
BUILDING ALARMS, STAY OFF.
REED RICHARDS, STAY SLEEPING.
OKAY, DOCTOR, WHERE DO YOU KEEP ALL OF YOUR SECRETS?
A DOOR TO NOTHING.
I NEED THIS DOOR TO OPEN.
MY...

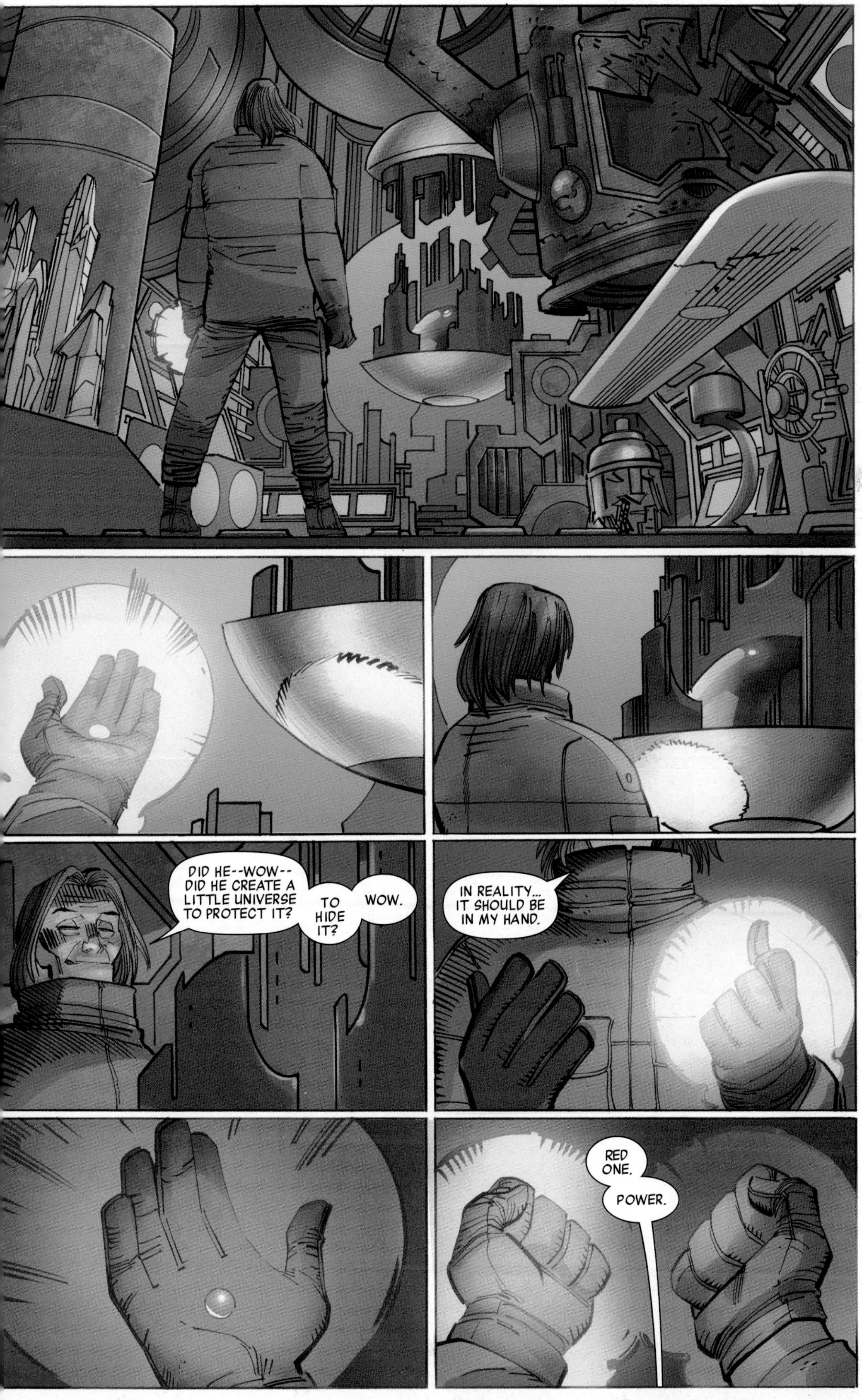
DID HE--WOW--
DID HE CREATE A
LITTLE UNIVERSE
TO PROTECT IT?
TO
HIDE
IT?
WOW.
IN REALITY...
IT SHOULD BE
IN MY HAND.
RED
ONE.
POWER.

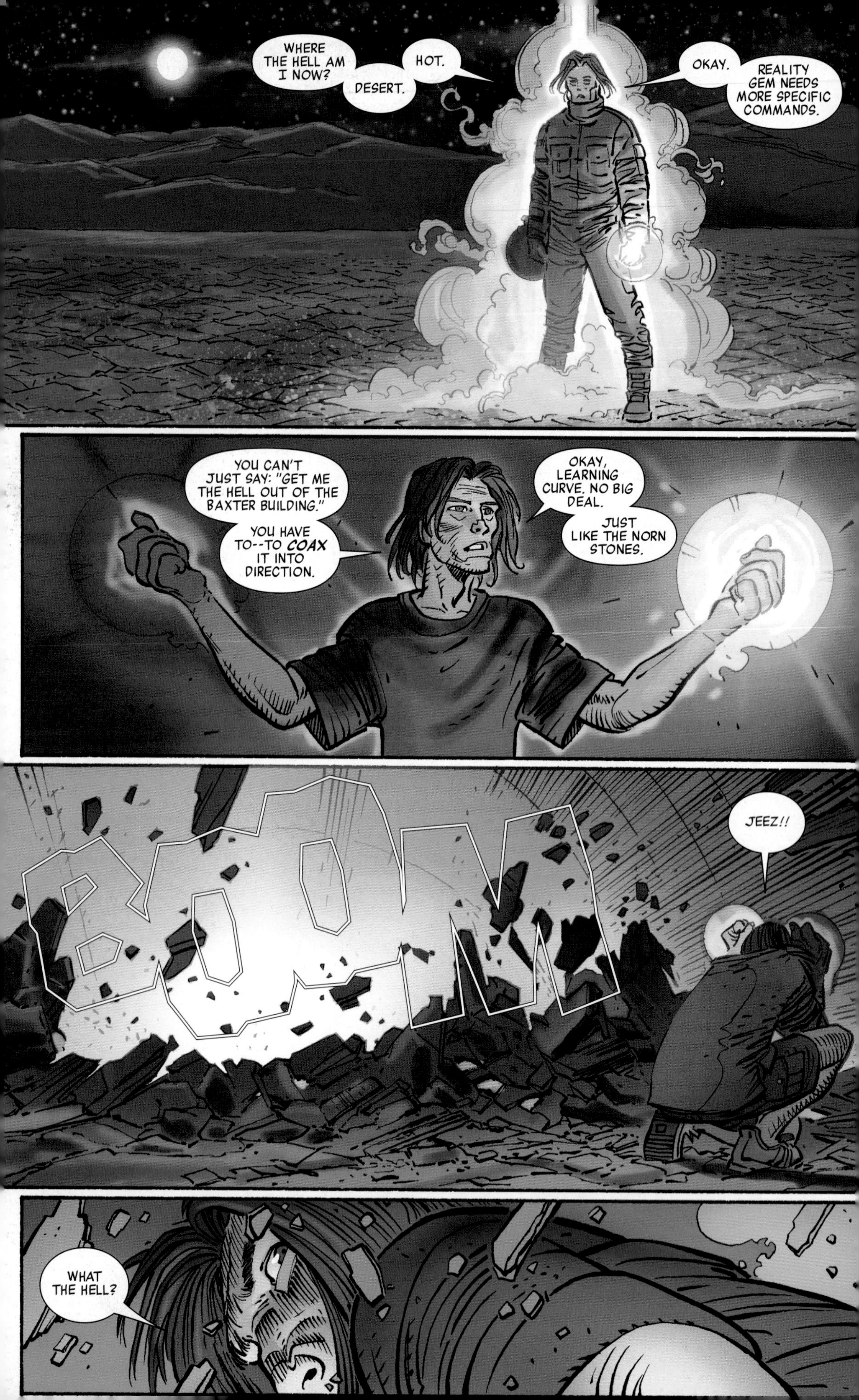
WHERE THE HELL AM I NOW?
DESERT.
HOT.
OKAY.
REALITY GEM NEEDS MORE SPECIFIC COMMANDS.
YOU CAN'T JUST SAY: "GET ME THE HELL OUT OF THE BAXTER BUILDING."
YOU HAVE TO--TO COAX IT INTO DIRECTION.
OKAY, LEARNING CURVE. NO BIG DEAL.
JUST LIKE THE NORN STONES.
BOOM
JEEZ!!
WHAT THE HELL?

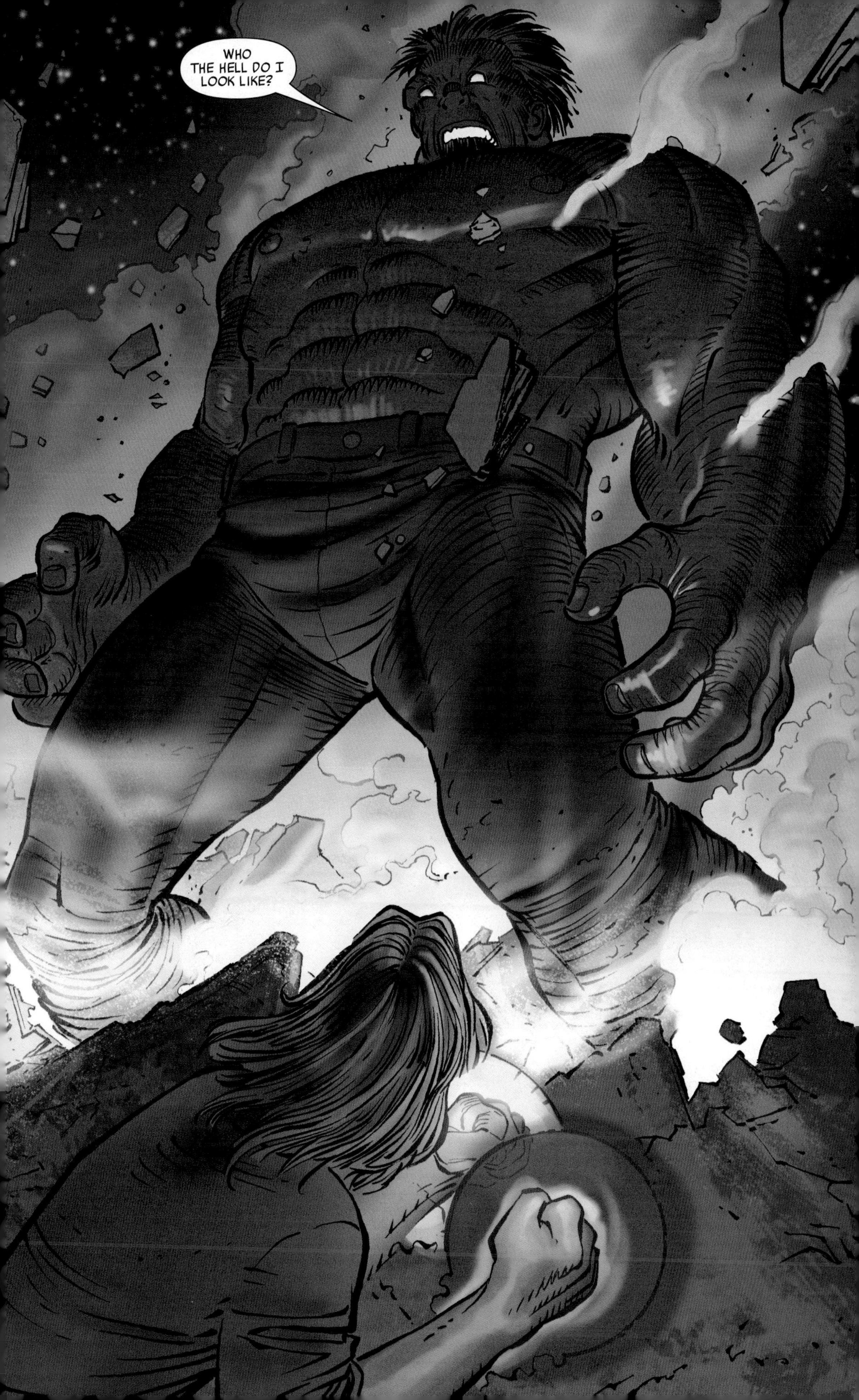
WHO THE HELL DO I LOOK LIKE?

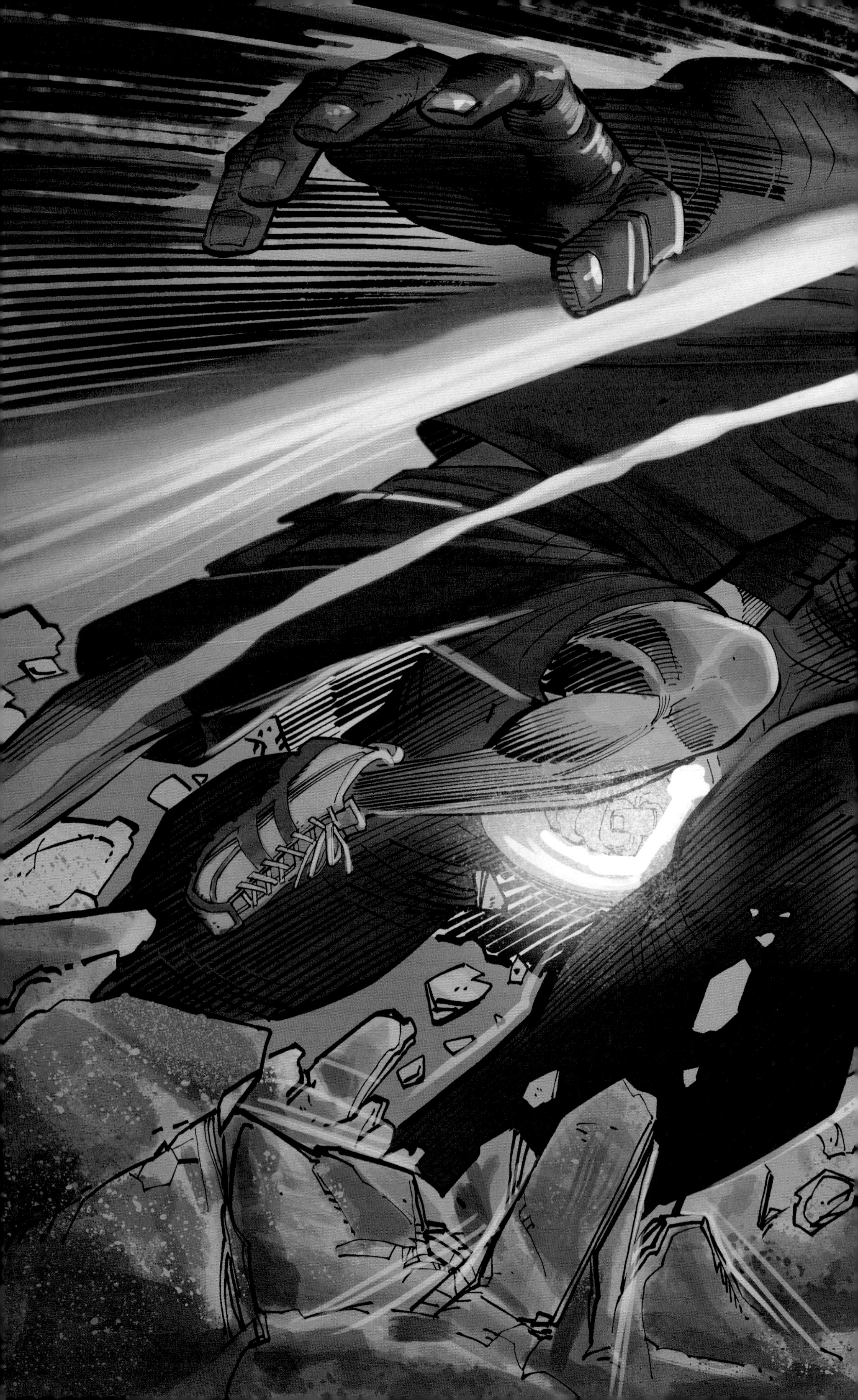

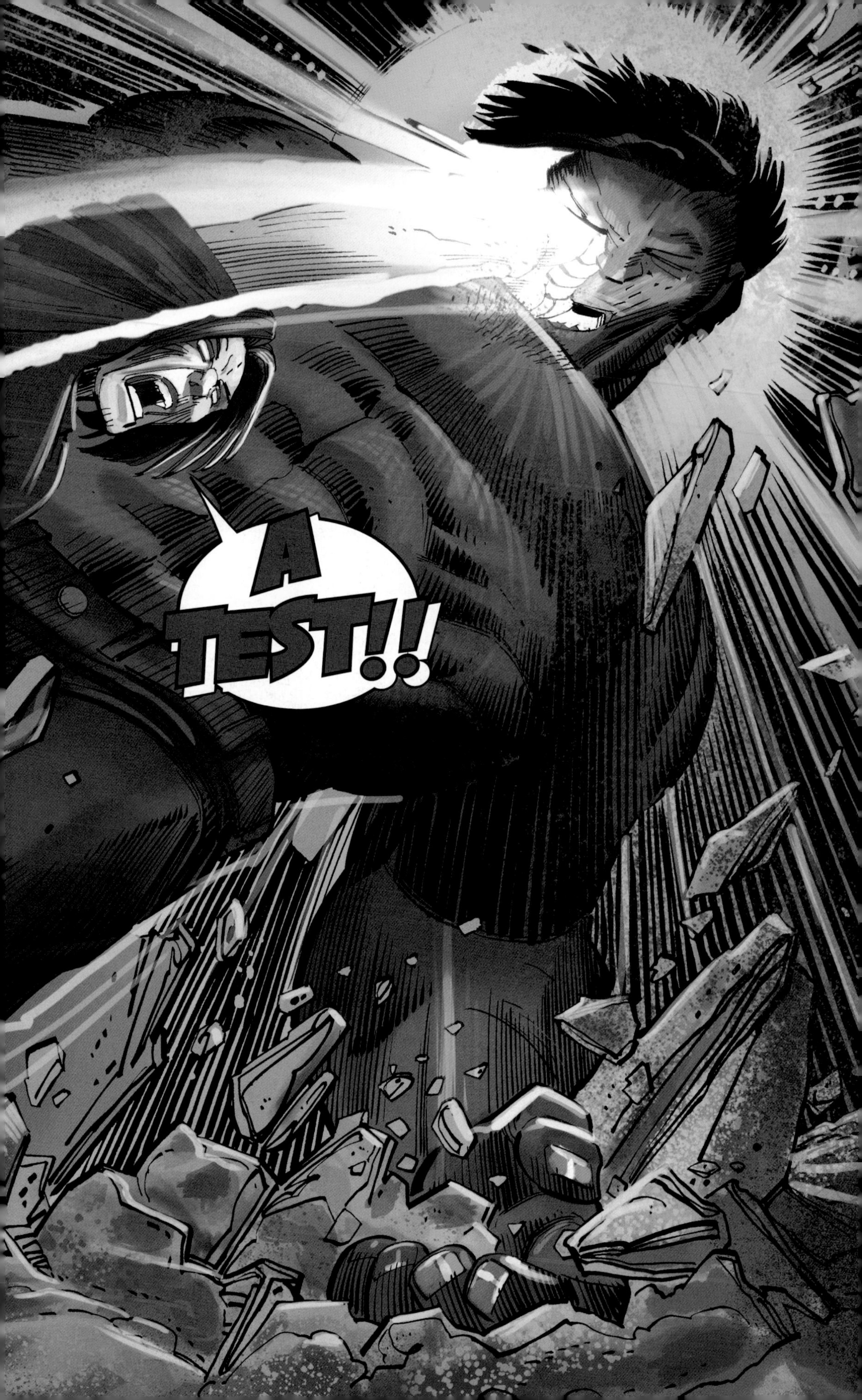
A TEST!!

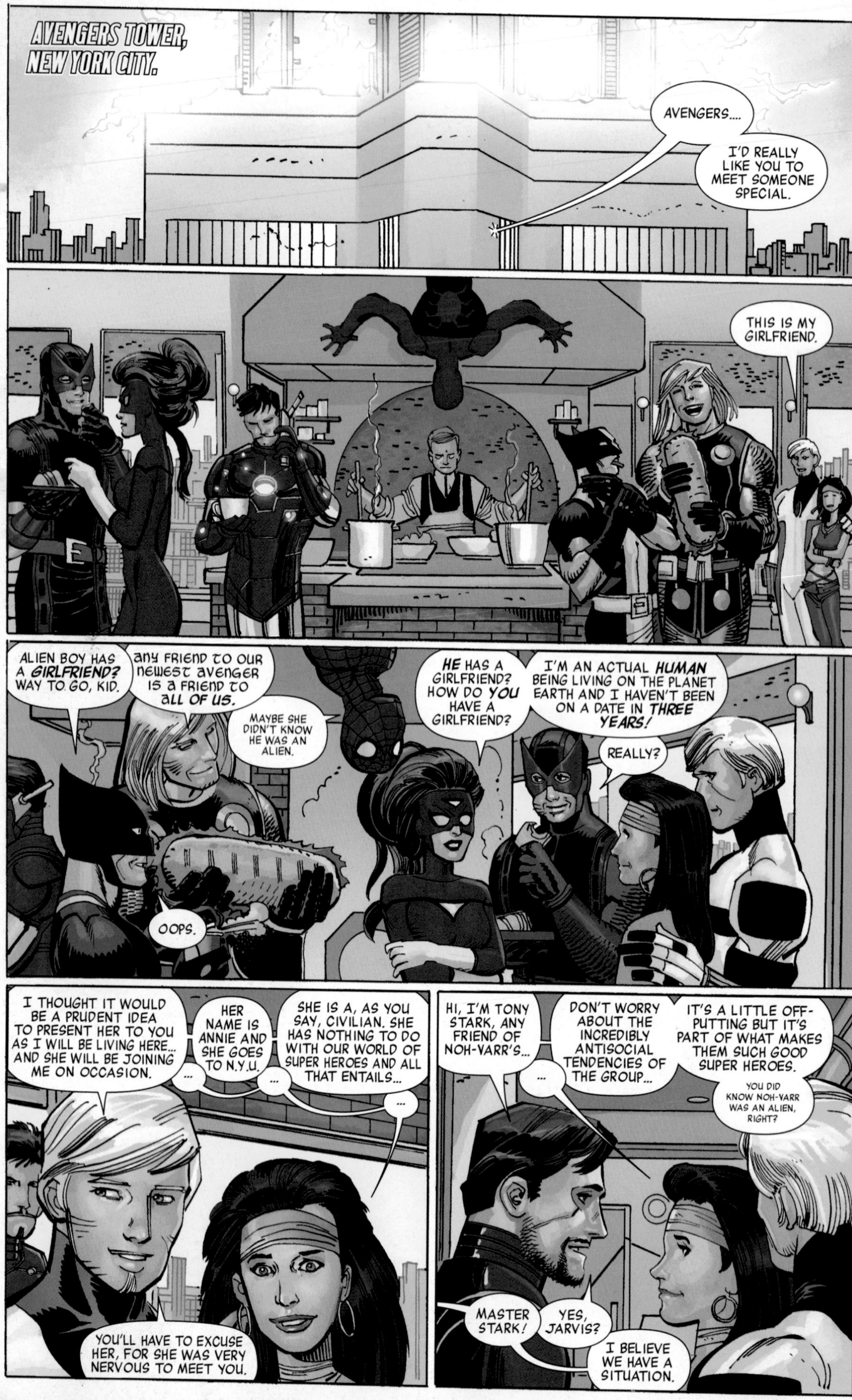
AVENGERS TOWER, NEW YORK CITY.
AVENGERS....
I'D REALLY LIKE YOU TO MEET SOMEONE SPECIAL.
THIS IS MY GIRLFRIEND.
ALIEN BOY HAS A GIRLFRIEND? WAY TO GO, KID.
any friend to our newest avenger is a friend to all of us.
MAYBE SHE DIDN'T KNOW HE WAS AN ALIEN.
HE HAS A GIRLFRIEND? HOW DO YOU HAVE A GIRLFRIEND?
I'M AN ACTUAL HUMAN BEING LIVING ON THE PLANET EARTH AND I HAVEN'T BEEN ON A DATE IN THREE YEARS!
REALLY?
OOPS.
I THOUGHT IT WOULD BE A PRUDENT IDEA TO PRESENT HER TO YOU AS I WILL BE LIVING HERE... AND SHE WILL BE JOINING ME ON OCCASION.
...
HER NAME IS ANNIE AND SHE GOES TO N.Y.U.
...
SHE IS A, AS YOU SAY, CIVILIAN. SHE HAS NOTHING TO DO WITH OUR WORLD OF SUPER HEROES AND ALL THAT ENTAILS...
...
YOU'LL HAVE TO EXCUSE HER, FOR SHE WAS VERY NERVOUS TO MEET YOU.
HI, I'M TONY STARK, ANY FRIEND OF NOH-VARR'S...
...
DON'T WORRY ABOUT THE INCREDIBLY ANTISOCIAL TENDENCIES OF THE GROUP...
IT'S A LITTLE OFF-PUTTING BUT IT'S PART OF WHAT MAKES THEM SUCH GOOD SUPER HEROES.
YOU DID KNOW NOH-VARR WAS AN ALIEN, RIGHT?
MASTER STARK!
YES, JARVIS?
I BELIEVE WE HAVE A SITUATION.

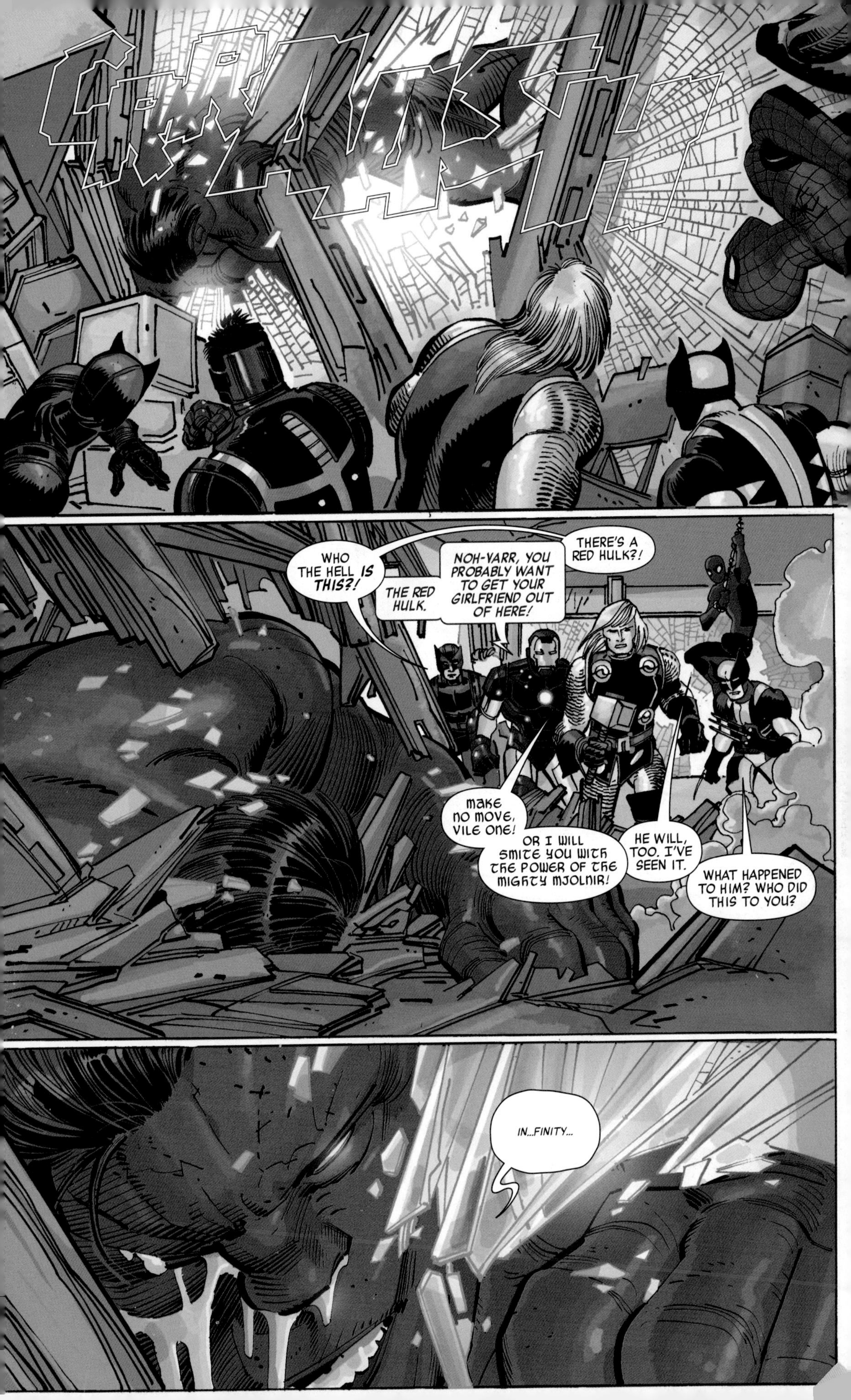
WHO THE HELL IS THIS?!
THE RED HULK.
NOH-VARR, YOU PROBABLY WANT TO GET YOUR GIRLFRIEND OUT OF HERE!
THERE'S A RED HULK?!
MAKE NO MOVE, VILE ONE!
OR I WILL SMITE YOU WITH THE POWER OF THE MIGHTY MJOLNIR!
HE WILL, TOO. I'VE SEEN IT.
WHAT HAPPENED TO HIM? WHO DID THIS TO YOU?
IN...FINITY...

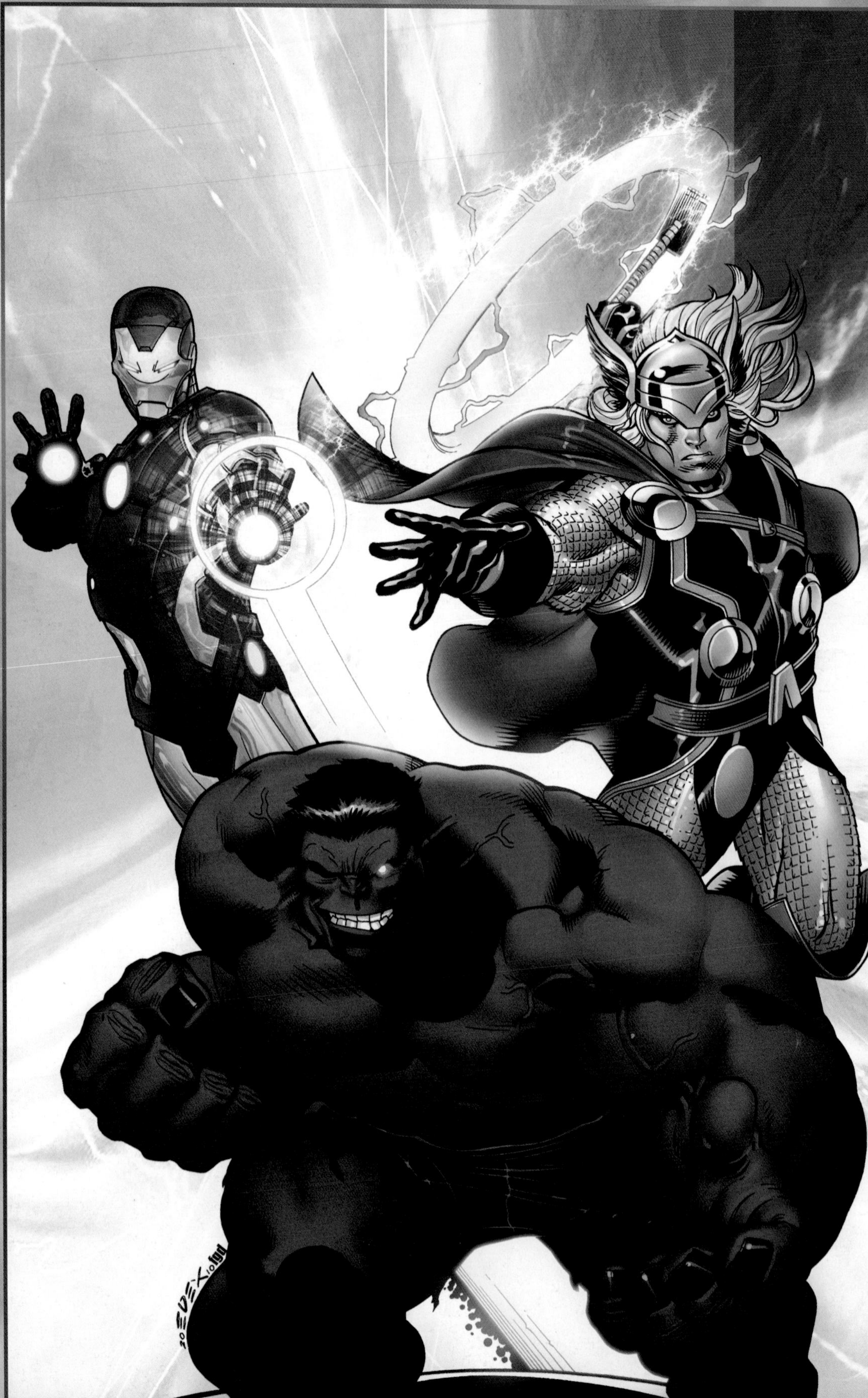

#7 VARIANT BY ED McGUINNESS

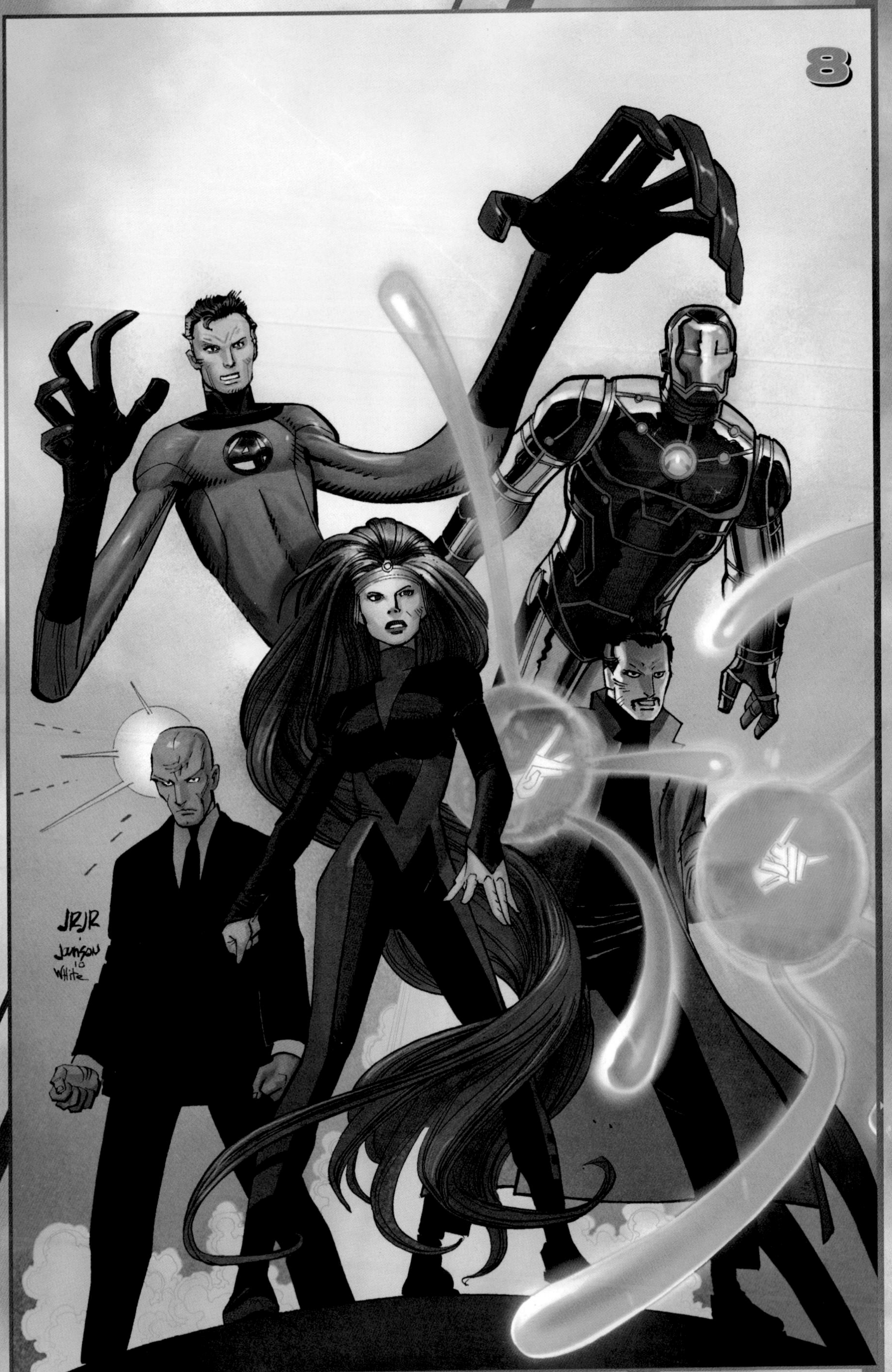
8
JRJR
JANSON
'10
White

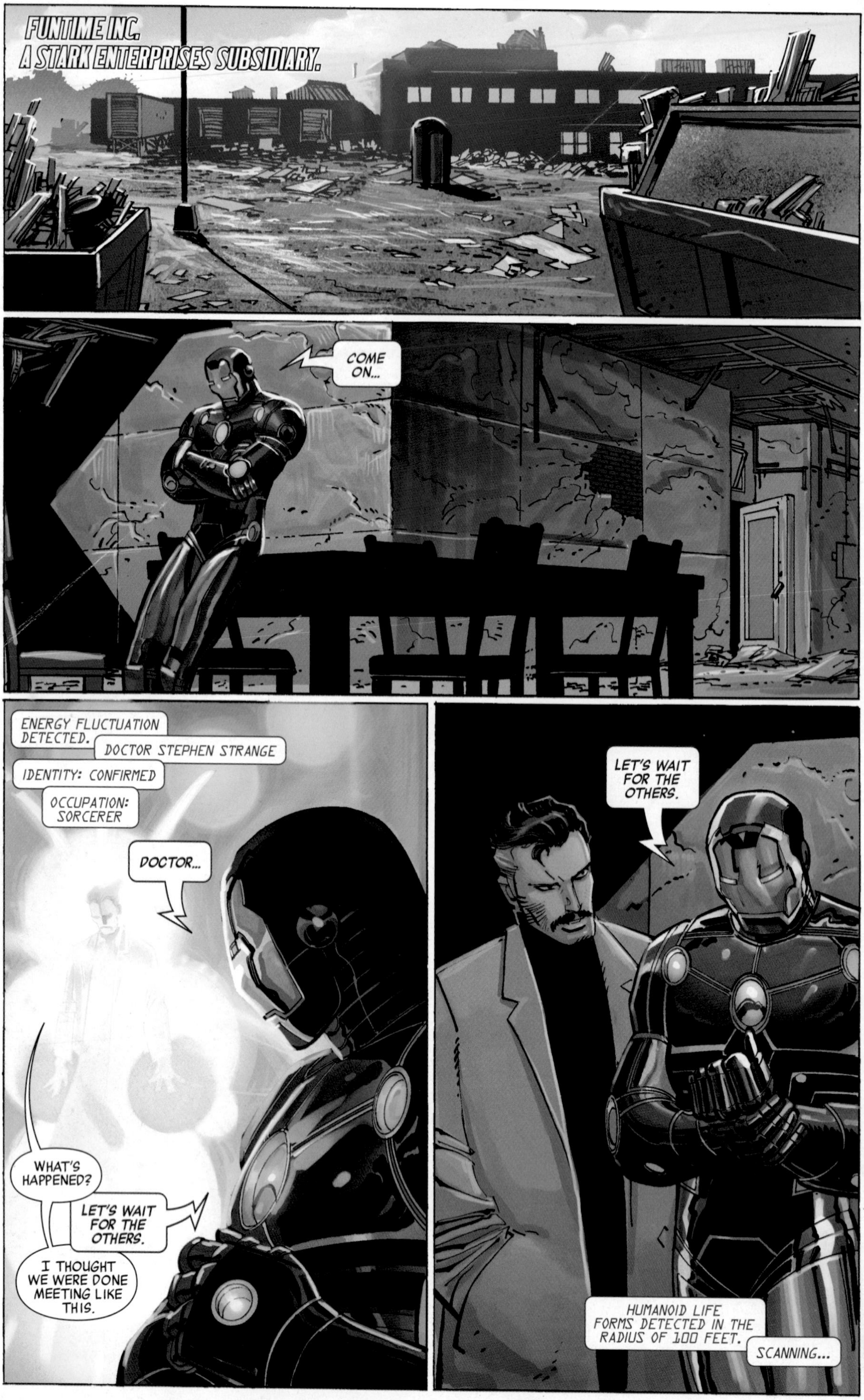
FUNTIME INC.
A STARK ENTERPRISES SUBSIDIARY.
COME ON...
ENERGY FLUCTUATION DETECTED.
DOCTOR STEPHEN STRANGE
IDENTITY: CONFIRMED
OCCUPATION: SORCERER
DOCTOR...
WHAT'S HAPPENED?
LET'S WAIT FOR THE OTHERS.
I THOUGHT WE WERE DONE MEETING LIKE THIS.
LET'S WAIT FOR THE OTHERS.
HUMANOID LIFE FORMS DETECTED IN THE RADIUS OF 100 FEET.
SCANNING...

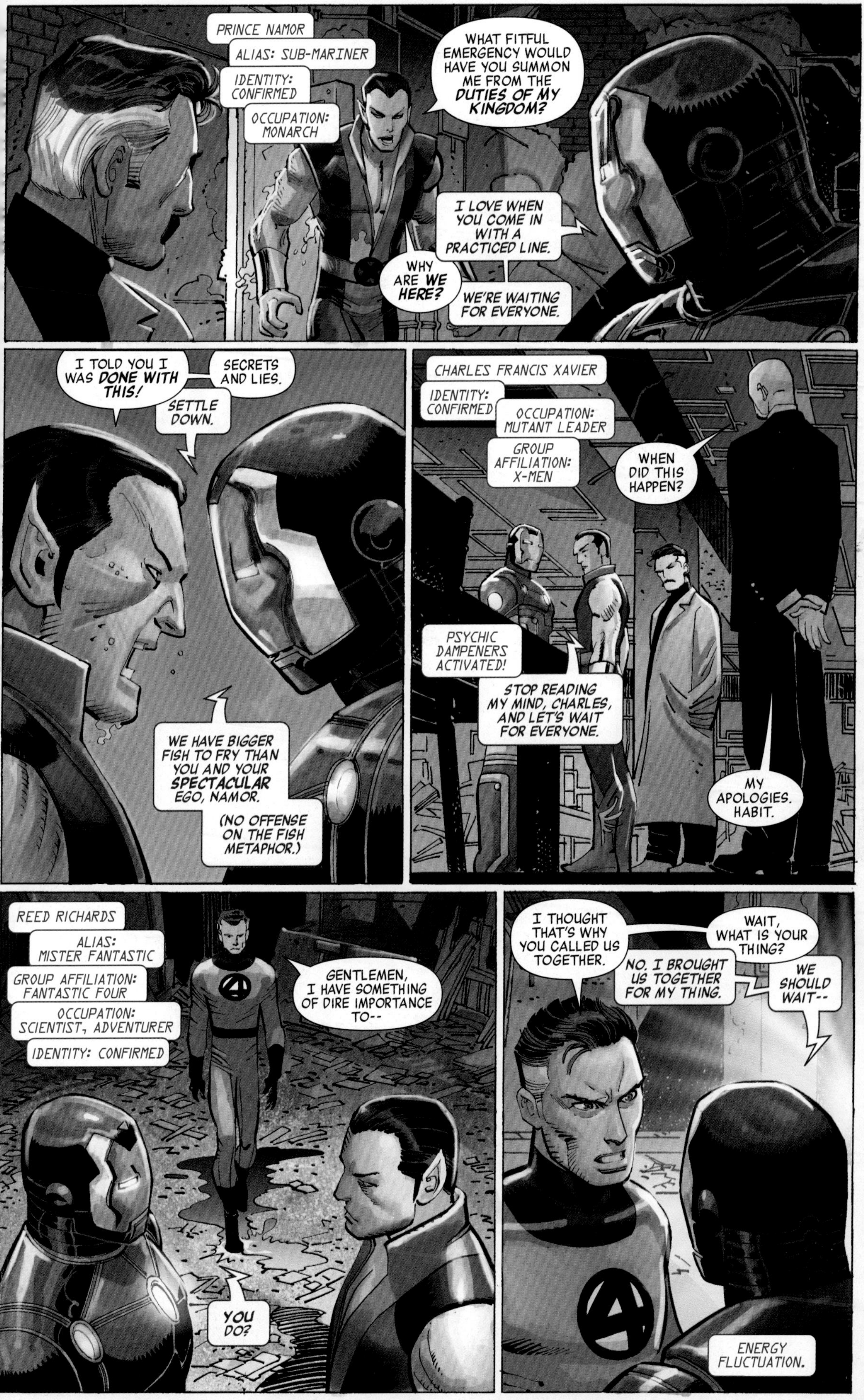
PRINCE NAMOR
ALIAS: SUB-MARINER
IDENTITY: CONFIRMED
OCCUPATION: MONARCH
WHAT FITFUL EMERGENCY WOULD HAVE YOU SUMMON ME FROM THE DUTIES OF MY KINGDOM?
I LOVE WHEN YOU COME IN WITH A PRACTICED LINE.
WHY ARE WE HERE?
WE'RE WAITING FOR EVERYONE.
I TOLD YOU I WAS DONE WITH THIS!
SECRETS AND LIES.
SETTLE DOWN.
WE HAVE BIGGER FISH TO FRY THAN YOU AND YOUR SPECTACULAR EGO, NAMOR.
(NO OFFENSE ON THE FISH METAPHOR.)
CHARLES FRANCIS XAVIER
IDENTITY: CONFIRMED
OCCUPATION: MUTANT LEADER
GROUP AFFILIATION: X-MEN
WHEN DID THIS HAPPEN?
PSYCHIC DAMPENERS ACTIVATED!
STOP READING MY MIND, CHARLES, AND LET'S WAIT FOR EVERYONE.
MY APOLOGIES. HABIT.
REED RICHARDS
ALIAS: MISTER FANTASTIC
GROUP AFFILIATION: FANTASTIC FOUR
OCCUPATION: SCIENTIST, ADVENTURER
IDENTITY: CONFIRMED
GENTLEMEN, I HAVE SOMETHING OF DIRE IMPORTANCE TO--
YOU DO?
I THOUGHT THAT'S WHY YOU CALLED US TOGETHER.
NO. I BROUGHT US TOGETHER FOR MY THING.
WAIT, WHAT IS YOUR THING?
WE SHOULD WAIT--
ENERGY FLUCTUATION.

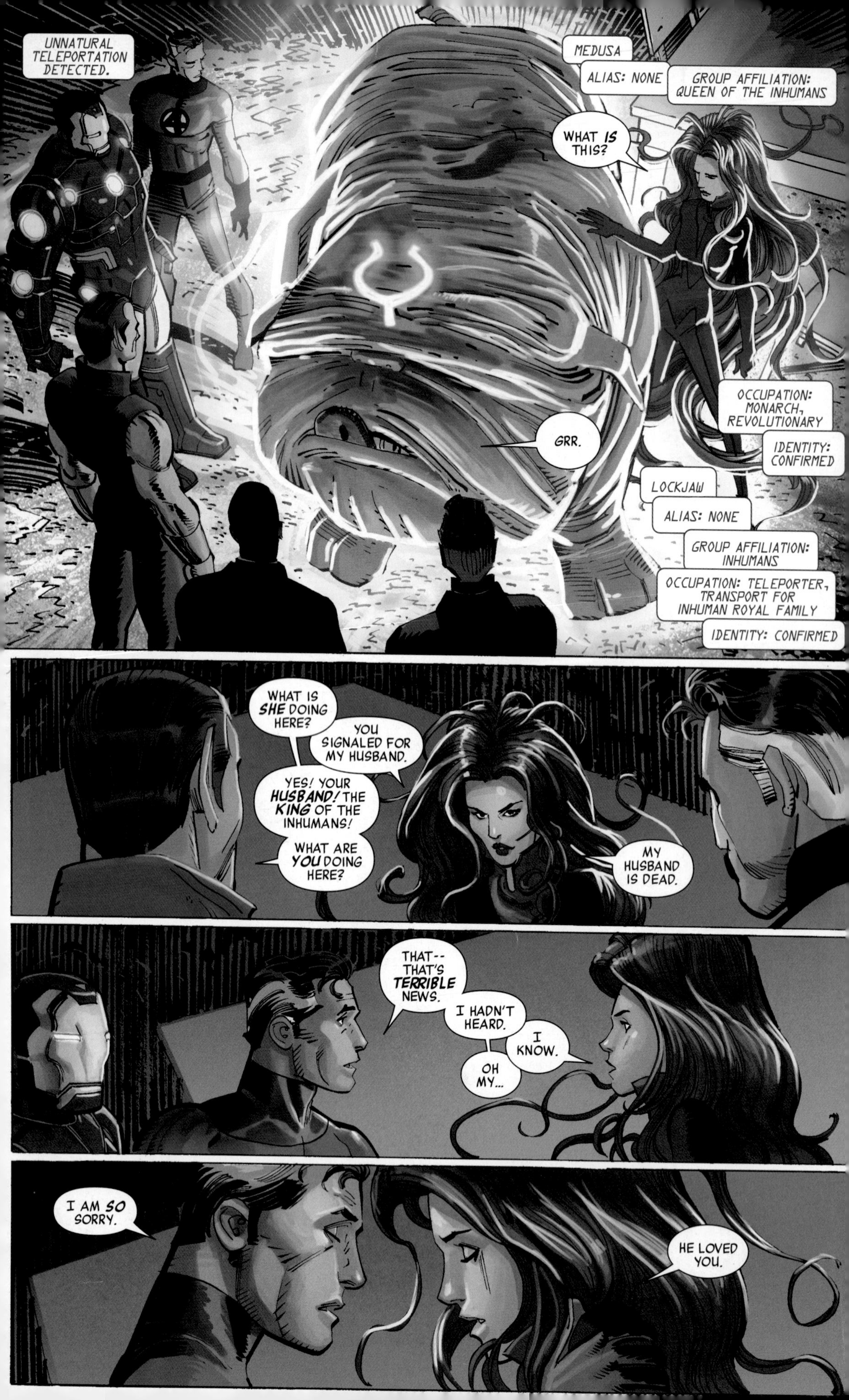
UNNATURAL TELEPORTATION DETECTED.
MEDUSA
ALIAS: NONE
GROUP AFFILIATION: QUEEN OF THE INHUMANS
WHAT IS THIS?
OCCUPATION: MONARCH, REVOLUTIONARY
IDENTITY: CONFIRMED
GRR.
LOCKJAW
ALIAS: NONE
GROUP AFFILIATION: INHUMANS
OCCUPATION: TELEPORTER, TRANSPORT FOR INHUMAN ROYAL FAMILY
IDENTITY: CONFIRMED
WHAT IS SHE DOING HERE?
YOU SIGNALED FOR MY HUSBAND.
YES! YOUR HUSBAND! THE KING OF THE INHUMANS!
WHAT ARE YOU DOING HERE?
MY HUSBAND IS DEAD.
THAT-- THAT'S TERRIBLE NEWS.
I HADN'T HEARD.
OH MY...
I KNOW.
I AM SO SORRY.
HE LOVED YOU.

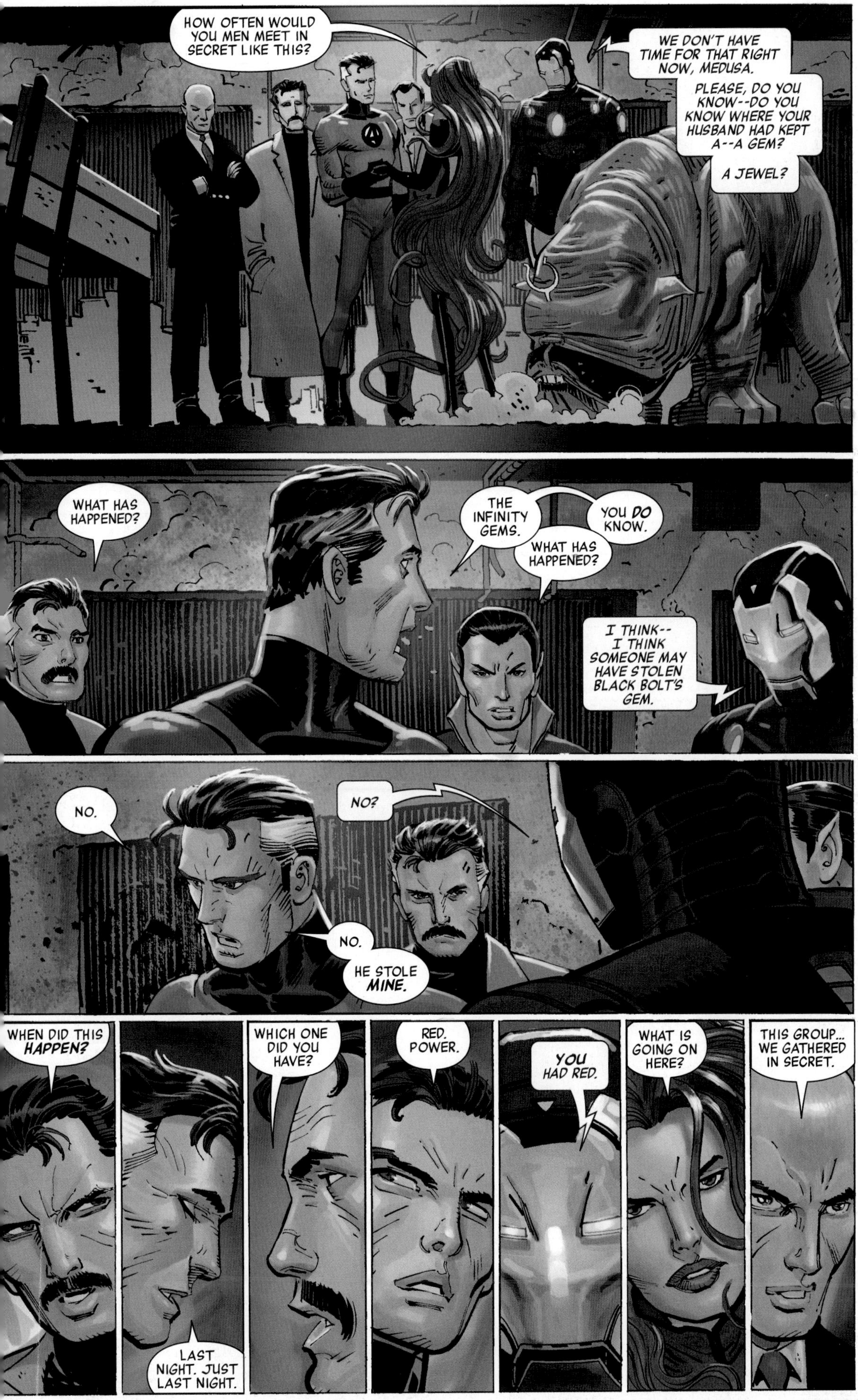

HOW OFTEN WOULD YOU MEN MEET IN SECRET LIKE THIS?
WE DON'T HAVE TIME FOR THAT RIGHT NOW, MEDUSA.
PLEASE, DO YOU KNOW--DO YOU KNOW WHERE YOUR HUSBAND HAD KEPT A--A GEM?
A JEWEL?
WHAT HAS HAPPENED?
THE INFINITY GEMS.
YOU DO KNOW.
WHAT HAS HAPPENED?
I THINK-- I THINK SOMEONE MAY HAVE STOLEN BLACK BOLT'S GEM.
NO.
NO?
NO.
HE STOLE MINE.
WHEN DID THIS HAPPEN?
LAST NIGHT. JUST LAST NIGHT.
WHICH ONE DID YOU HAVE?
RED. POWER.
YOU HAD RED.
WHAT IS GOING ON HERE?
THIS GROUP... WE GATHERED IN SECRET.

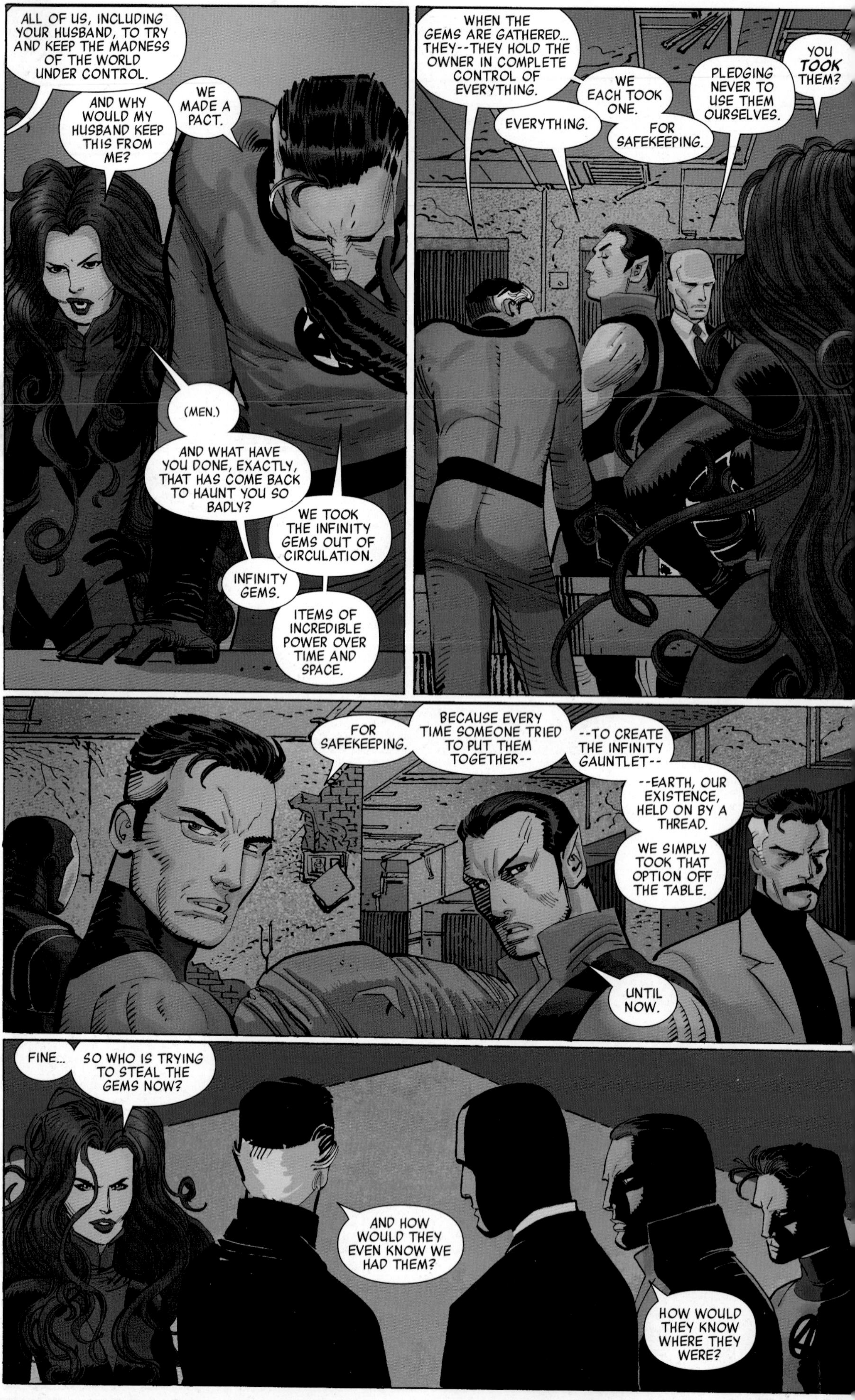
ALL OF US, INCLUDING YOUR HUSBAND, TO TRY AND KEEP THE MADNESS OF THE WORLD UNDER CONTROL.
AND WHY WOULD MY HUSBAND KEEP THIS FROM ME?
WE MADE A PACT.
(MEN.)
AND WHAT HAVE YOU DONE, EXACTLY, THAT HAS COME BACK TO HAUNT YOU SO BADLY?
WE TOOK THE INFINITY GEMS OUT OF CIRCULATION.
INFINITY GEMS.
ITEMS OF INCREDIBLE POWER OVER TIME AND SPACE.
WHEN THE GEMS ARE GATHERED... THEY--THEY HOLD THE OWNER IN COMPLETE CONTROL OF EVERYTHING.
EVERYTHING.
WE EACH TOOK ONE.
FOR SAFEKEEPING.
PLEDGING NEVER TO USE THEM OURSELVES.
YOU *TOOK* THEM?
FOR SAFEKEEPING.
BECAUSE EVERY TIME SOMEONE TRIED TO PUT THEM TOGETHER--
--TO CREATE THE INFINITY GAUNTLET--
--EARTH, OUR EXISTENCE, HELD ON BY A THREAD.
WE SIMPLY TOOK THAT OPTION OFF THE TABLE.
UNTIL NOW.
FINE...
SO WHO IS TRYING TO STEAL THE GEMS NOW?
AND HOW WOULD THEY EVEN KNOW WE HAD THEM?
HOW WOULD THEY KNOW WHERE THEY WERE?

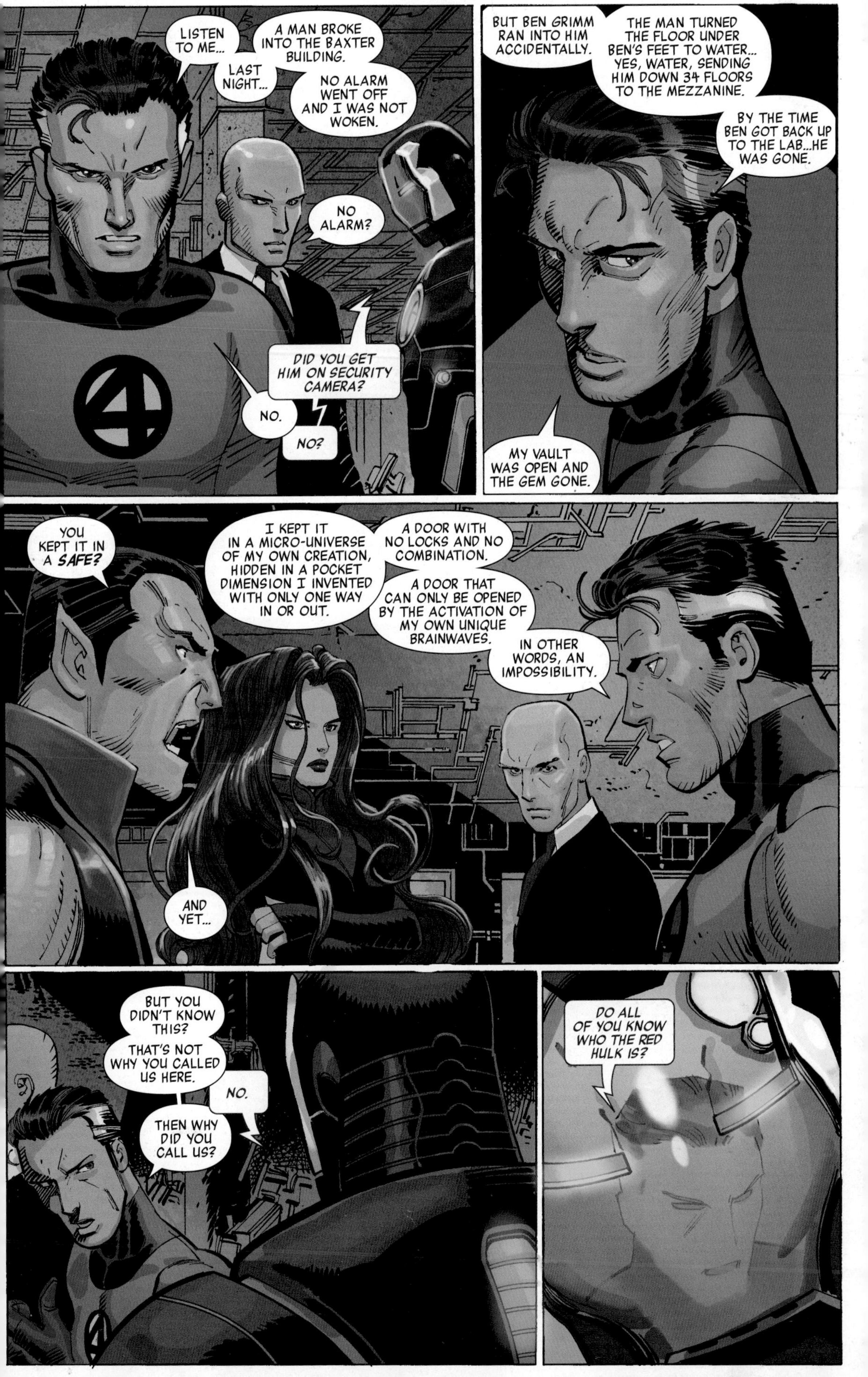
LISTEN TO ME...
LAST NIGHT...
A MAN BROKE INTO THE BAXTER BUILDING.
NO ALARM WENT OFF AND I WAS NOT WOKEN.
NO ALARM?
DID YOU GET HIM ON SECURITY CAMERA?
NO.
NO?
BUT BEN GRIMM RAN INTO HIM ACCIDENTALLY.
THE MAN TURNED THE FLOOR UNDER BEN'S FEET TO WATER... YES, WATER, SENDING HIM DOWN 34 FLOORS TO THE MEZZANINE.
BY THE TIME BEN GOT BACK UP TO THE LAB...HE WAS GONE.
MY VAULT WAS OPEN AND THE GEM GONE.
YOU KEPT IT IN A *SAFE?*
I KEPT IT IN A MICRO-UNIVERSE OF MY OWN CREATION, HIDDEN IN A POCKET DIMENSION I INVENTED WITH ONLY ONE WAY IN OR OUT.
A DOOR WITH NO LOCKS AND NO COMBINATION.
A DOOR THAT CAN ONLY BE OPENED BY THE ACTIVATION OF MY OWN UNIQUE BRAINWAVES.
IN OTHER WORDS, AN IMPOSSIBILITY.
AND YET...
BUT YOU DIDN'T KNOW THIS?
THAT'S NOT WHY YOU CALLED US HERE.
NO.
THEN WHY DID YOU CALL US?
DO ALL OF YOU KNOW WHO THE RED HULK IS?

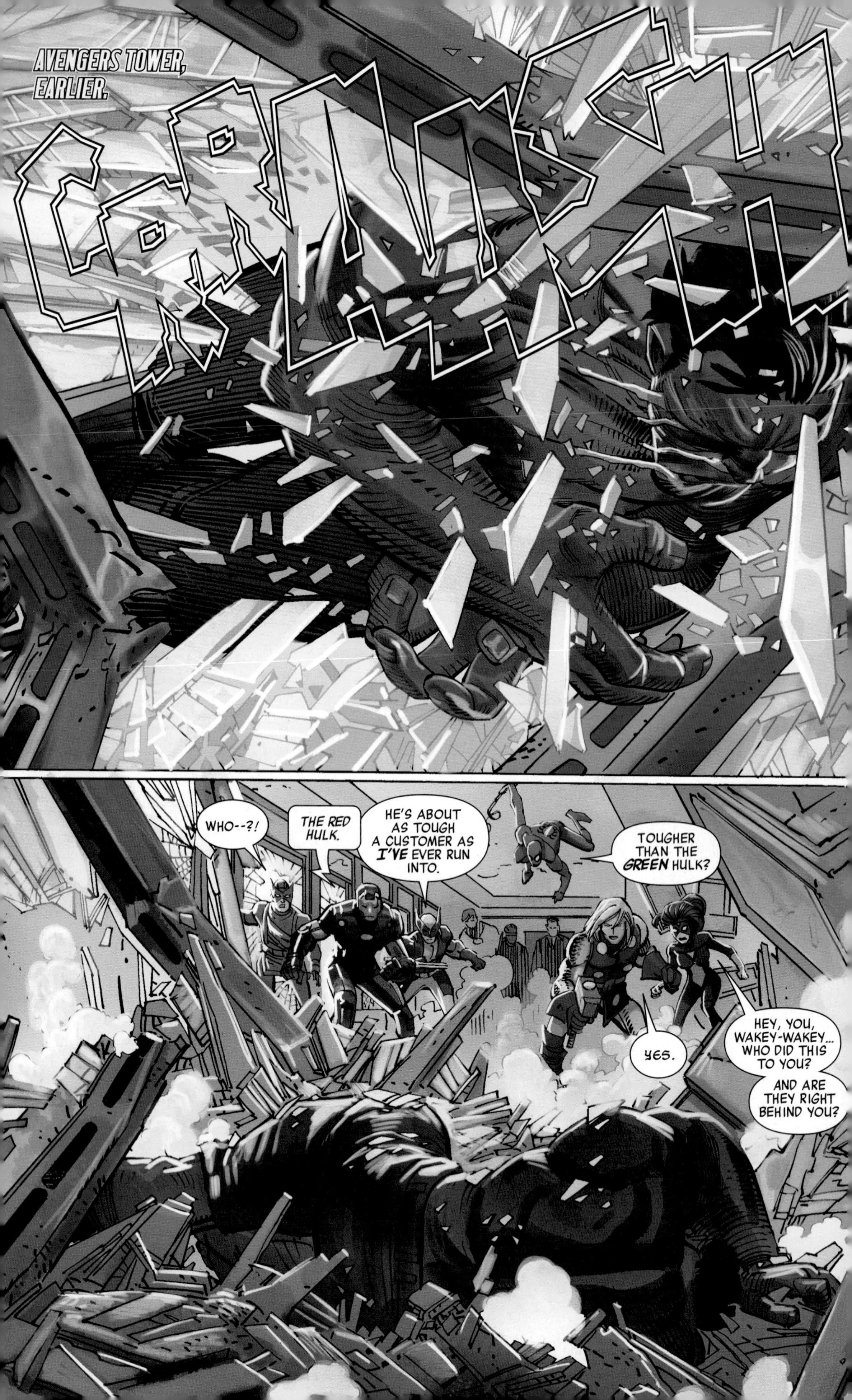
AVENGERS TOWER, EARLIER.
CRAASSH
WHO--?!
THE RED HULK.
HE'S ABOUT AS TOUGH A CUSTOMER AS I'VE EVER RUN INTO.
TOUGHER THAN THE GREEN HULK?
YES.
HEY, YOU, WAKEY-WAKEY... WHO DID THIS TO YOU?
AND ARE THEY RIGHT BEHIND YOU?

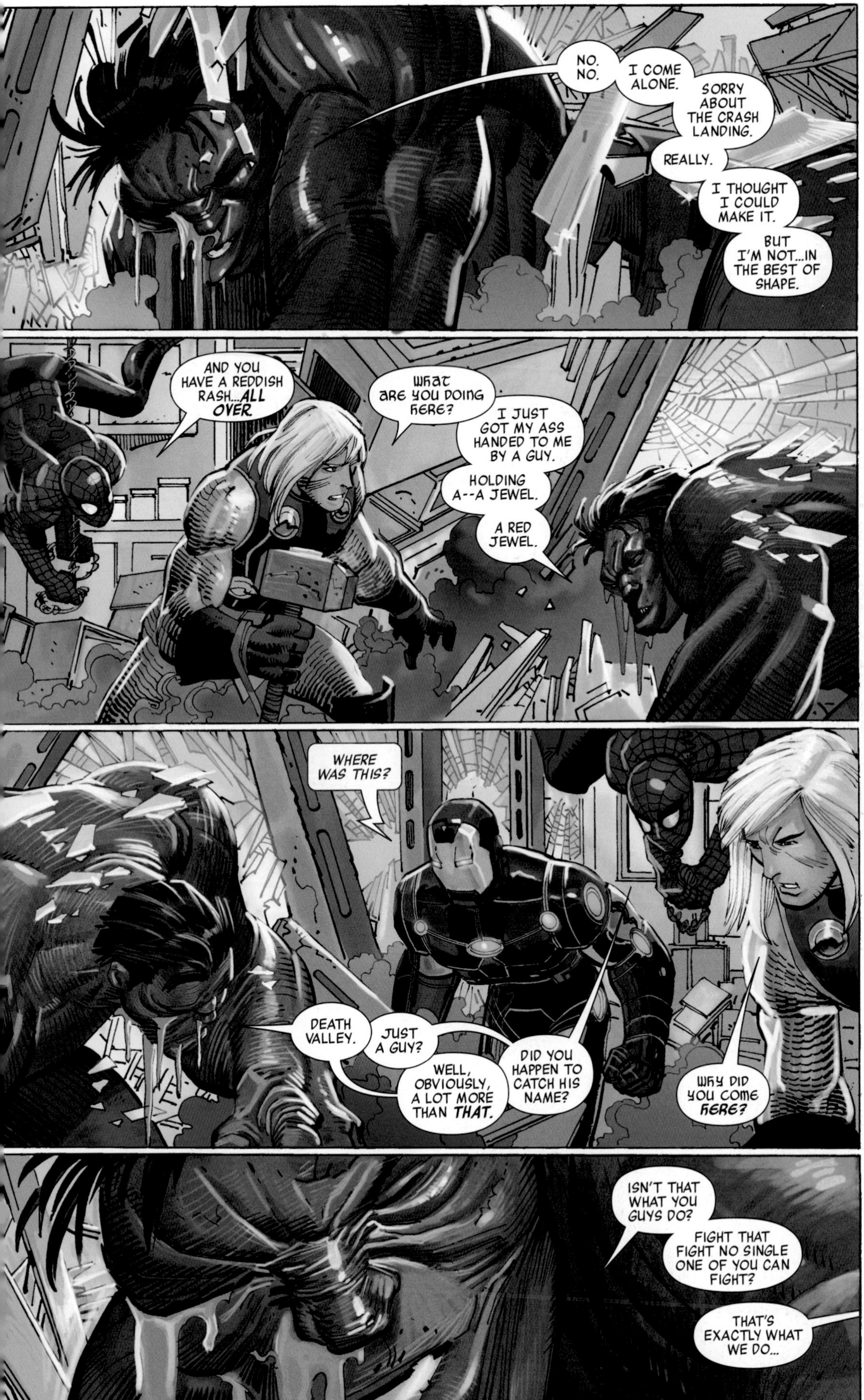
NO. NO.
I COME ALONE.
SORRY ABOUT THE CRASH LANDING.
REALLY.
I THOUGHT I COULD MAKE IT.
BUT I'M NOT...IN THE BEST OF SHAPE.
AND YOU HAVE A REDDISH RASH...ALL OVER.
WHAT ARE YOU DOING HERE?
I JUST GOT MY ASS HANDED TO ME BY A GUY.
HOLDING A--A JEWEL.
A RED JEWEL.
WHERE WAS THIS?
DEATH VALLEY.
JUST A GUY?
WELL, OBVIOUSLY, A LOT MORE THAN THAT.
DID YOU HAPPEN TO CATCH HIS NAME?
WHY DID YOU COME HERE?
ISN'T THAT WHAT YOU GUYS DO?
FIGHT THAT FIGHT NO SINGLE ONE OF YOU CAN FIGHT?
THAT'S EXACTLY WHAT WE DO...

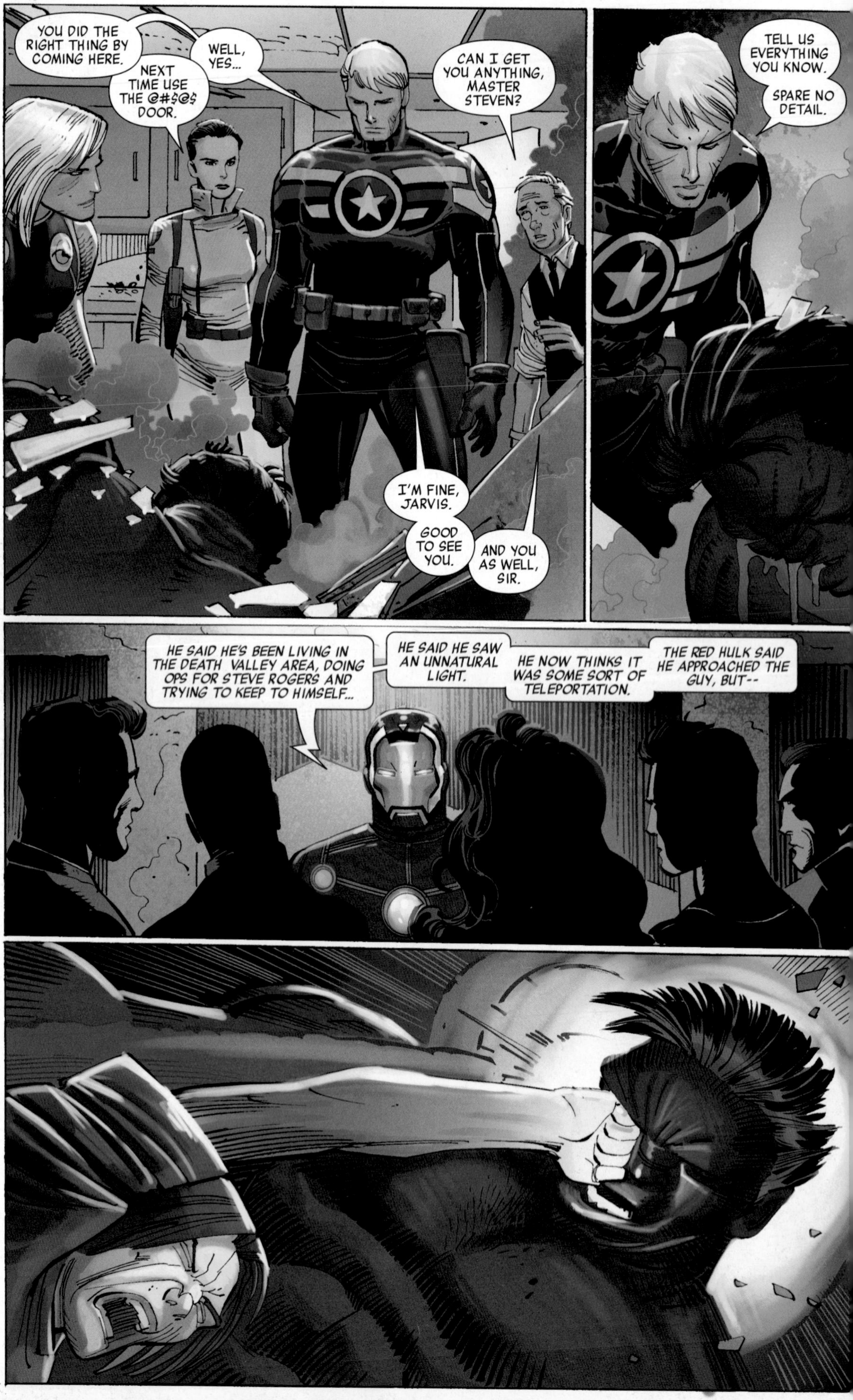
YOU DID THE RIGHT THING BY COMING HERE.
NEXT TIME USE THE @#$@$ DOOR.
WELL, YES...
CAN I GET YOU ANYTHING, MASTER STEVEN?
I'M FINE, JARVIS.
GOOD TO SEE YOU.
AND YOU AS WELL, SIR.
TELL US EVERYTHING YOU KNOW.
SPARE NO DETAIL.
HE SAID HE'S BEEN LIVING IN THE DEATH VALLEY AREA, DOING OPS FOR STEVE ROGERS AND TRYING TO KEEP TO HIMSELF...
HE SAID HE SAW AN UNNATURAL LIGHT.
HE NOW THINKS IT WAS SOME SORT OF TELEPORTATION.
THE RED HULK SAID HE APPROACHED THE GUY, BUT--

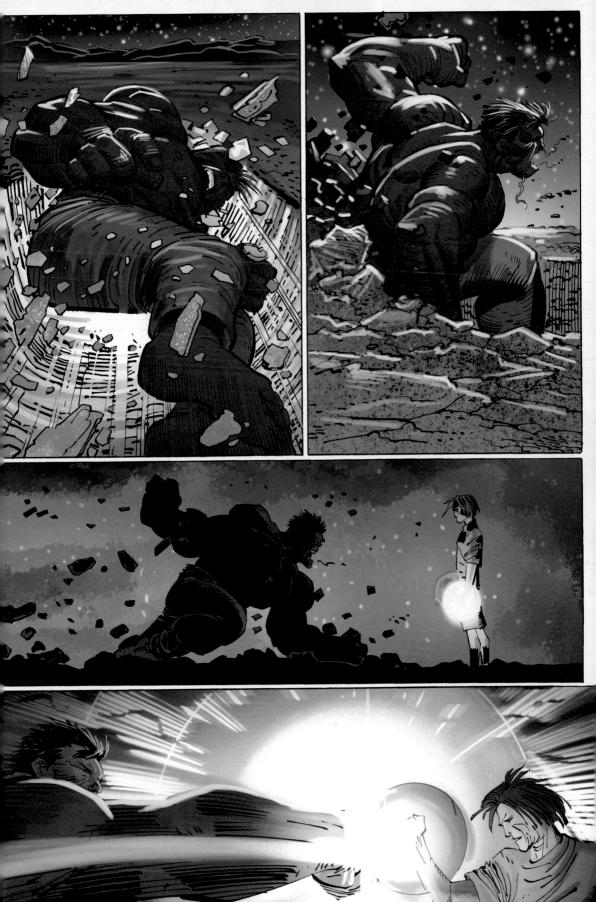

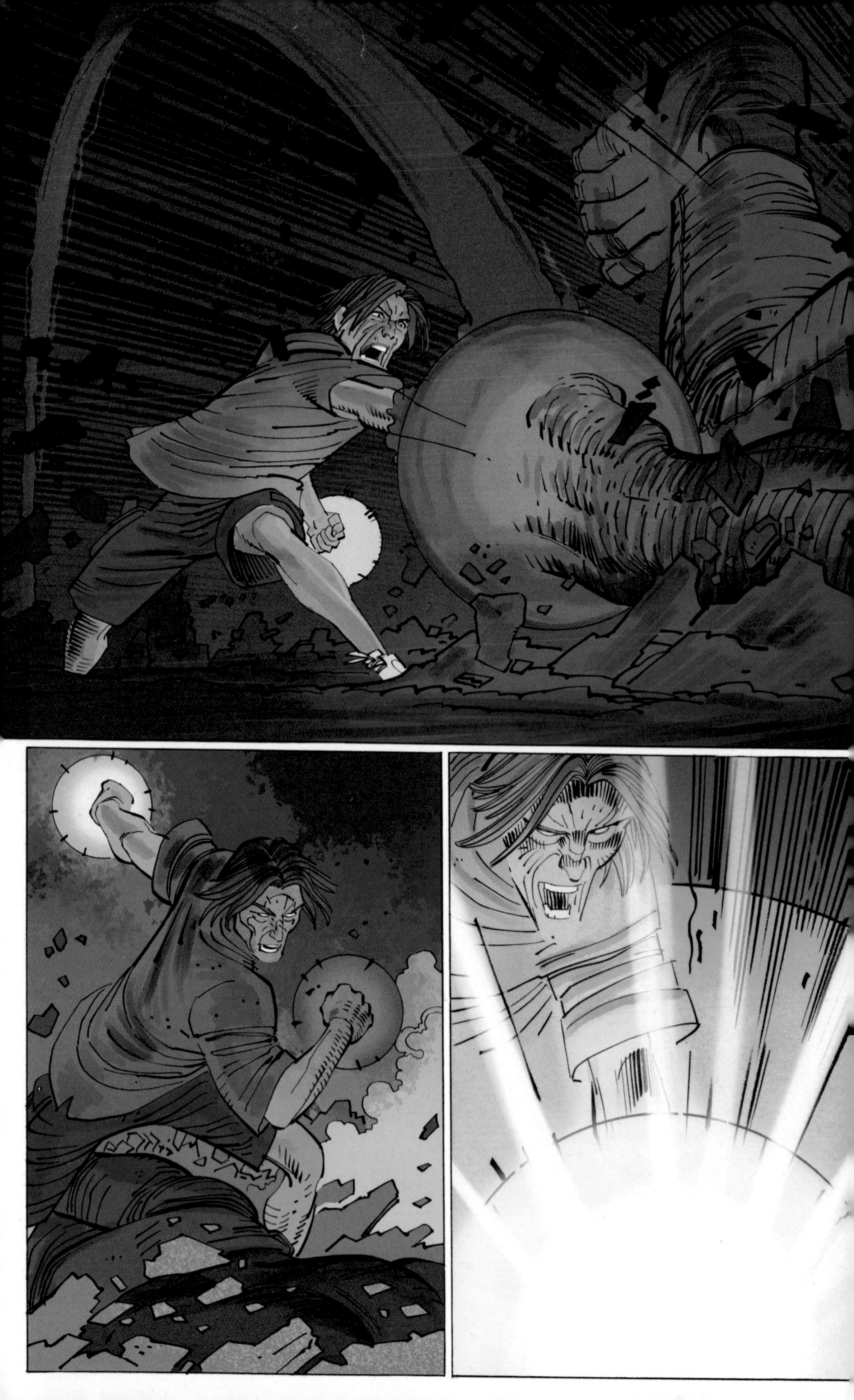

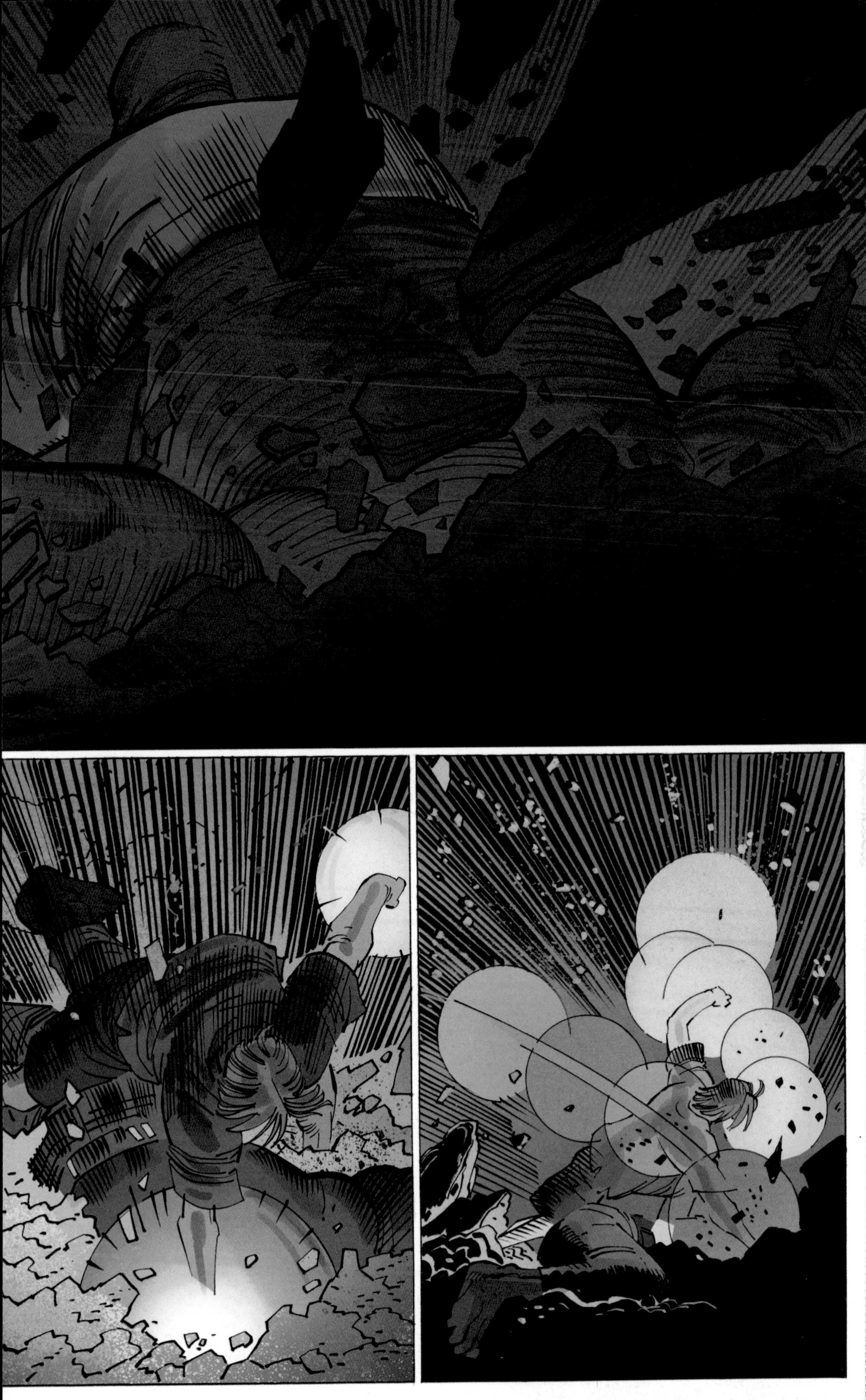

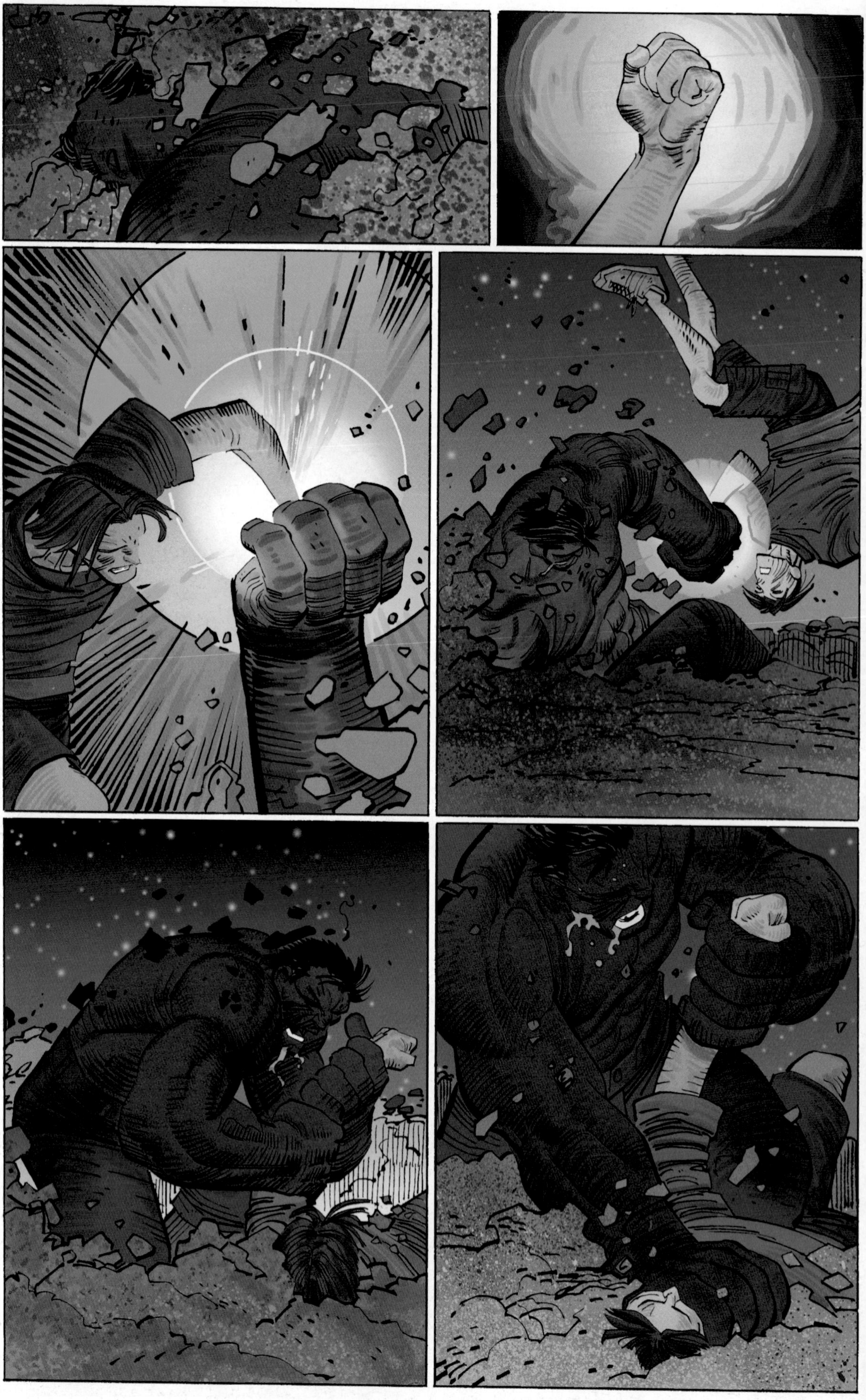

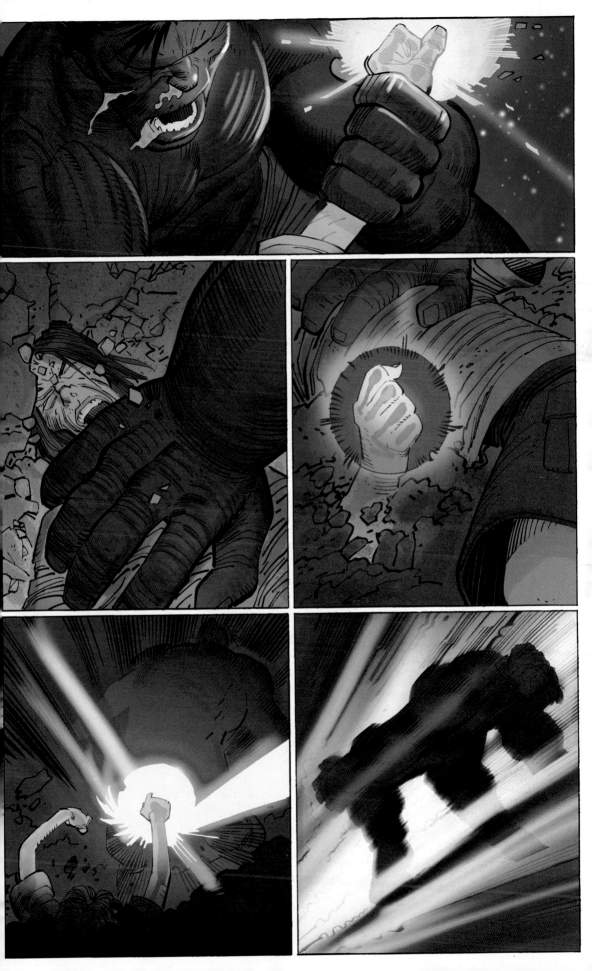

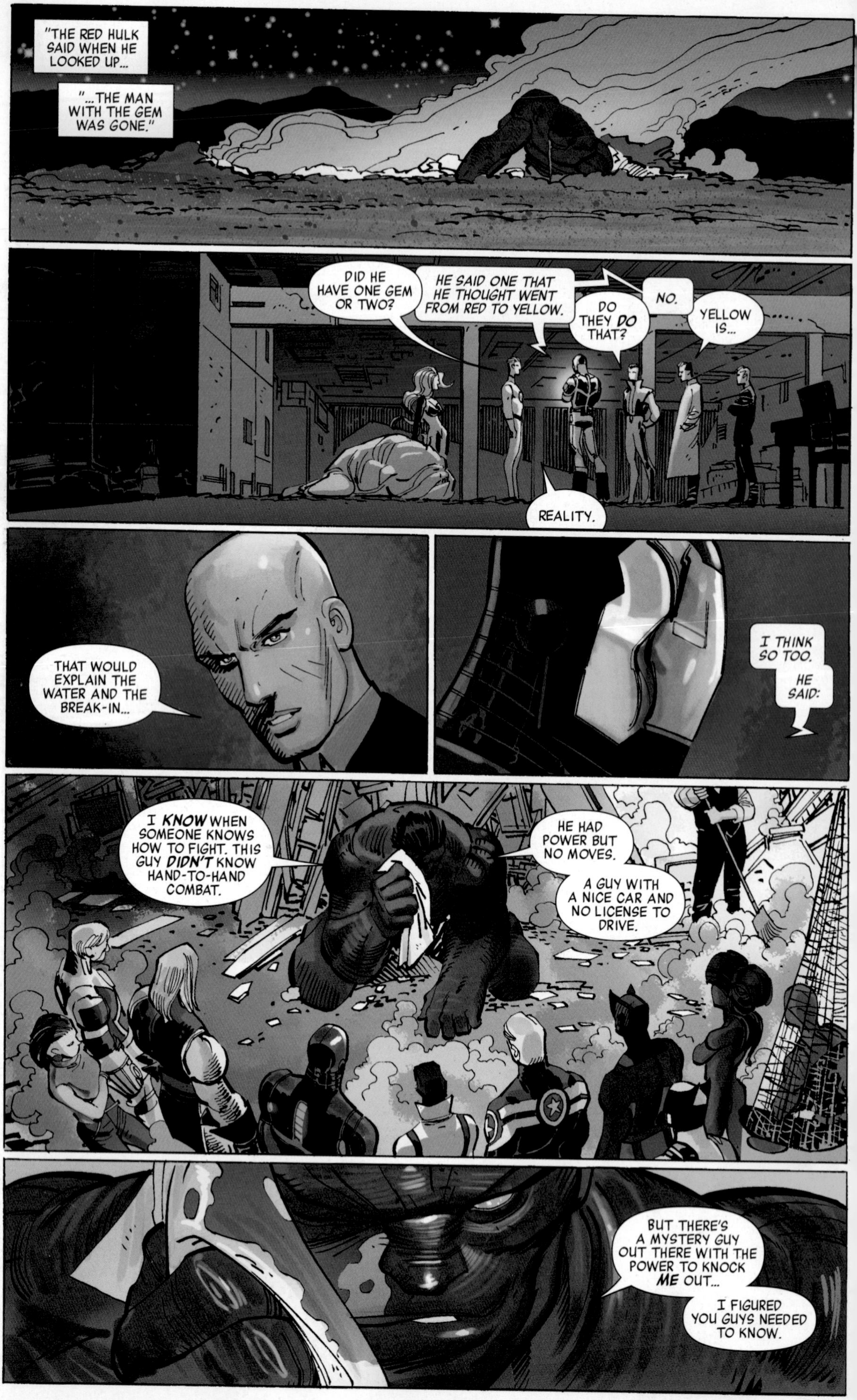
"THE RED HULK SAID WHEN HE LOOKED UP...
"...THE MAN WITH THE GEM WAS GONE."
DID HE HAVE ONE GEM OR TWO?
HE SAID ONE THAT HE THOUGHT WENT FROM RED TO YELLOW.
NO.
DO THEY DO THAT?
YELLOW IS...
REALITY.
THAT WOULD EXPLAIN THE WATER AND THE BREAK-IN...
I THINK SO TOO.
HE SAID:
I KNOW WHEN SOMEONE KNOWS HOW TO FIGHT. THIS GUY DIDN'T KNOW HAND-TO-HAND COMBAT.
HE HAD POWER BUT NO MOVES.
A GUY WITH A NICE CAR AND NO LICENSE TO DRIVE.
BUT THERE'S A MYSTERY GUY OUT THERE WITH THE POWER TO KNOCK ME OUT...
I FIGURED YOU GUYS NEEDED TO KNOW.

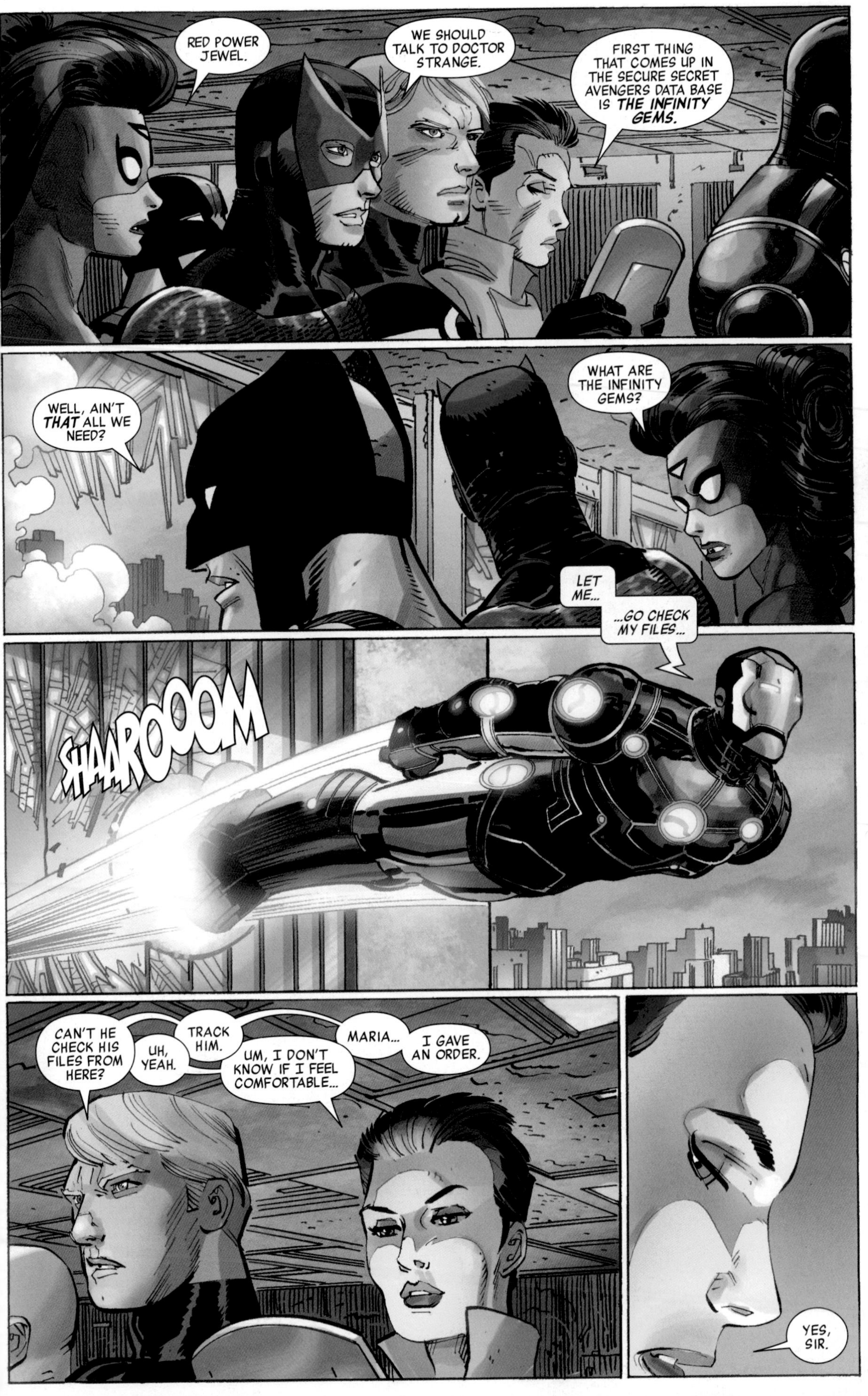
RED POWER JEWEL.
WE SHOULD TALK TO DOCTOR STRANGE.
FIRST THING THAT COMES UP IN THE SECURE SECRET AVENGERS DATA BASE IS THE INFINITY GEMS.
WELL, AIN'T THAT ALL WE NEED?
WHAT ARE THE INFINITY GEMS?
LET ME...
...GO CHECK MY FILES...
SHAAROOOM
CAN'T HE CHECK HIS FILES FROM HERE?
UH, YEAH.
TRACK HIM.
UM, I DON'T KNOW IF I FEEL COMFORTABLE...
MARIA...
I GAVE AN ORDER.
YES, SIR.

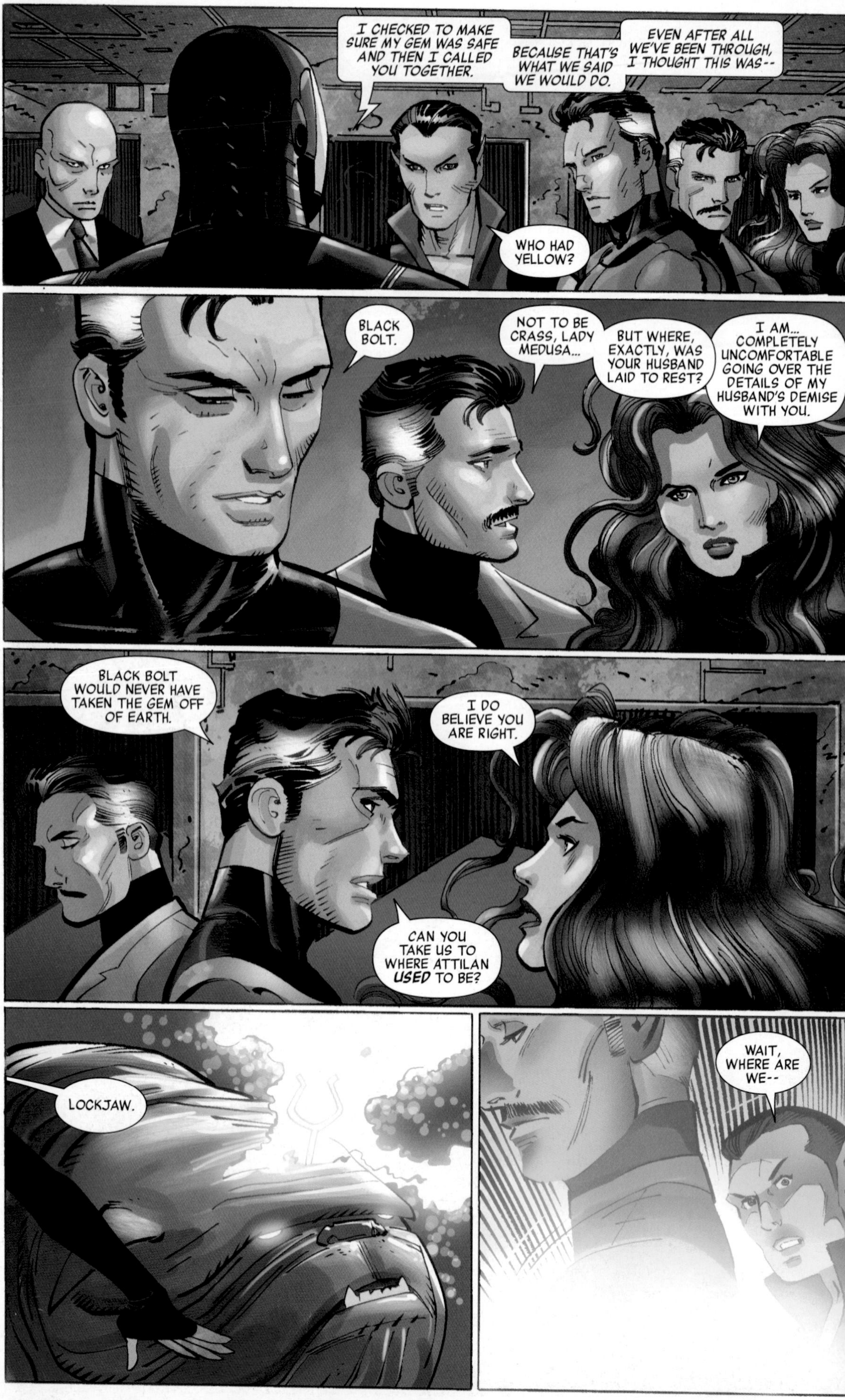
I CHECKED TO MAKE SURE MY GEM WAS SAFE AND THEN I CALLED YOU TOGETHER.
BECAUSE THAT'S WHAT WE SAID WE WOULD DO.
EVEN AFTER ALL WE'VE BEEN THROUGH, I THOUGHT THIS WAS--
WHO HAD YELLOW?
BLACK BOLT.
NOT TO BE CRASS, LADY MEDUSA...
BUT WHERE, EXACTLY, WAS YOUR HUSBAND LAID TO REST?
I AM... COMPLETELY UNCOMFORTABLE GOING OVER THE DETAILS OF MY HUSBAND'S DEMISE WITH YOU.
BLACK BOLT WOULD NEVER HAVE TAKEN THE GEM OFF OF EARTH.
I DO BELIEVE YOU ARE RIGHT.
CAN YOU TAKE US TO WHERE ATTILAN *USED* TO BE?
LOCKJAW.
WAIT, WHERE ARE WE--

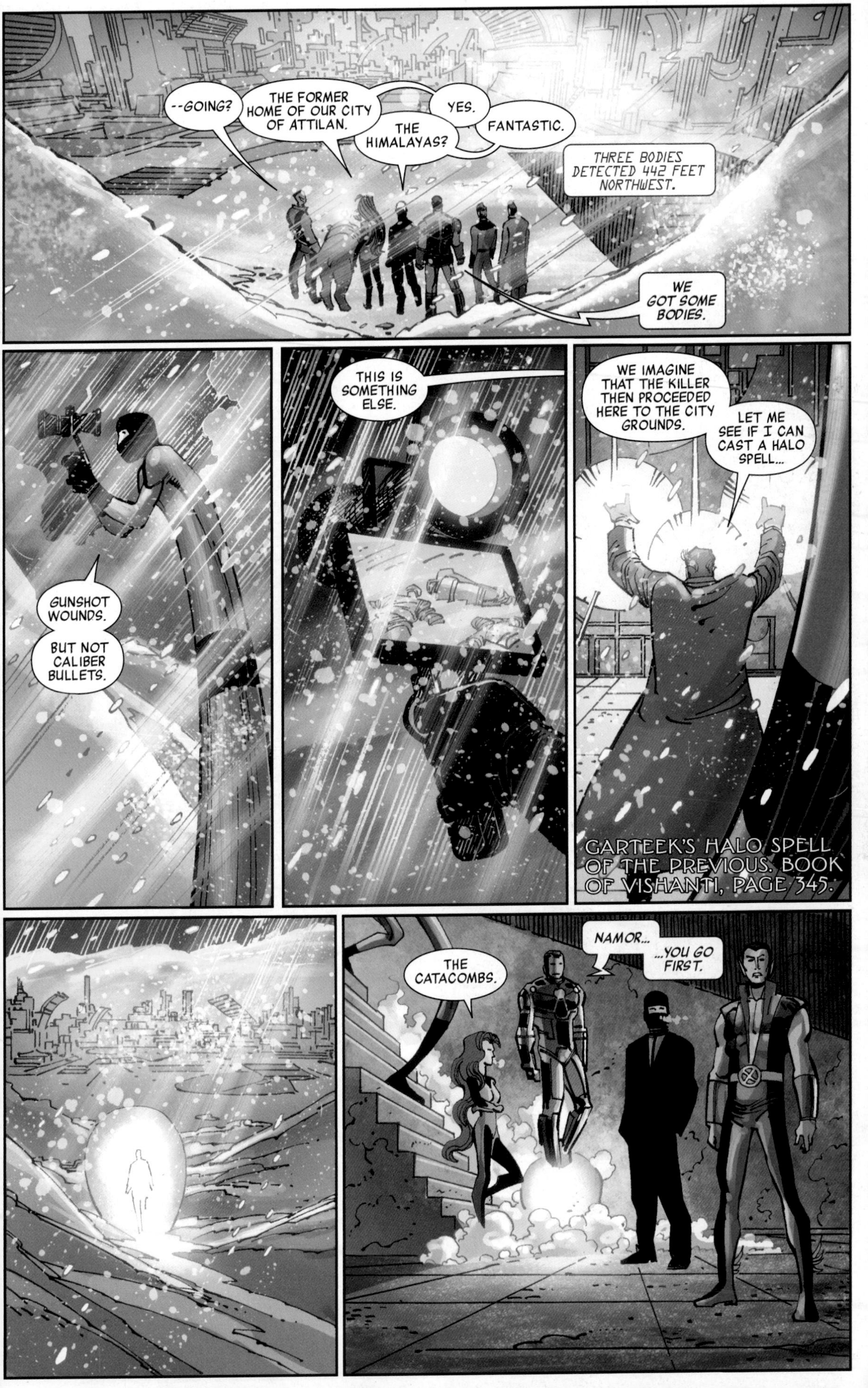
--GOING?
THE FORMER HOME OF OUR CITY OF ATTILAN.
THE HIMALAYAS?
YES.
FANTASTIC.
THREE BODIES DETECTED 442 FEET NORTHWEST.
WE GOT SOME BODIES.
GUNSHOT WOUNDS.
BUT NOT CALIBER BULLETS.
THIS IS SOMETHING ELSE.
WE IMAGINE THAT THE KILLER THEN PROCEEDED HERE TO THE CITY GROUNDS.
LET ME SEE IF I CAN CAST A HALO SPELL...
GARTEEK'S HALO SPELL OF THE PREVIOUS. BOOK OF VISHANTI, PAGE 345.
THE CATACOMBS.
NAMOR...
...YOU GO FIRST.

THERE ARE NO MIND WAVES DOWN HERE. ANIMAL, HUMAN OR INHUMAN...

I KNOW. I WAS MAKING A BAD JOKE.

(I CAN'T REMEMBER YOU MAKING ANY OTHER KIND.)

THIS IS WHERE THE ROYAL FAMILY WOULD JAIL ITS INSURGENTS.

THIS WAY.

WELL...

WE HAVE ANOTHER CRIME SCENE.

SCANNING...

MMRRFF...

THIS IS THE MURDER WEAPON.

ION CHARGE PULSE TECHNOLOGY. VERY NEW.

IT'S A HYDRA WEAPON.

HYDRA IS BEHIND THIS?!

NOT NECESSARILY. SOMEONE WITH A HYDRA *WEAPON*.

AND THEN THERE'S THIS...

THIS IS A.I.M. TECHNOLOGY. THIS IS AN ENVIRONMENTAL ENERGY SOURCE SCANNER.

WHICH MEANS?

A SUPER-HIGH-TECH PIECE OF EQUIPMENT-- LIKE--LIKE THE THING YOU USE TO LOOK FOR METAL ON THE BEACH.

WHO MAKES THEM? WHERE CAN YOU GET ONE?

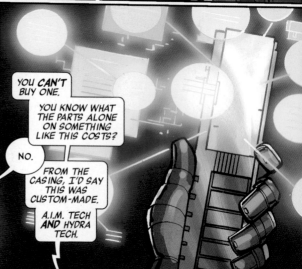

YOU *CAN'T* BUY ONE.

YOU KNOW WHAT THE PARTS ALONE ON SOMETHING LIKE THIS COSTS?

NO.

FROM THE CASING, I'D SAY THIS WAS CUSTOM-MADE.

A.I.M. TECH *AND* HYDRA TECH.

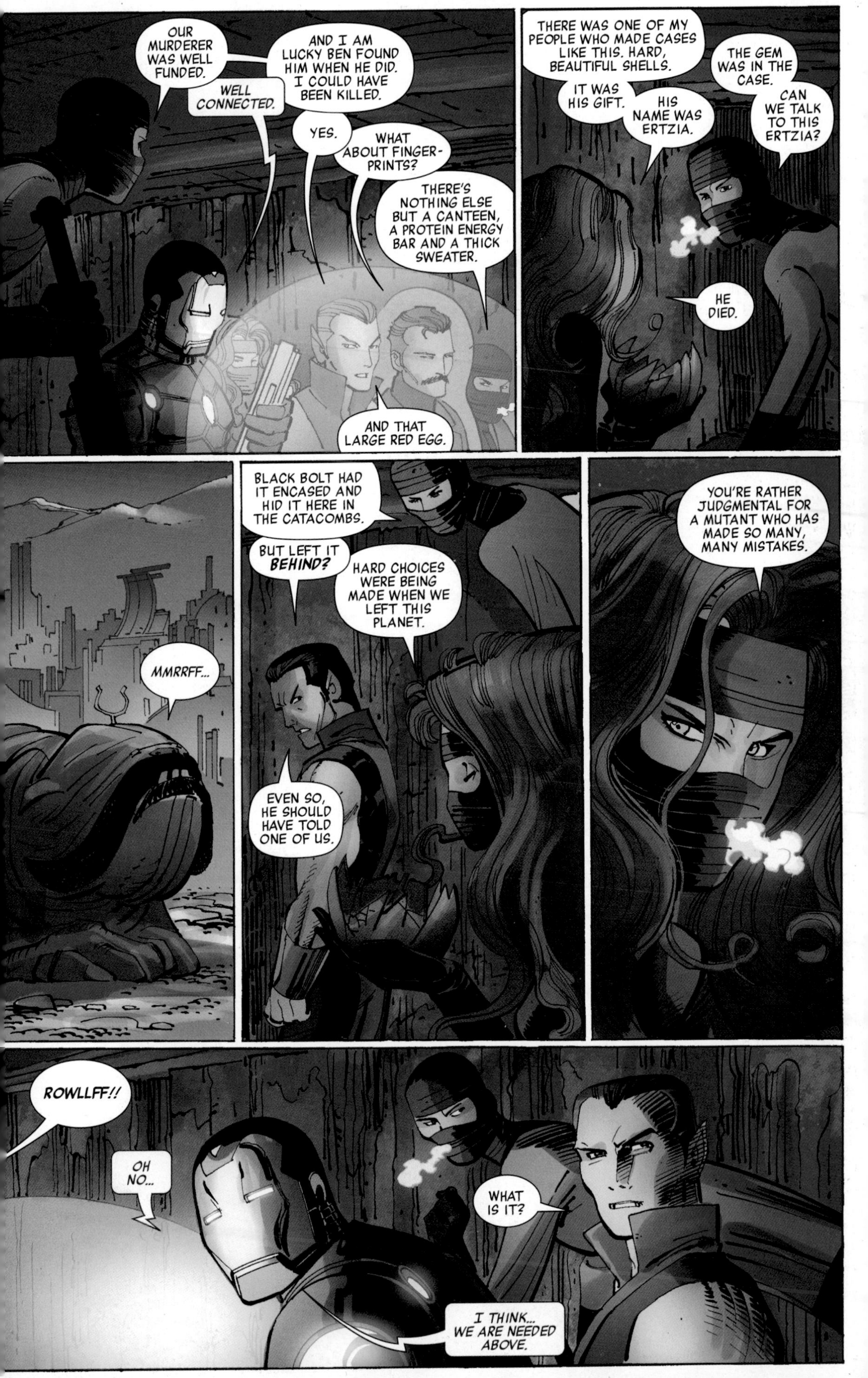
OUR MURDERER WAS WELL FUNDED.
WELL CONNECTED.
AND I AM LUCKY BEN FOUND HIM WHEN HE DID. I COULD HAVE BEEN KILLED.
YES.
WHAT ABOUT FINGER-PRINTS?
THERE'S NOTHING ELSE BUT A CANTEEN, A PROTEIN ENERGY BAR AND A THICK SWEATER.
AND THAT LARGE RED EGG.
THERE WAS ONE OF MY PEOPLE WHO MADE CASES LIKE THIS. HARD, BEAUTIFUL SHELLS.
IT WAS HIS GIFT.
HIS NAME WAS ERTZIA.
THE GEM WAS IN THE CASE.
CAN WE TALK TO THIS ERTZIA?
HE DIED.
MMRRFF...
BLACK BOLT HAD IT ENCASED AND HID IT HERE IN THE CATACOMBS.
BUT LEFT IT BEHIND?
HARD CHOICES WERE BEING MADE WHEN WE LEFT THIS PLANET.
EVEN SO, HE SHOULD HAVE TOLD ONE OF US.
YOU'RE RATHER JUDGMENTAL FOR A MUTANT WHO HAS MADE SO MANY, MANY MISTAKES.
ROWLLFF!!
OH NO...
WHAT IS IT?
I THINK... WE ARE NEEDED ABOVE.

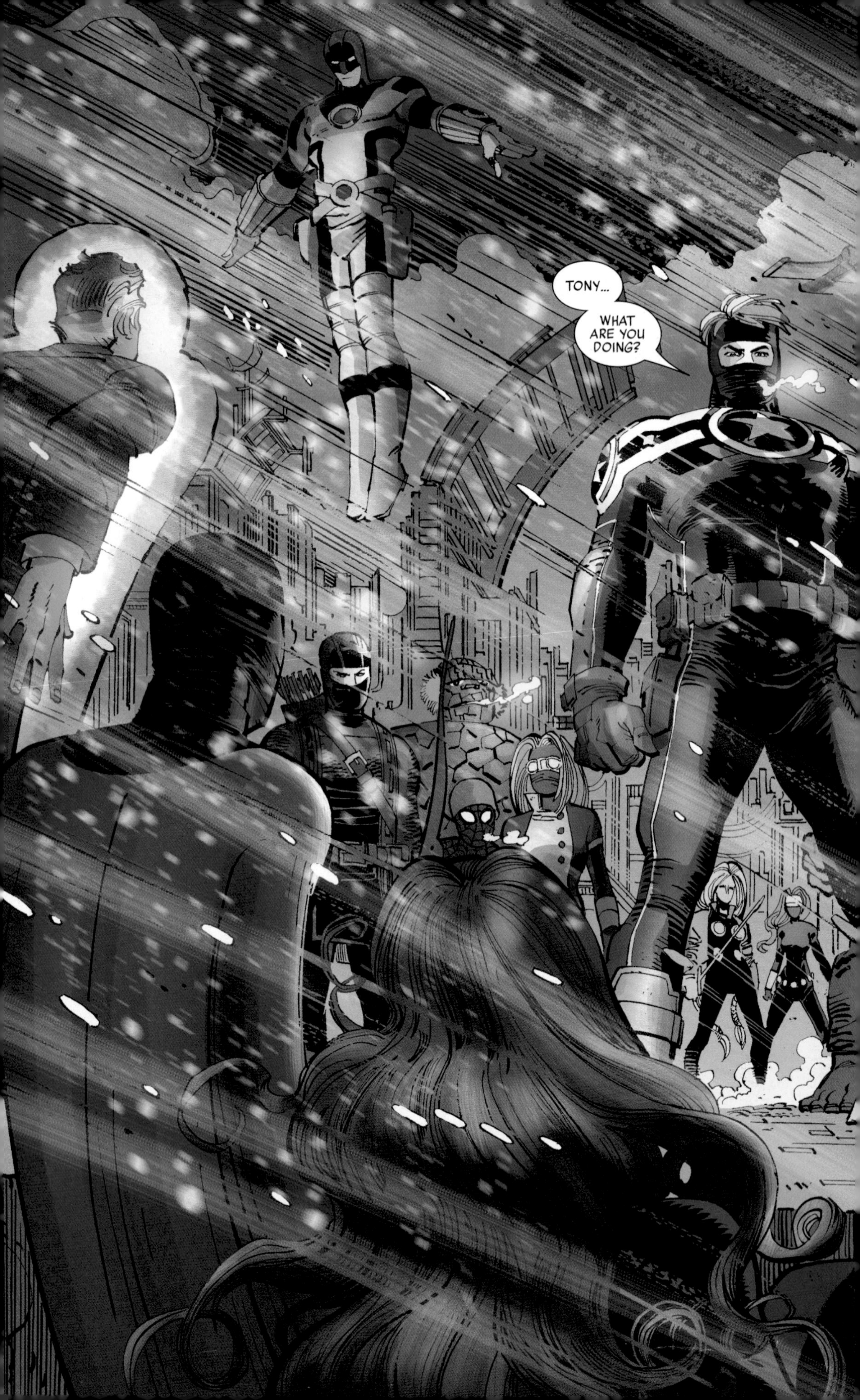
TONY...
WHAT ARE YOU DOING?

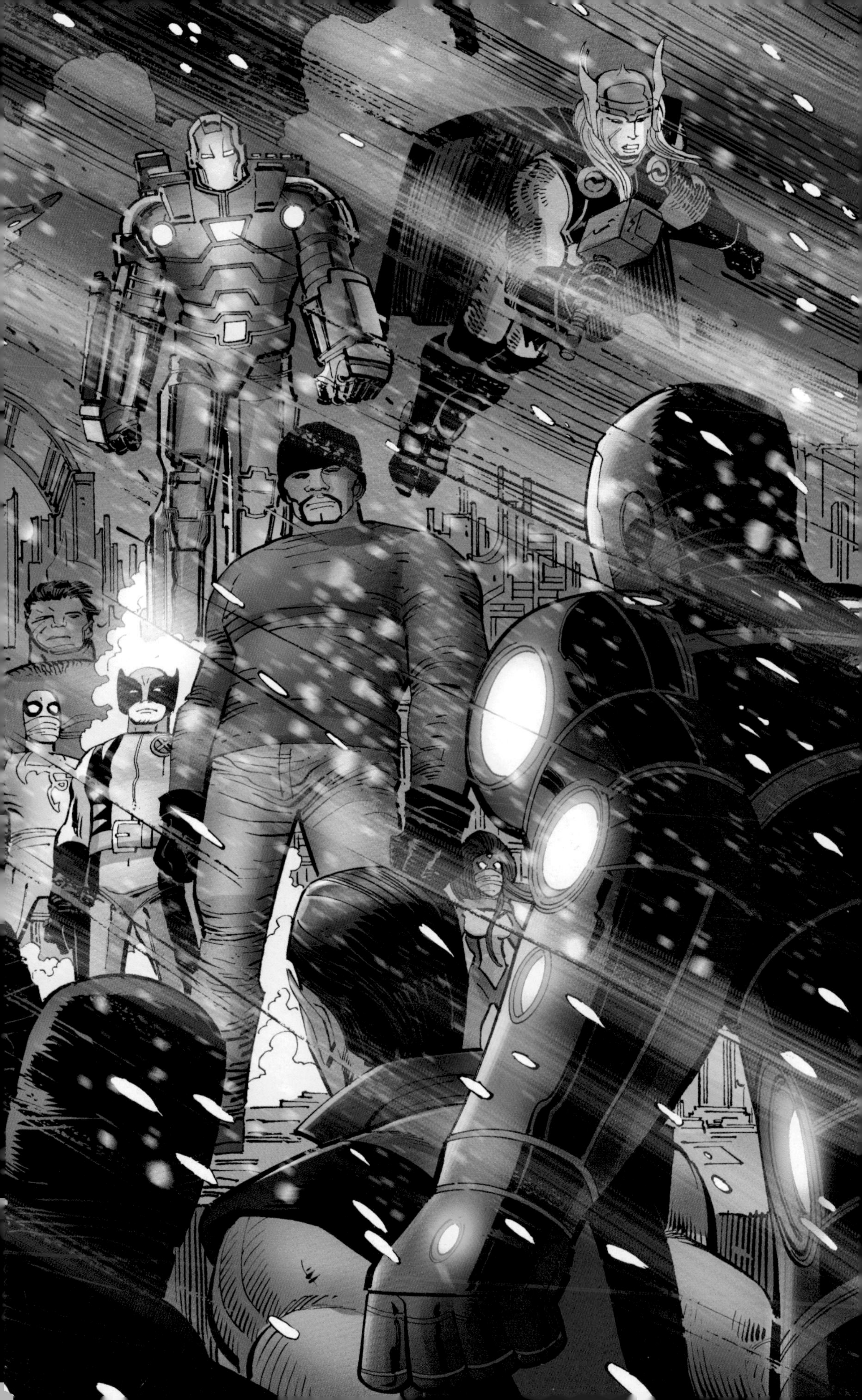

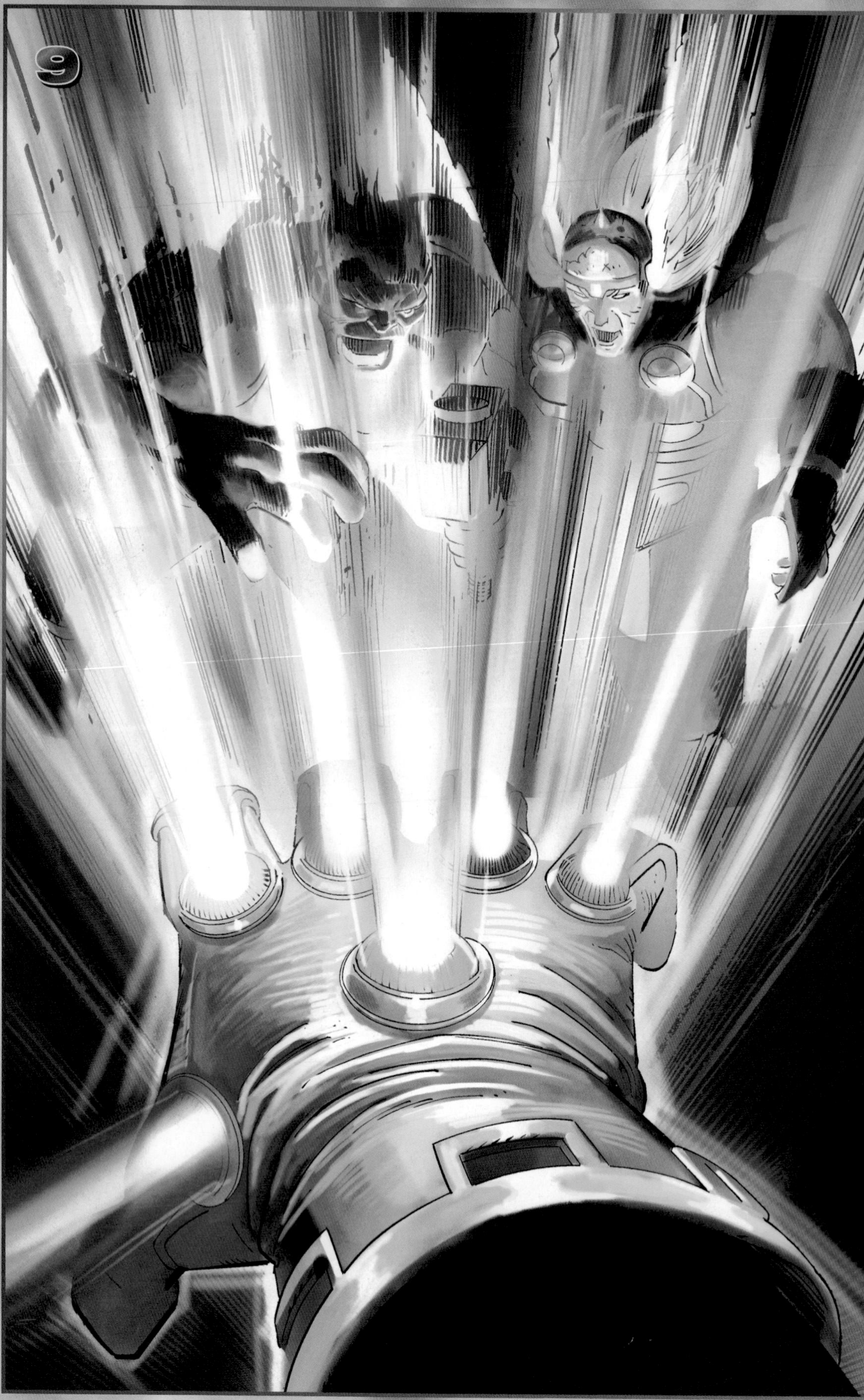
9

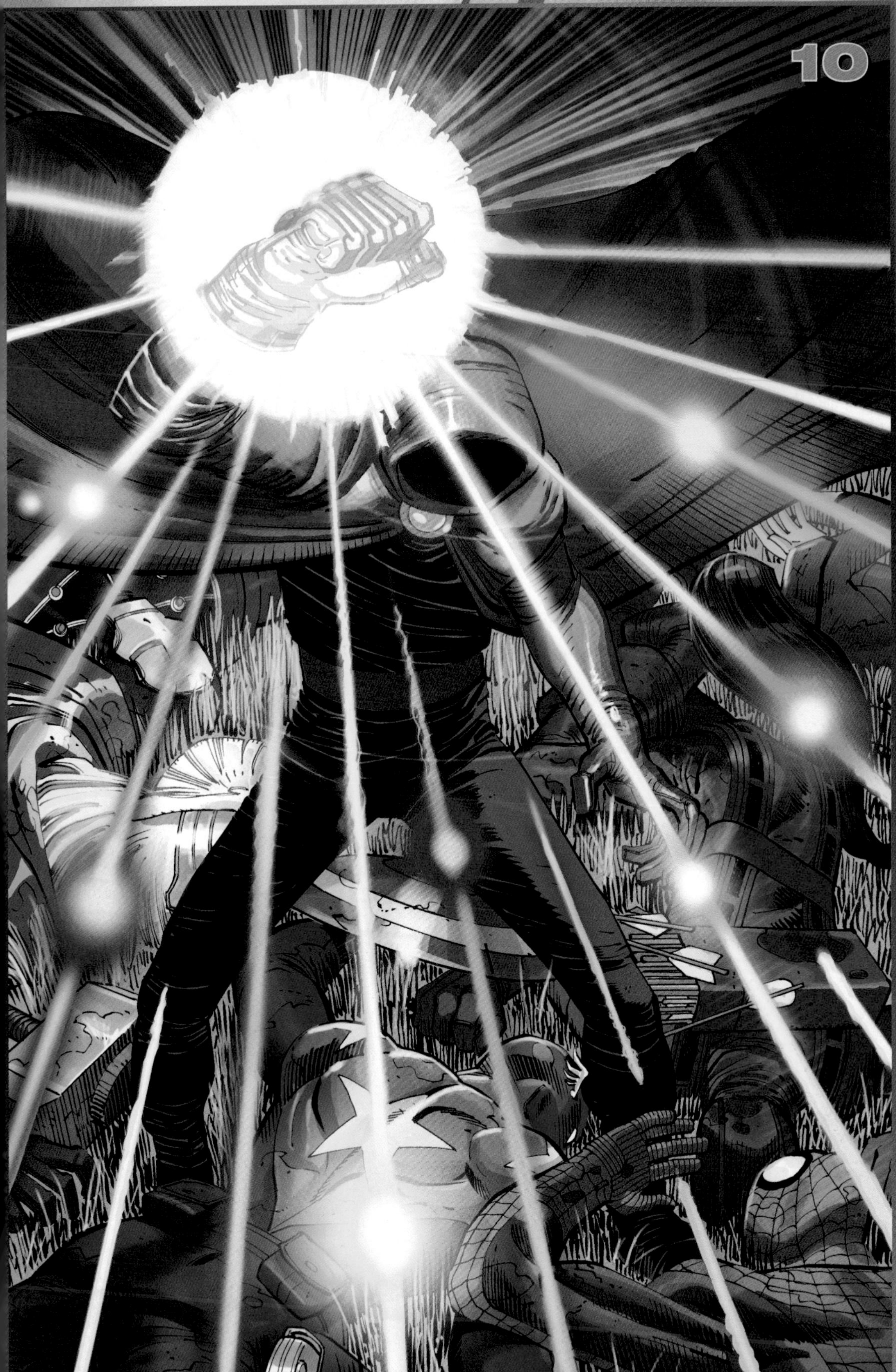
10

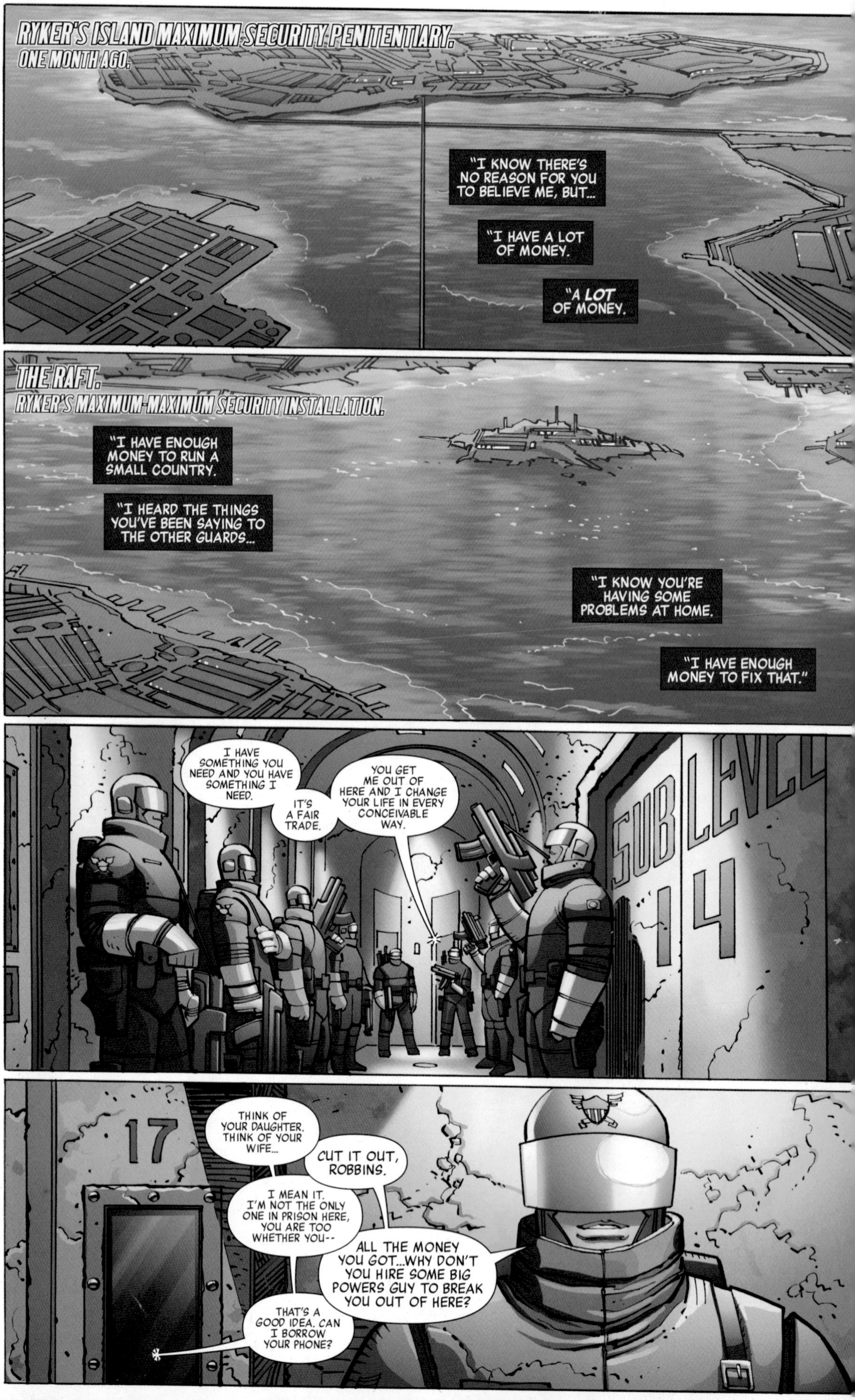

RYKER'S ISLAND MAXIMUM SECURITY PENITENTIARY.
ONE MONTH AGO.
"I KNOW THERE'S NO REASON FOR YOU TO BELIEVE ME, BUT...
"I HAVE A LOT OF MONEY.
"A LOT OF MONEY.
THE RAFT.
RYKER'S MAXIMUM-MAXIMUM SECURITY INSTALLATION.
"I HAVE ENOUGH MONEY TO RUN A SMALL COUNTRY.
"I HEARD THE THINGS YOU'VE BEEN SAYING TO THE OTHER GUARDS...
"I KNOW YOU'RE HAVING SOME PROBLEMS AT HOME.
"I HAVE ENOUGH MONEY TO FIX THAT."
I HAVE SOMETHING YOU NEED AND YOU HAVE SOMETHING I NEED.
IT'S A FAIR TRADE.
YOU GET ME OUT OF HERE AND I CHANGE YOUR LIFE IN EVERY CONCEIVABLE WAY.
SUB LEVEL 14
17
THINK OF YOUR DAUGHTER. THINK OF YOUR WIFE...
CUT IT OUT, ROBBINS.
I MEAN IT. I'M NOT THE ONLY ONE IN PRISON HERE, YOU ARE TOO WHETHER YOU--
ALL THE MONEY YOU GOT...WHY DON'T YOU HIRE SOME BIG POWERS GUY TO BREAK YOU OUT OF HERE?
THAT'S A GOOD IDEA. CAN I BORROW YOUR PHONE?

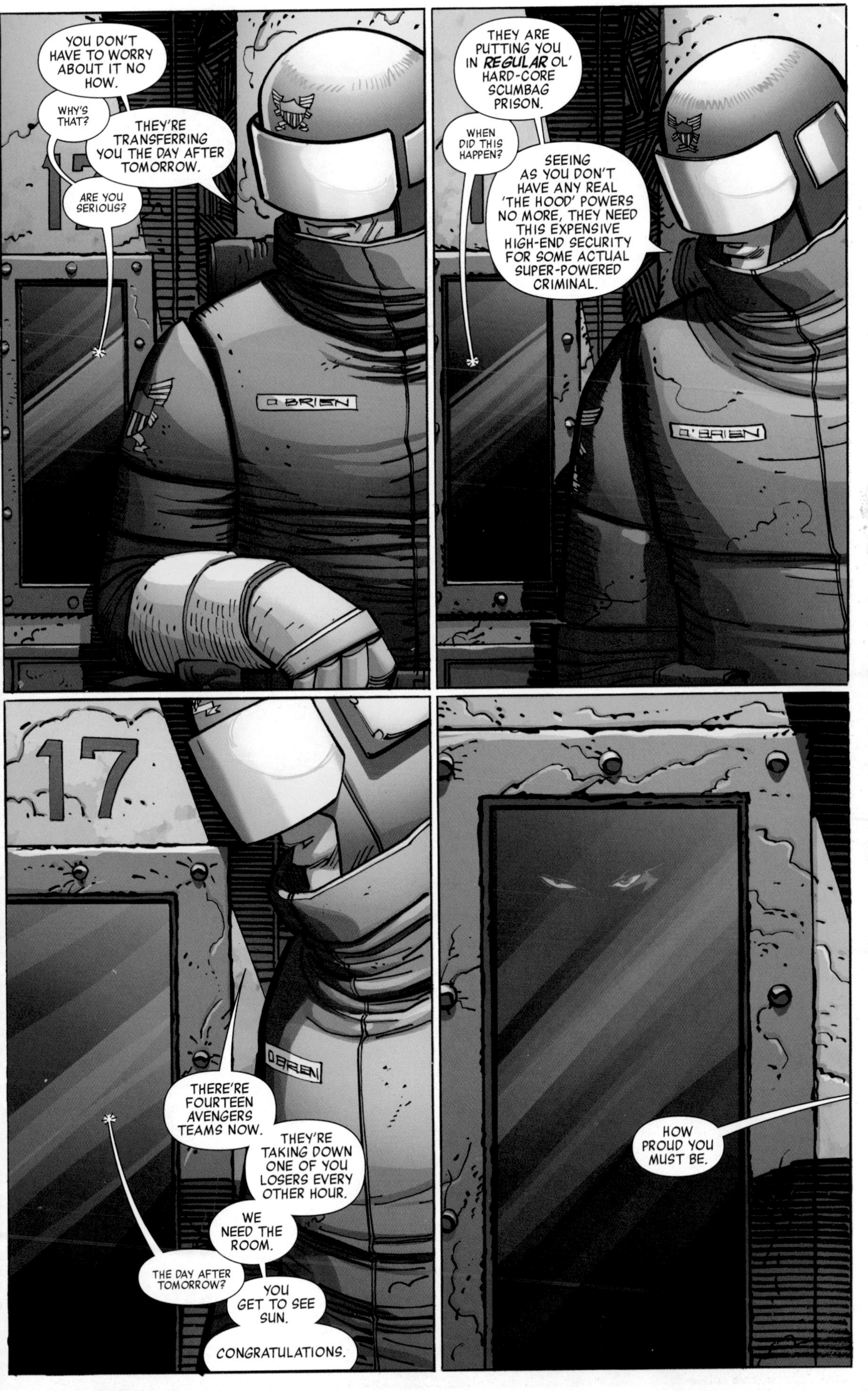
YOU DON'T HAVE TO WORRY ABOUT IT NO HOW.
WHY'S THAT?
THEY'RE TRANSFERRING YOU THE DAY AFTER TOMORROW.
ARE YOU SERIOUS?
O'BRIEN
THEY ARE PUTTING YOU IN *REGULAR* OL' HARD-CORE SCUMBAG PRISON.
WHEN DID THIS HAPPEN?
SEEING AS YOU DON'T HAVE ANY REAL 'THE HOOD' POWERS NO MORE, THEY NEED THIS EXPENSIVE HIGH-END SECURITY FOR SOME ACTUAL SUPER-POWERED CRIMINAL.
O'BRIEN
17
O'BRIEN
THERE'RE FOURTEEN AVENGERS TEAMS NOW.
THEY'RE TAKING DOWN ONE OF YOU LOSERS EVERY OTHER HOUR.
WE NEED THE ROOM.
THE DAY AFTER TOMORROW?
YOU GET TO SEE SUN.
CONGRATULATIONS.
HOW PROUD YOU MUST BE.

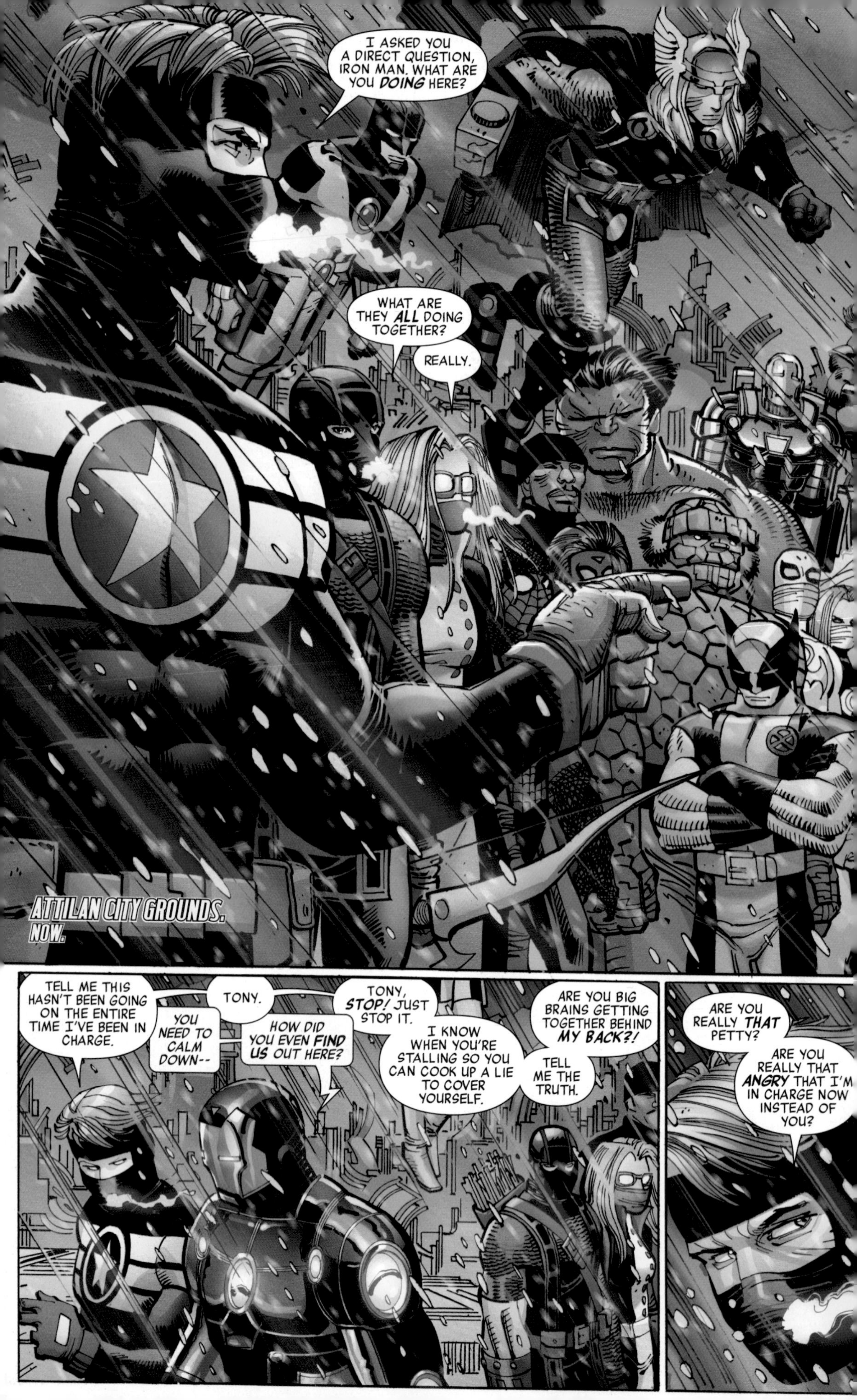
I ASKED YOU A DIRECT QUESTION, IRON MAN. WHAT ARE YOU *DOING* HERE?
WHAT ARE THEY *ALL* DOING TOGETHER?
REALLY.
ATTILAN CITY GROUNDS. NOW.
TELL ME THIS HASN'T BEEN GOING ON THE ENTIRE TIME I'VE BEEN IN CHARGE.
TONY.
YOU NEED TO CALM DOWN--
HOW DID YOU EVEN *FIND US* OUT HERE?
TONY, *STOP!* JUST STOP IT.
I KNOW WHEN YOU'RE STALLING SO YOU CAN COOK UP A LIE TO COVER YOURSELF.
ARE YOU BIG BRAINS GETTING TOGETHER BEHIND *MY BACK?!*
TELL ME THE TRUTH.
ARE YOU REALLY *THAT* PETTY?
ARE YOU REALLY THAT *ANGRY* THAT I'M IN CHARGE NOW INSTEAD OF YOU?

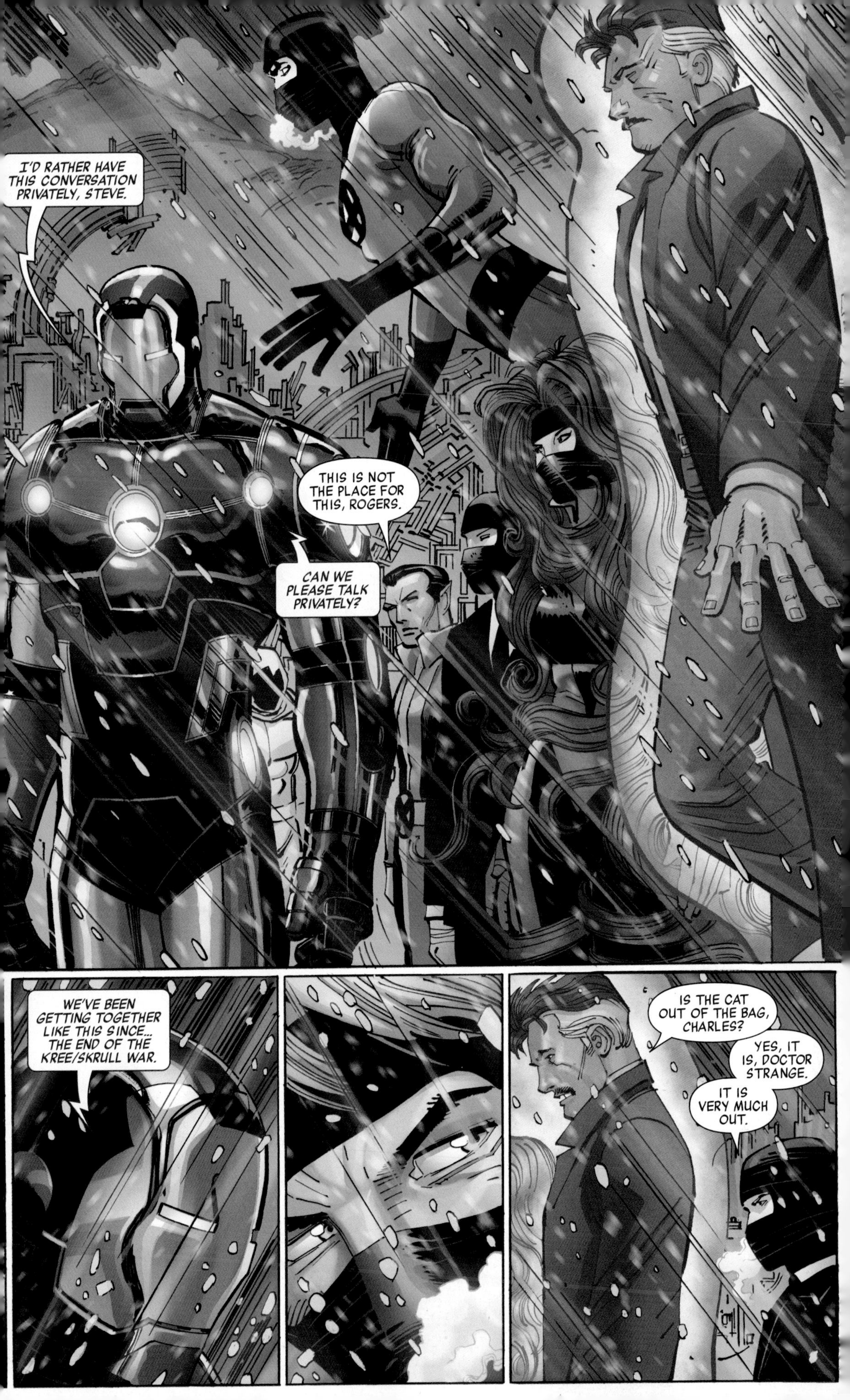
I'D RATHER HAVE THIS CONVERSATION PRIVATELY, STEVE.
THIS IS NOT THE PLACE FOR THIS, ROGERS.
CAN WE PLEASE TALK PRIVATELY?
WE'VE BEEN GETTING TOGETHER LIKE THIS SINCE... THE END OF THE KREE/SKRULL WAR.
IS THE CAT OUT OF THE BAG, CHARLES?
YES, IT IS, DOCTOR STRANGE.
IT IS VERY MUCH OUT.

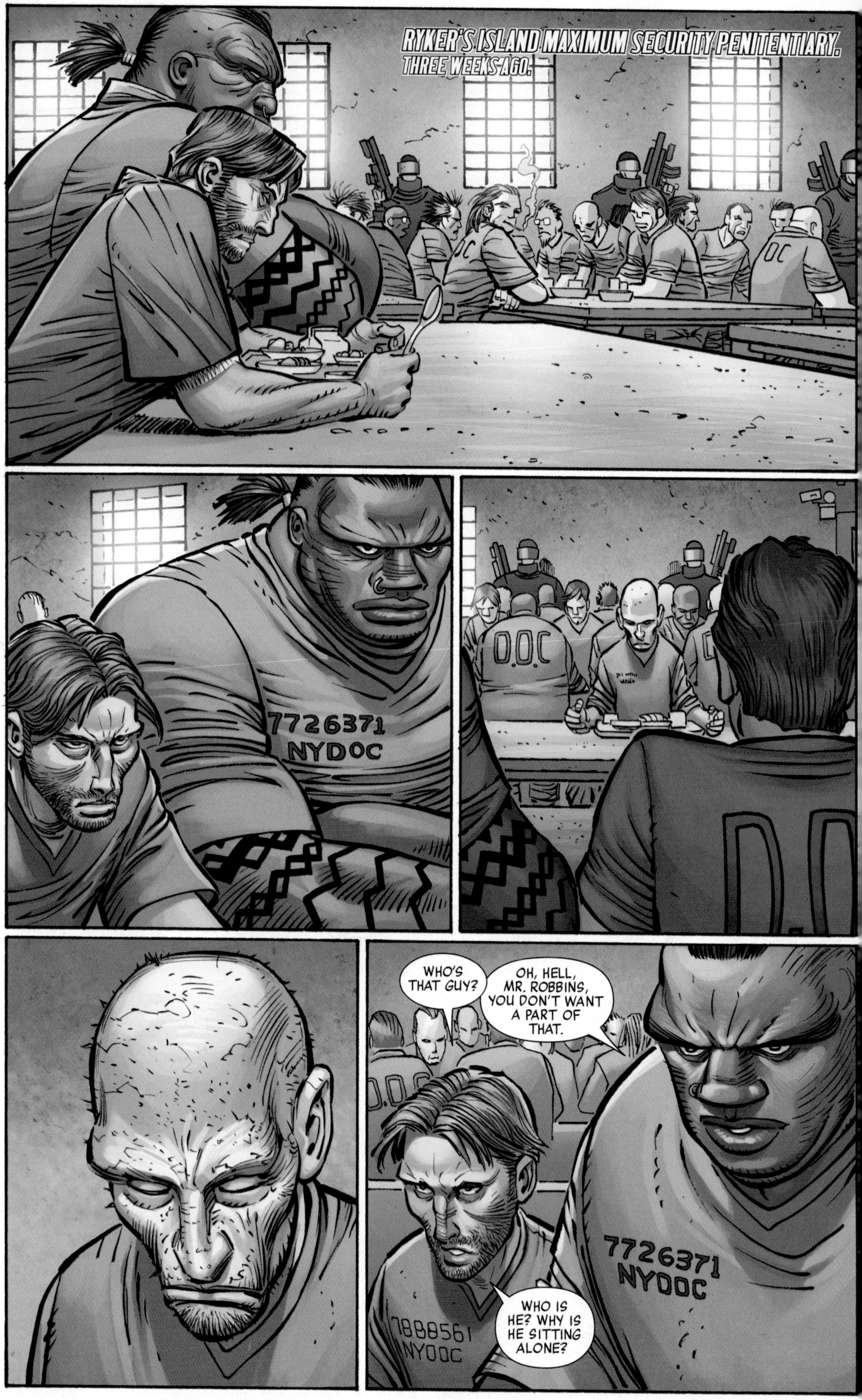
RYKER'S ISLAND MAXIMUM SECURITY PENITENTIARY.
THREE WEEKS AGO.
7726371 NYDOC
WHO'S THAT GUY?
OH, HELL, MR. ROBBINS, YOU DON'T WANT A PART OF THAT.
7726371 NYDOC
7888561 NYDOC
WHO IS HE? WHY IS HE SITTING ALONE?

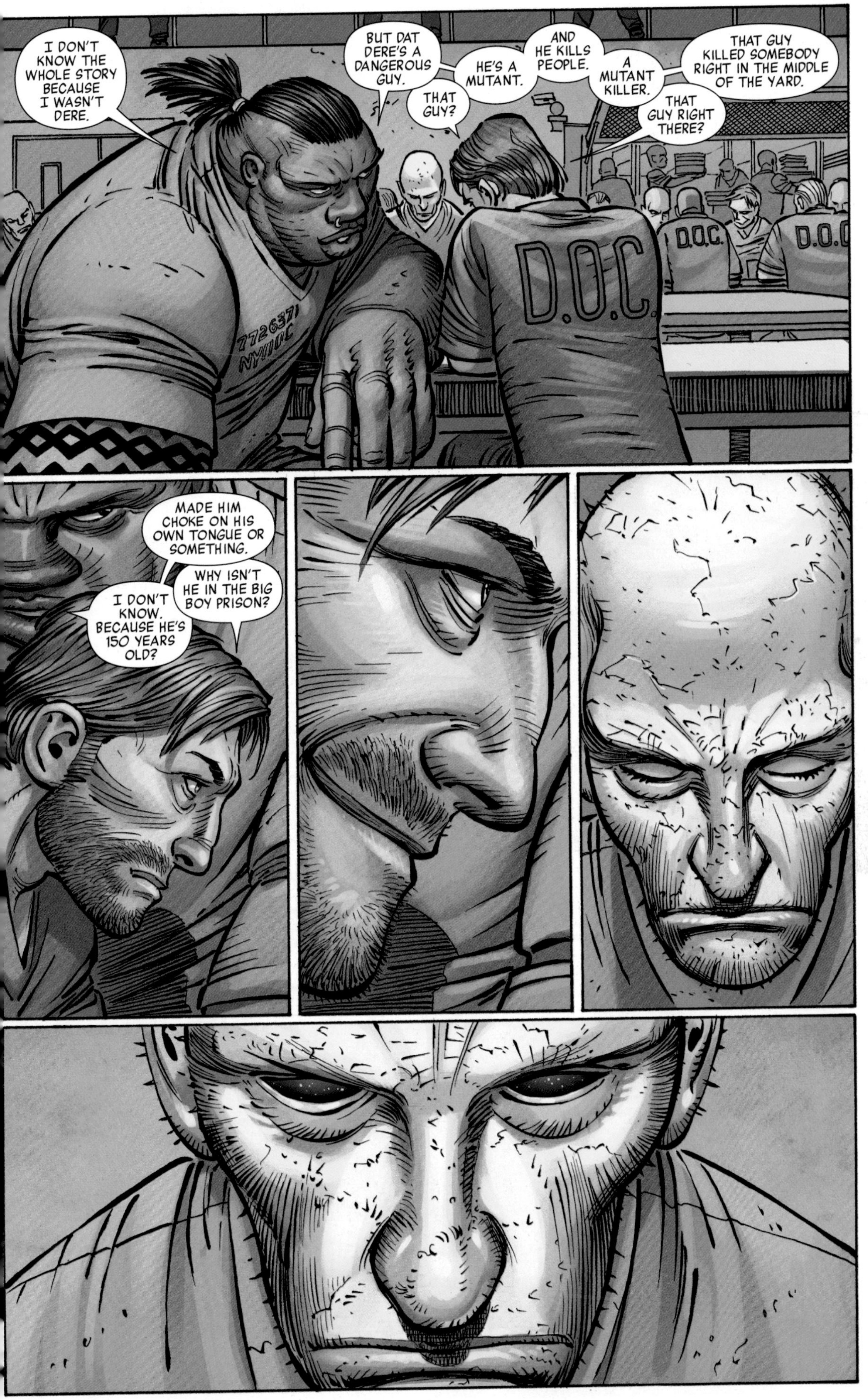
I DON'T KNOW THE WHOLE STORY BECAUSE I WASN'T DERE.
BUT DAT DERE'S A DANGEROUS GUY.
THAT GUY?
HE'S A MUTANT.
AND HE KILLS PEOPLE.
A MUTANT KILLER.
THAT GUY KILLED SOMEBODY RIGHT IN THE MIDDLE OF THE YARD.
THAT GUY RIGHT THERE?
7726371 NY/DOC
D.O.C.
D.O.C.
D.O.C
MADE HIM CHOKE ON HIS OWN TONGUE OR SOMETHING.
WHY ISN'T HE IN THE BIG BOY PRISON?
I DON'T KNOW. BECAUSE HE'S 150 YEARS OLD?

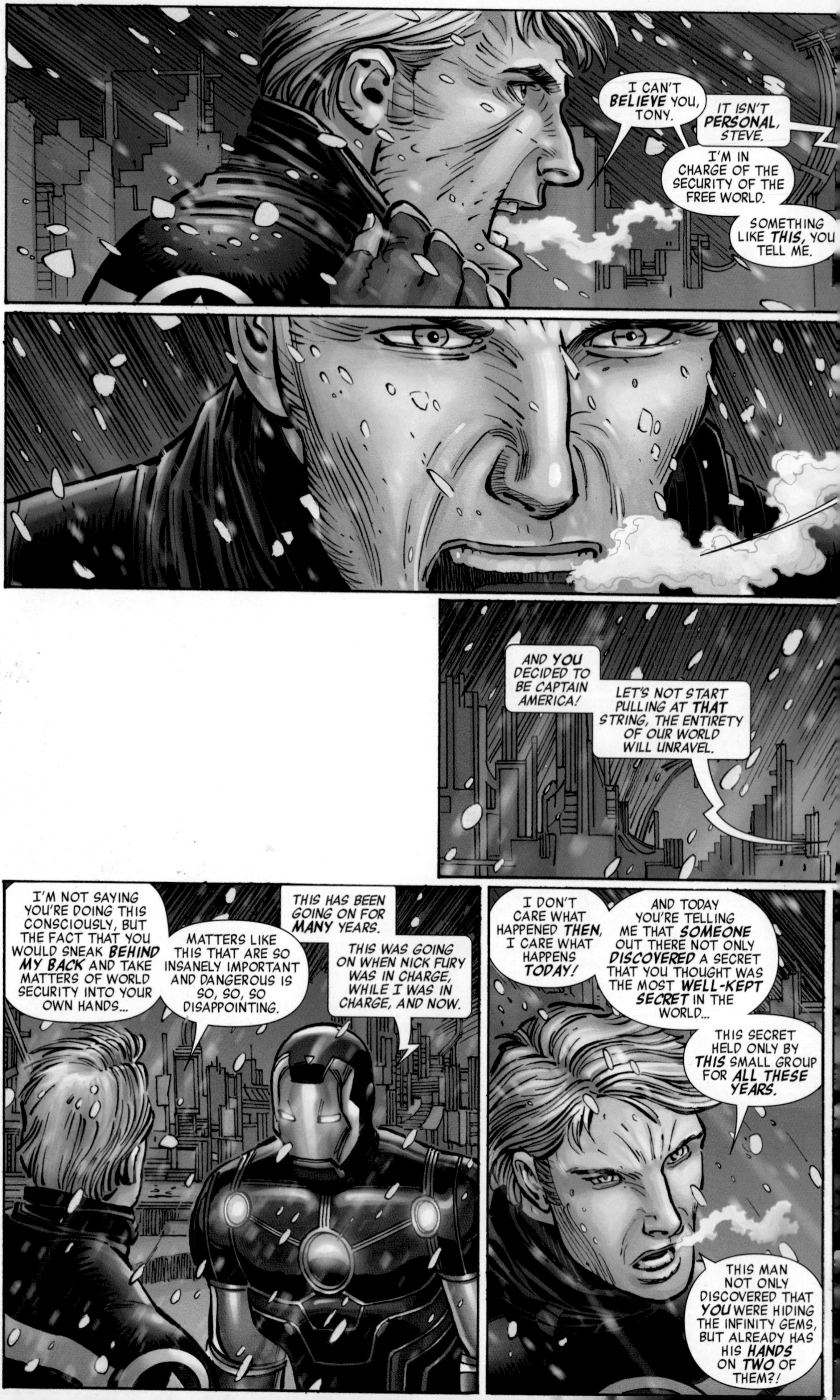
I CAN'T BELIEVE YOU, TONY.
IT ISN'T PERSONAL, STEVE.
I'M IN CHARGE OF THE SECURITY OF THE FREE WORLD.
SOMETHING LIKE THIS, YOU TELL ME.
AND YOU DECIDED TO BE CAPTAIN AMERICA!
LET'S NOT START PULLING AT THAT STRING, THE ENTIRETY OF OUR WORLD WILL UNRAVEL.
I'M NOT SAYING YOU'RE DOING THIS CONSCIOUSLY, BUT THE FACT THAT YOU WOULD SNEAK BEHIND MY BACK AND TAKE MATTERS OF WORLD SECURITY INTO YOUR OWN HANDS...
MATTERS LIKE THIS THAT ARE SO INSANELY IMPORTANT AND DANGEROUS IS SO, SO, SO DISAPPOINTING.
THIS HAS BEEN GOING ON FOR MANY YEARS.
THIS WAS GOING ON WHEN NICK FURY WAS IN CHARGE, WHILE I WAS IN CHARGE, AND NOW.
I DON'T CARE WHAT HAPPENED THEN, I CARE WHAT HAPPENS TODAY!
AND TODAY YOU'RE TELLING ME THAT SOMEONE OUT THERE NOT ONLY DISCOVERED A SECRET THAT YOU THOUGHT WAS THE MOST WELL-KEPT SECRET IN THE WORLD...
THIS SECRET HELD ONLY BY THIS SMALL GROUP FOR ALL THESE YEARS.
THIS MAN NOT ONLY DISCOVERED THAT YOU WERE HIDING THE INFINITY GEMS, BUT ALREADY HAS HIS HANDS ON TWO OF THEM?!

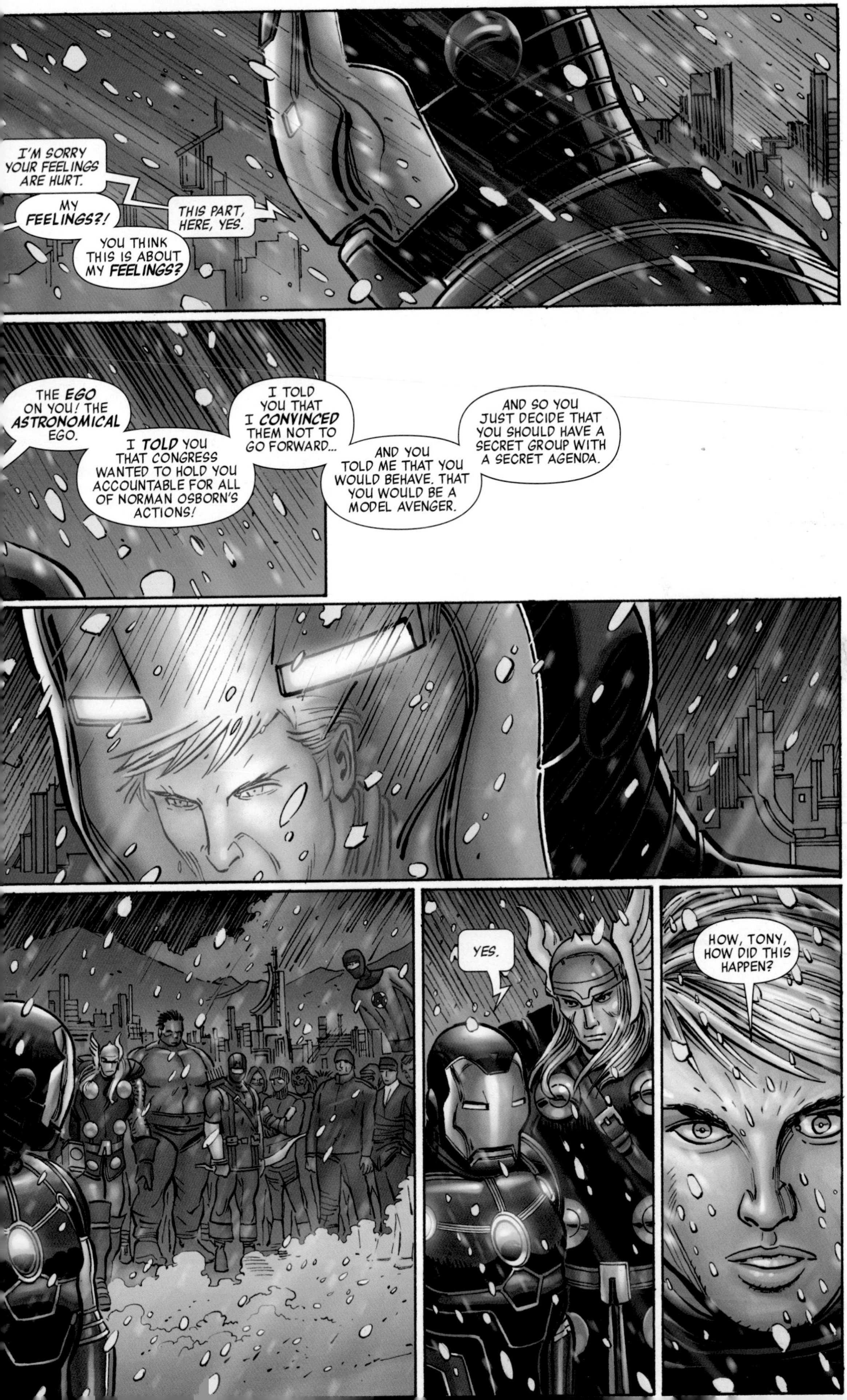
I'M SORRY YOUR FEELINGS ARE HURT.
MY FEELINGS?!
THIS PART, HERE, YES.
YOU THINK THIS IS ABOUT MY FEELINGS?
THE EGO ON YOU! THE ASTRONOMICAL EGO.
I TOLD YOU THAT CONGRESS WANTED TO HOLD YOU ACCOUNTABLE FOR ALL OF NORMAN OSBORN'S ACTIONS!
I TOLD YOU THAT I CONVINCED THEM NOT TO GO FORWARD...
AND YOU TOLD ME THAT YOU WOULD BEHAVE. THAT YOU WOULD BE A MODEL AVENGER.
AND SO YOU JUST DECIDE THAT YOU SHOULD HAVE A SECRET GROUP WITH A SECRET AGENDA.
YES.
HOW, TONY, HOW DID THIS HAPPEN?

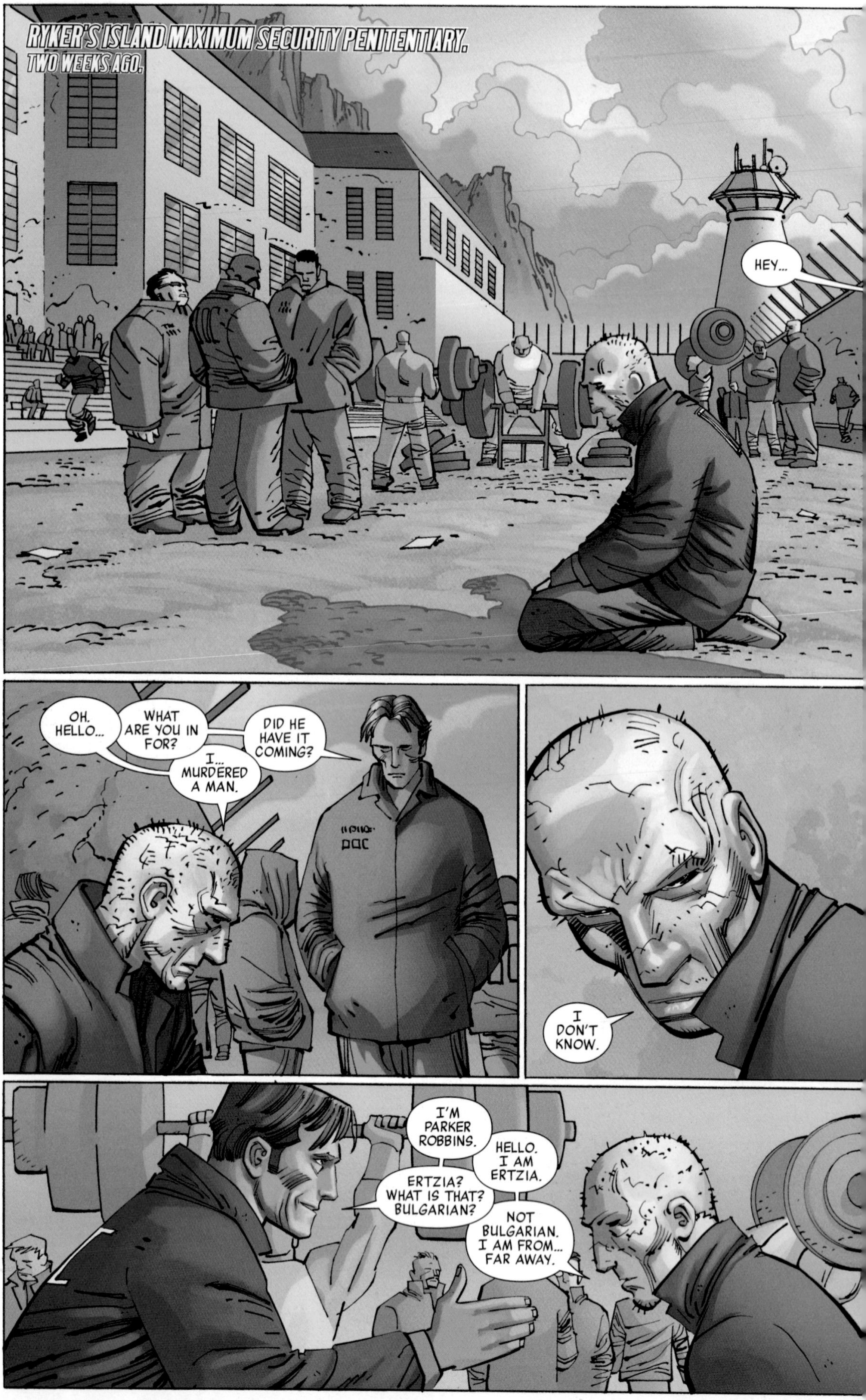
RYKER'S ISLAND MAXIMUM SECURITY PENITENTIARY.
TWO WEEKS AGO.
HEY...
OH. HELLO...
WHAT ARE YOU IN FOR?
I... MURDERED A MAN.
DID HE HAVE IT COMING?
I DON'T KNOW.
I'M PARKER ROBBINS.
HELLO. I AM ERTZIA.
ERTZIA? WHAT IS THAT? BULGARIAN?
NOT BULGARIAN. I AM FROM... FAR AWAY.

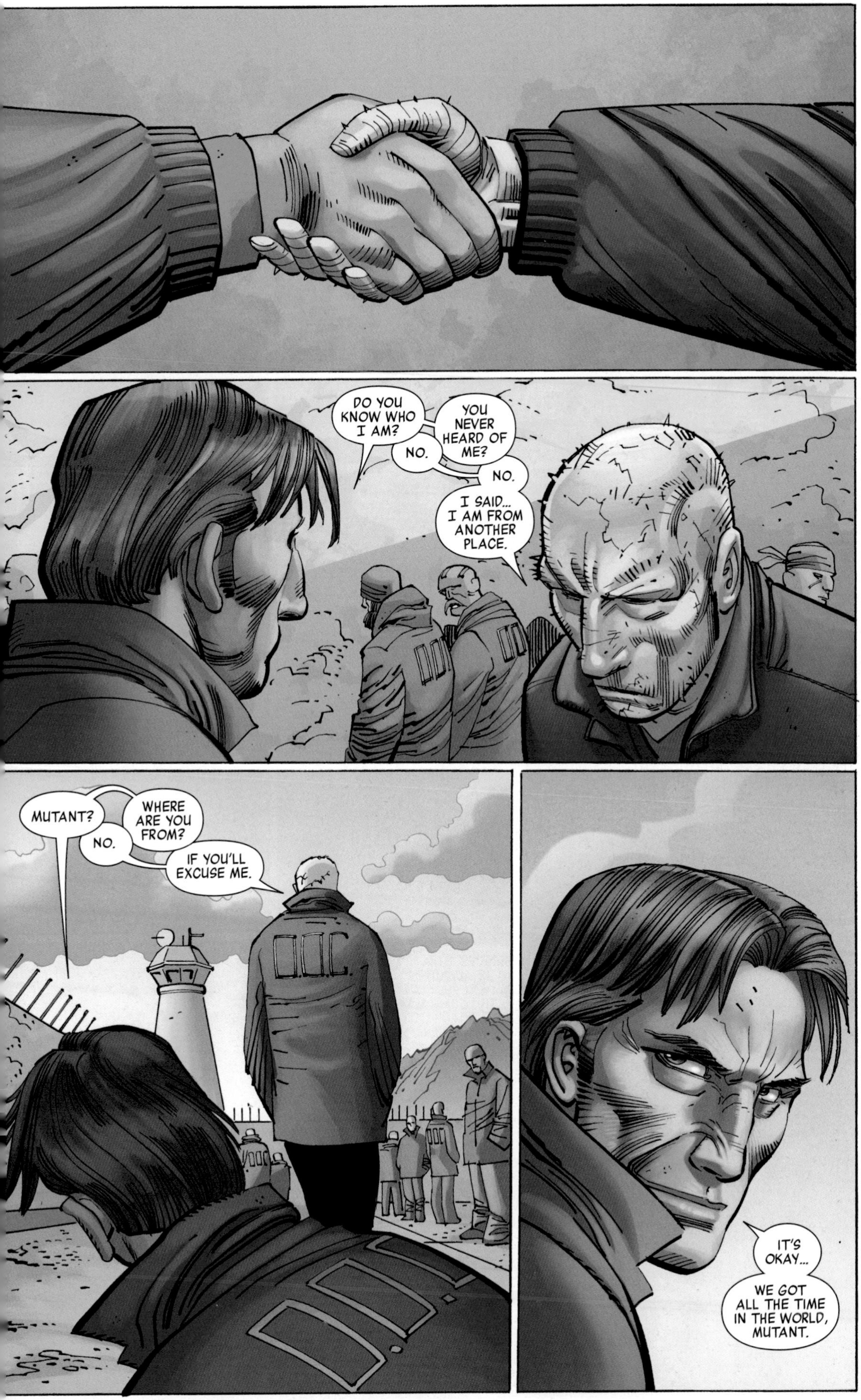
DO YOU KNOW WHO I AM?
NO.
YOU NEVER HEARD OF ME?
NO.
I SAID... I AM FROM ANOTHER PLACE.
MUTANT?
NO.
WHERE ARE YOU FROM?
IF YOU'LL EXCUSE ME.
IT'S OKAY...
WE GOT ALL THE TIME IN THE WORLD, MUTANT.

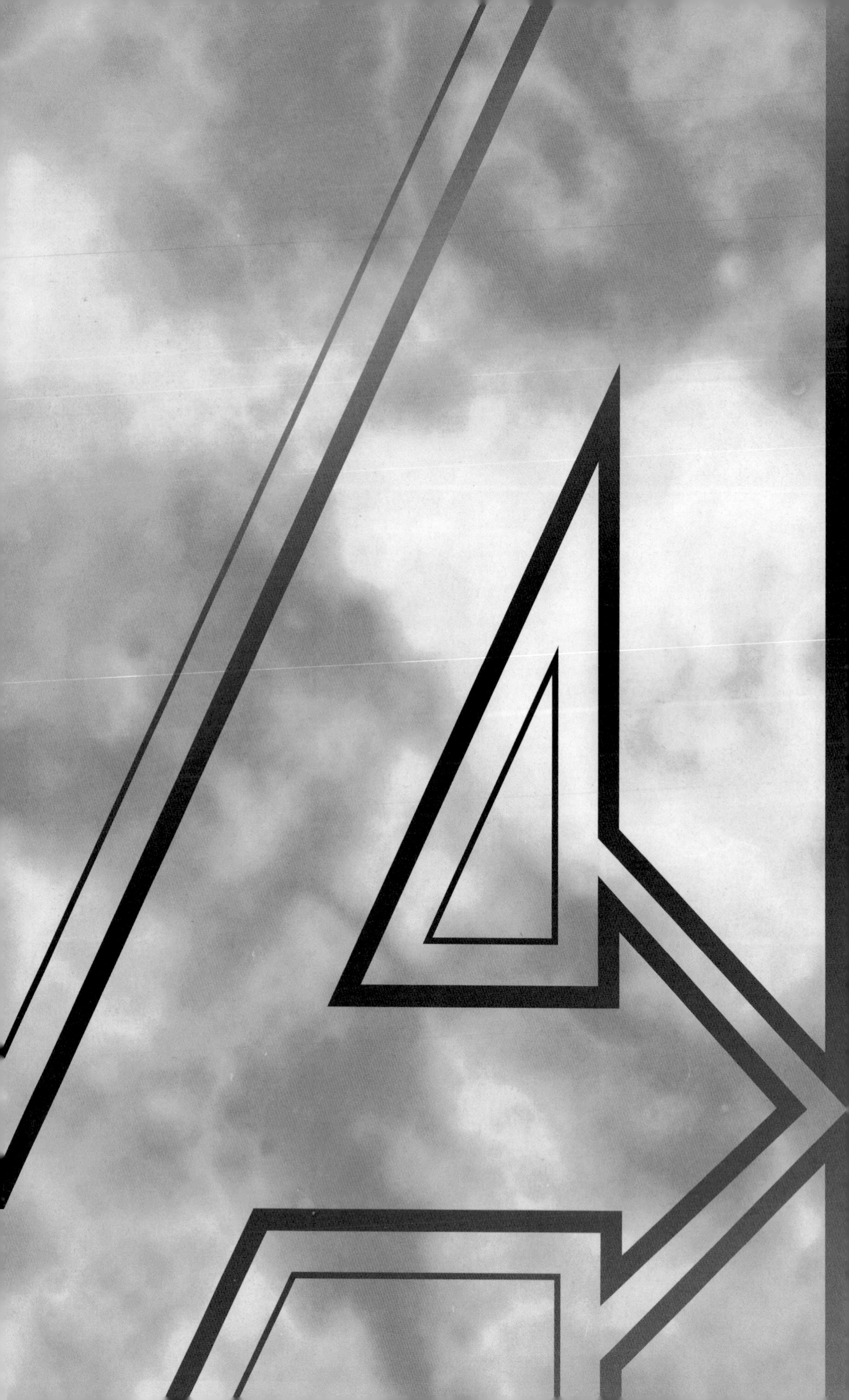

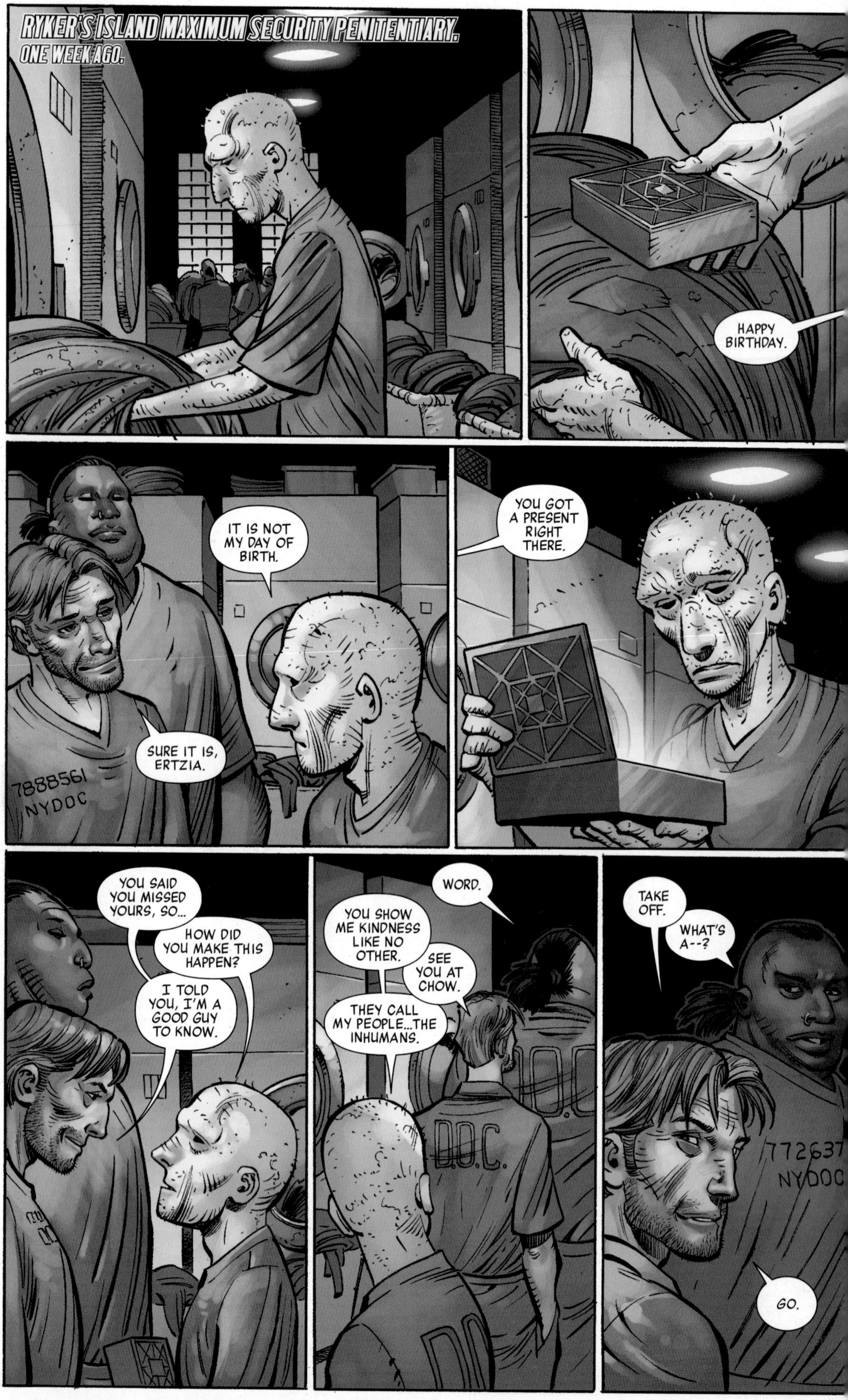
RYKER'S ISLAND MAXIMUM SECURITY PENITENTIARY.
ONE WEEK AGO.
HAPPY BIRTHDAY.
IT IS NOT MY DAY OF BIRTH.
SURE IT IS, ERTZIA.
7888561 NYDOC
YOU GOT A PRESENT RIGHT THERE.
YOU SAID YOU MISSED YOURS, SO...
HOW DID YOU MAKE THIS HAPPEN?
I TOLD YOU, I'M A GOOD GUY TO KNOW.
WORD.
YOU SHOW ME KINDNESS LIKE NO OTHER.
SEE YOU AT CHOW.
THEY CALL MY PEOPLE...THE INHUMANS.
D.O.C.
TAKE OFF.
WHAT'S A--?
772637 NYDOC
GO.

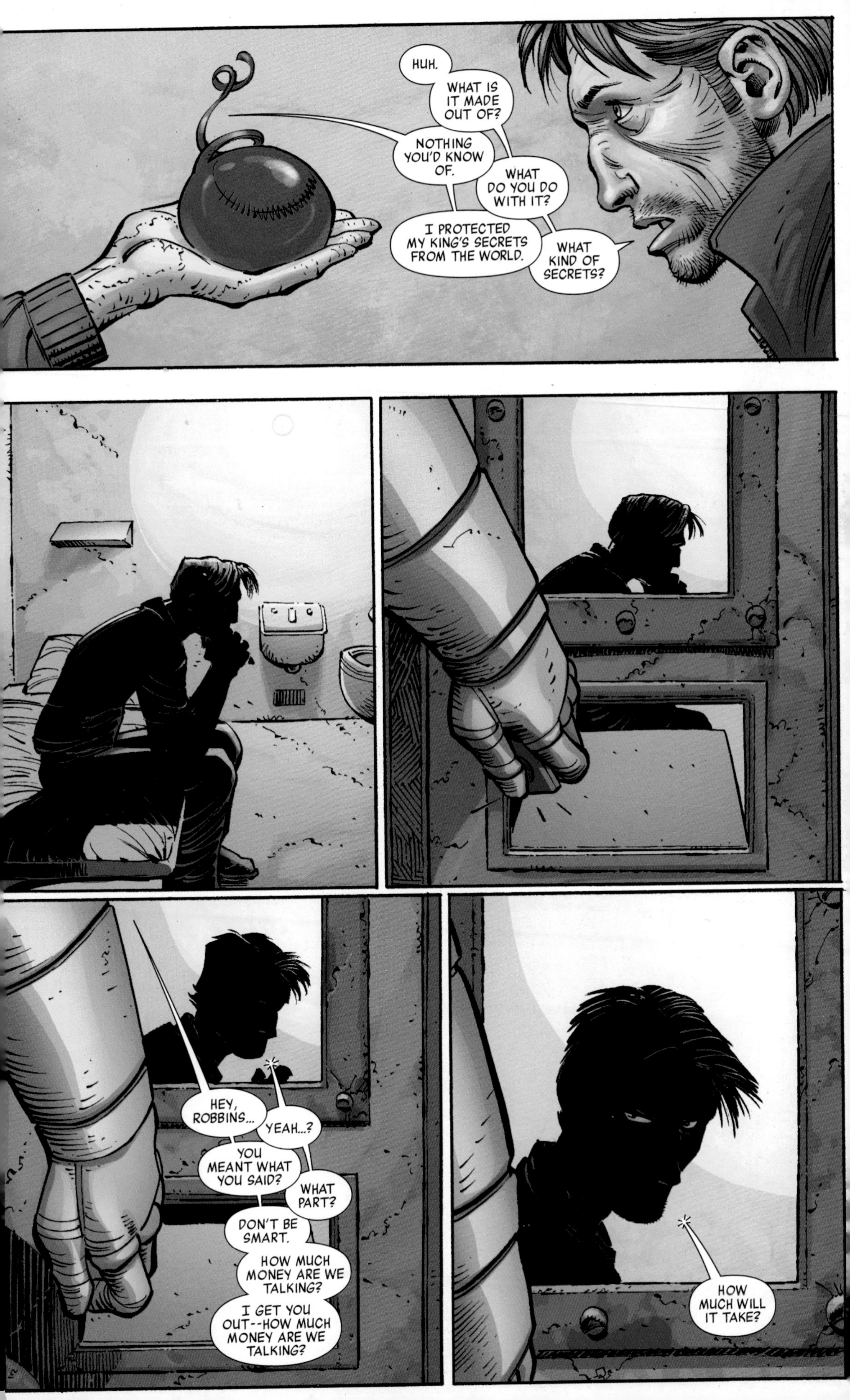
HUH.
WHAT IS IT MADE OUT OF?
NOTHING YOU'D KNOW OF.
WHAT DO YOU DO WITH IT?
I PROTECTED MY KING'S SECRETS FROM THE WORLD.
WHAT KIND OF SECRETS?
HEY, ROBBINS...
YEAH...?
YOU MEANT WHAT YOU SAID?
WHAT PART?
DON'T BE SMART.
HOW MUCH MONEY ARE WE TALKING?
I GET YOU OUT--HOW MUCH MONEY ARE WE TALKING?
HOW MUCH WILL IT TAKE?

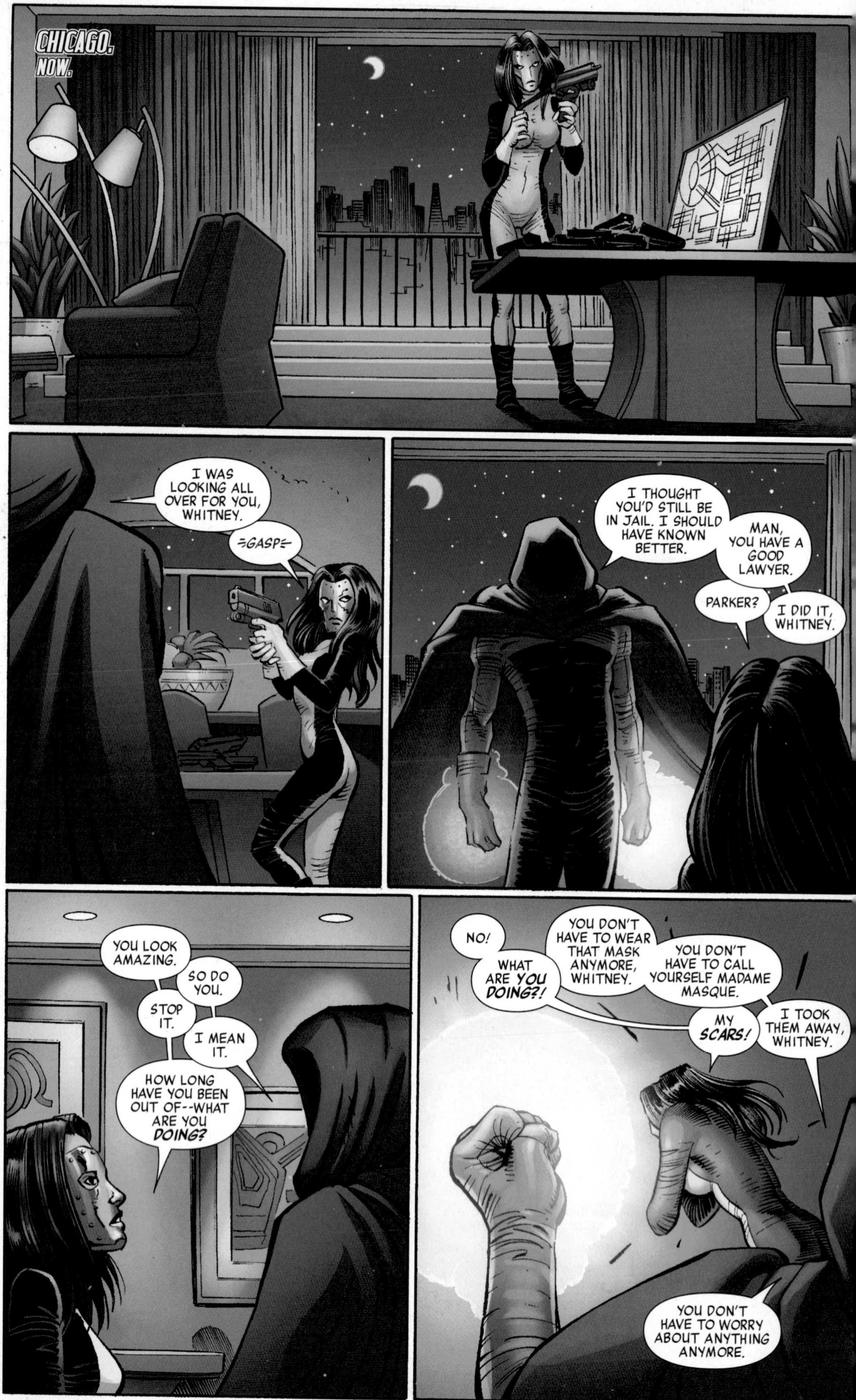
CHICAGO. NOW.
I WAS LOOKING ALL OVER FOR YOU, WHITNEY.
=GASP=
I THOUGHT YOU'D STILL BE IN JAIL. I SHOULD HAVE KNOWN BETTER.
MAN, YOU HAVE A GOOD LAWYER.
PARKER?
I DID IT, WHITNEY.
YOU LOOK AMAZING.
SO DO YOU.
STOP IT.
I MEAN IT.
HOW LONG HAVE YOU BEEN OUT OF--WHAT ARE YOU DOING?
NO!
WHAT ARE YOU DOING?!
YOU DON'T HAVE TO WEAR THAT MASK ANYMORE, WHITNEY.
YOU DON'T HAVE TO CALL YOURSELF MADAME MASQUE.
MY SCARS!
I TOOK THEM AWAY, WHITNEY.
YOU DON'T HAVE TO WORRY ABOUT ANYTHING ANYMORE.

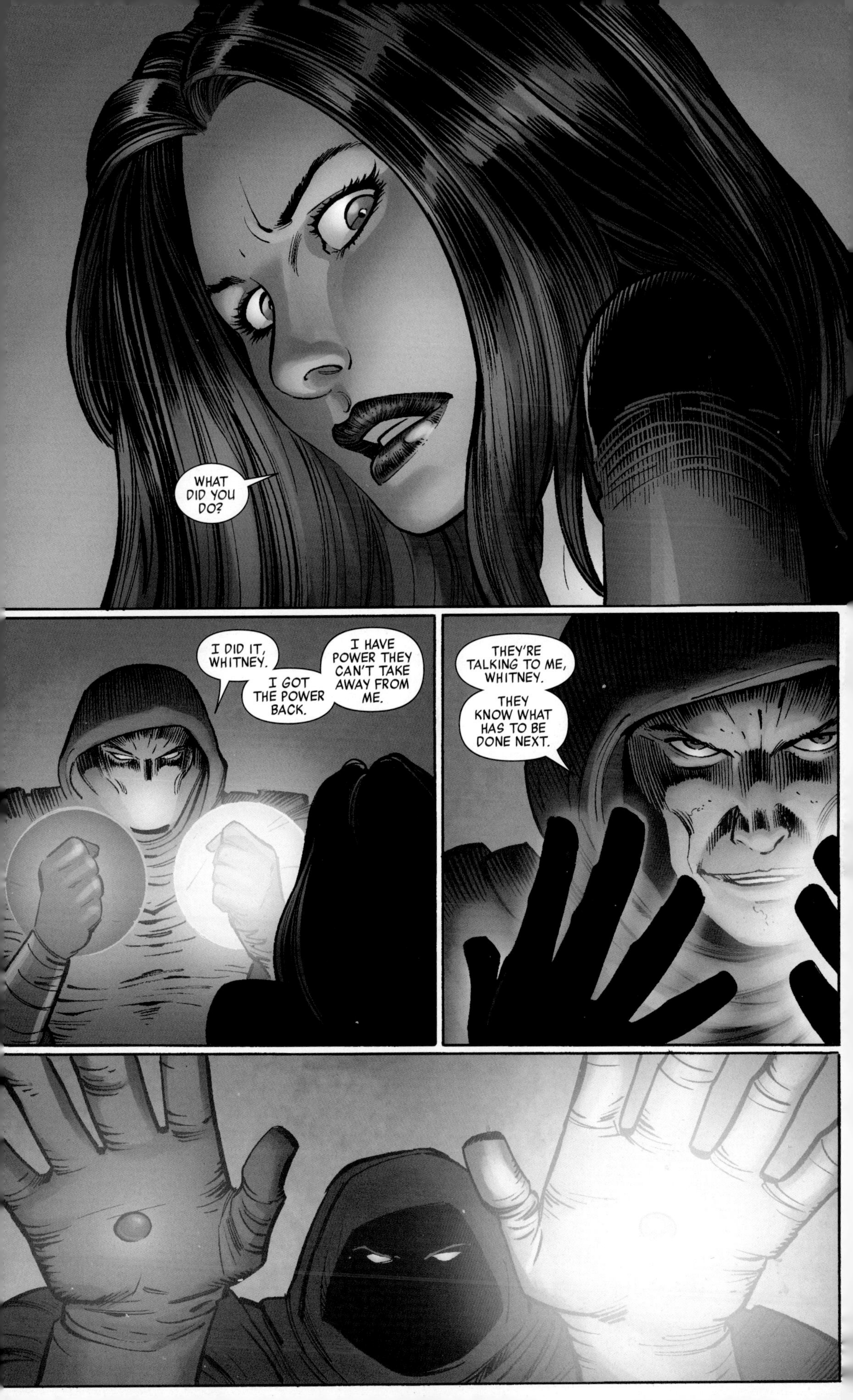
WHAT DID YOU DO?
I DID IT, WHITNEY.
I GOT THE POWER BACK.
I HAVE POWER THEY CAN'T TAKE AWAY FROM ME.
THEY'RE TALKING TO ME, WHITNEY.
THEY KNOW WHAT HAS TO BE DONE NEXT.

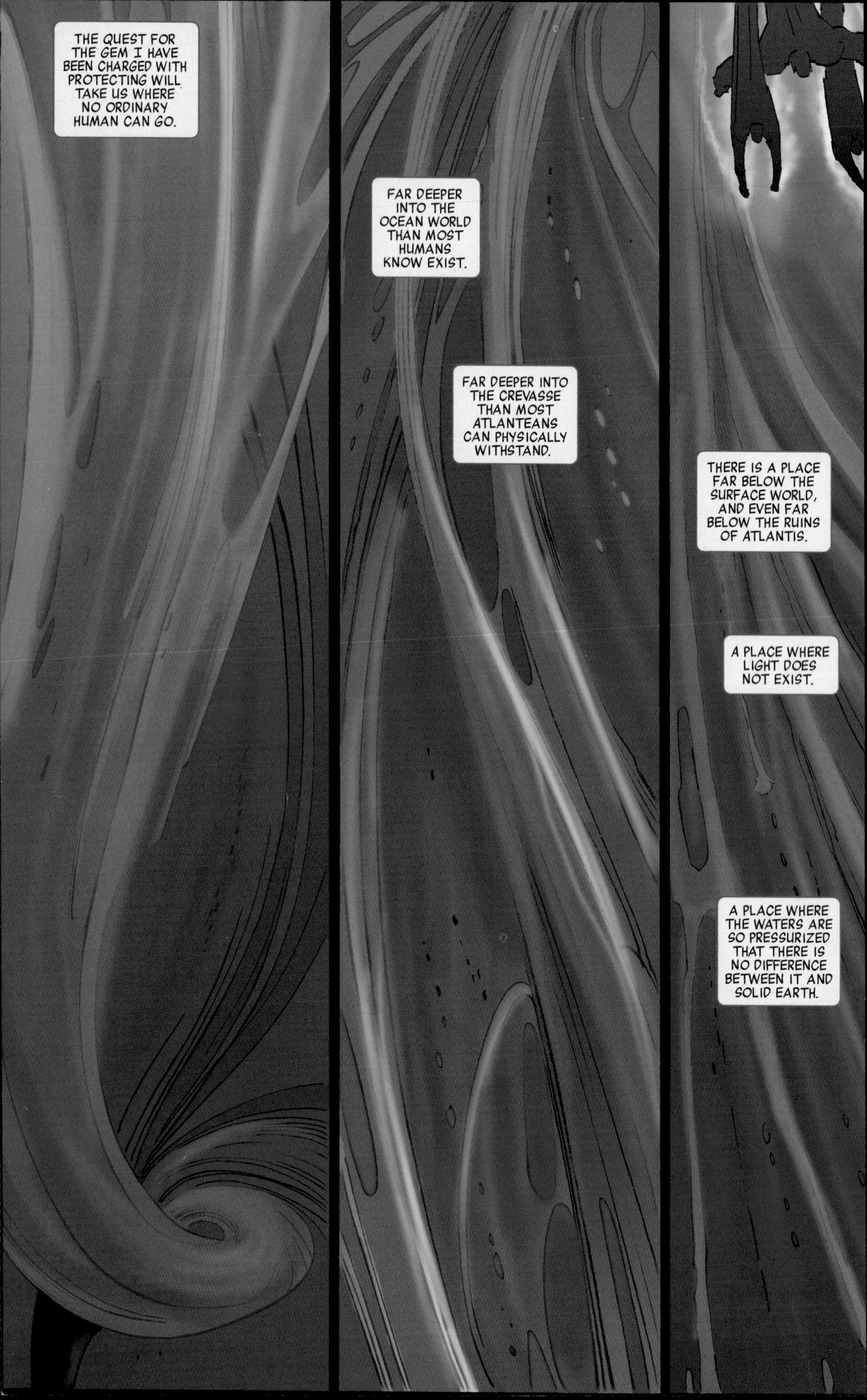
THE QUEST FOR THE GEM I HAVE BEEN CHARGED WITH PROTECTING WILL TAKE US WHERE NO ORDINARY HUMAN CAN GO.
FAR DEEPER INTO THE OCEAN WORLD THAN MOST HUMANS KNOW EXIST.
FAR DEEPER INTO THE CREVASSE THAN MOST ATLANTEANS CAN PHYSICALLY WITHSTAND.
THERE IS A PLACE FAR BELOW THE SURFACE WORLD, AND EVEN FAR BELOW THE RUINS OF ATLANTIS.
A PLACE WHERE LIGHT DOES NOT EXIST.
A PLACE WHERE THE WATERS ARE SO PRESSURIZED THAT THERE IS NO DIFFERENCE BETWEEN IT AND SOLID EARTH.

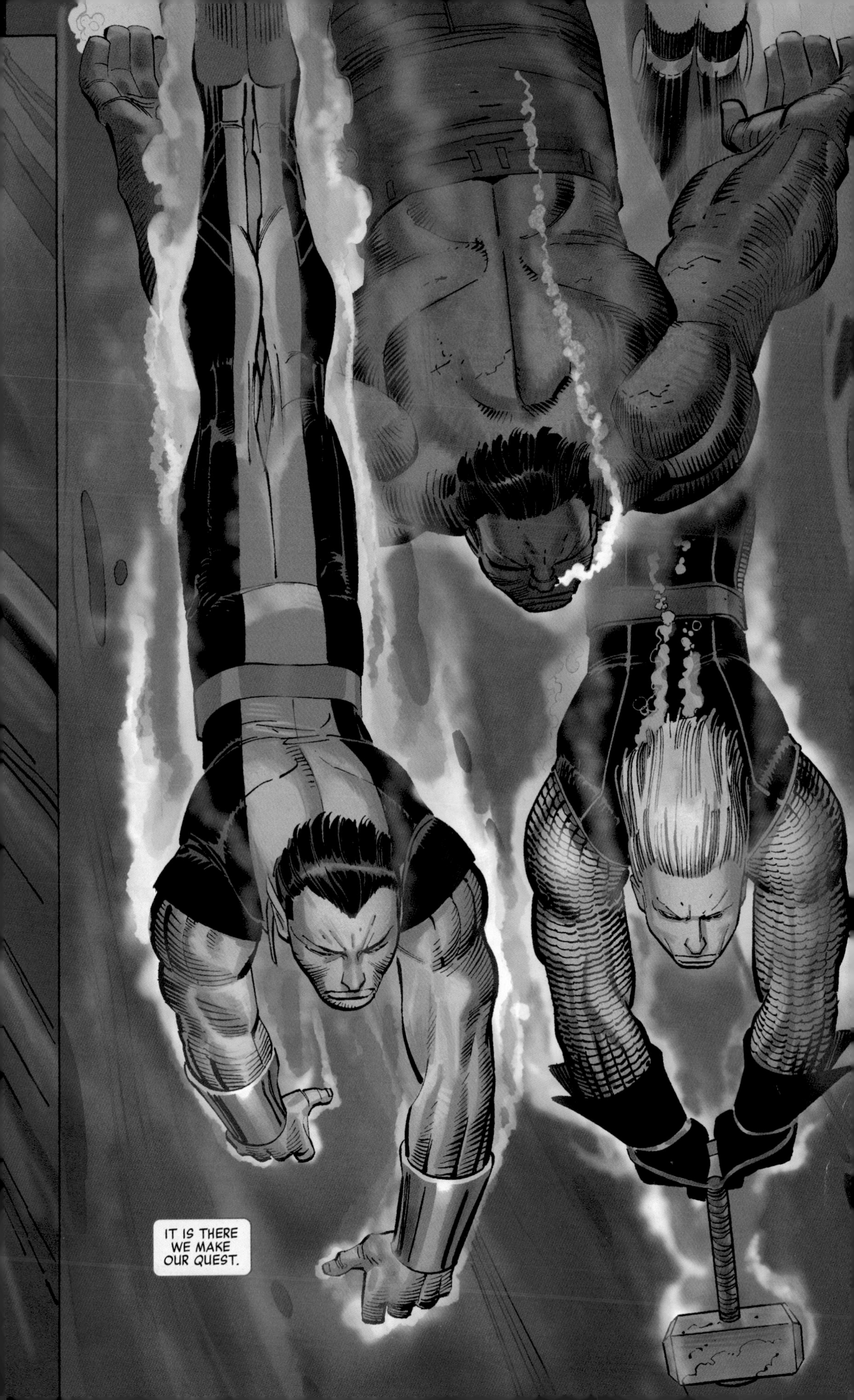
IT IS THERE WE MAKE OUR QUEST.

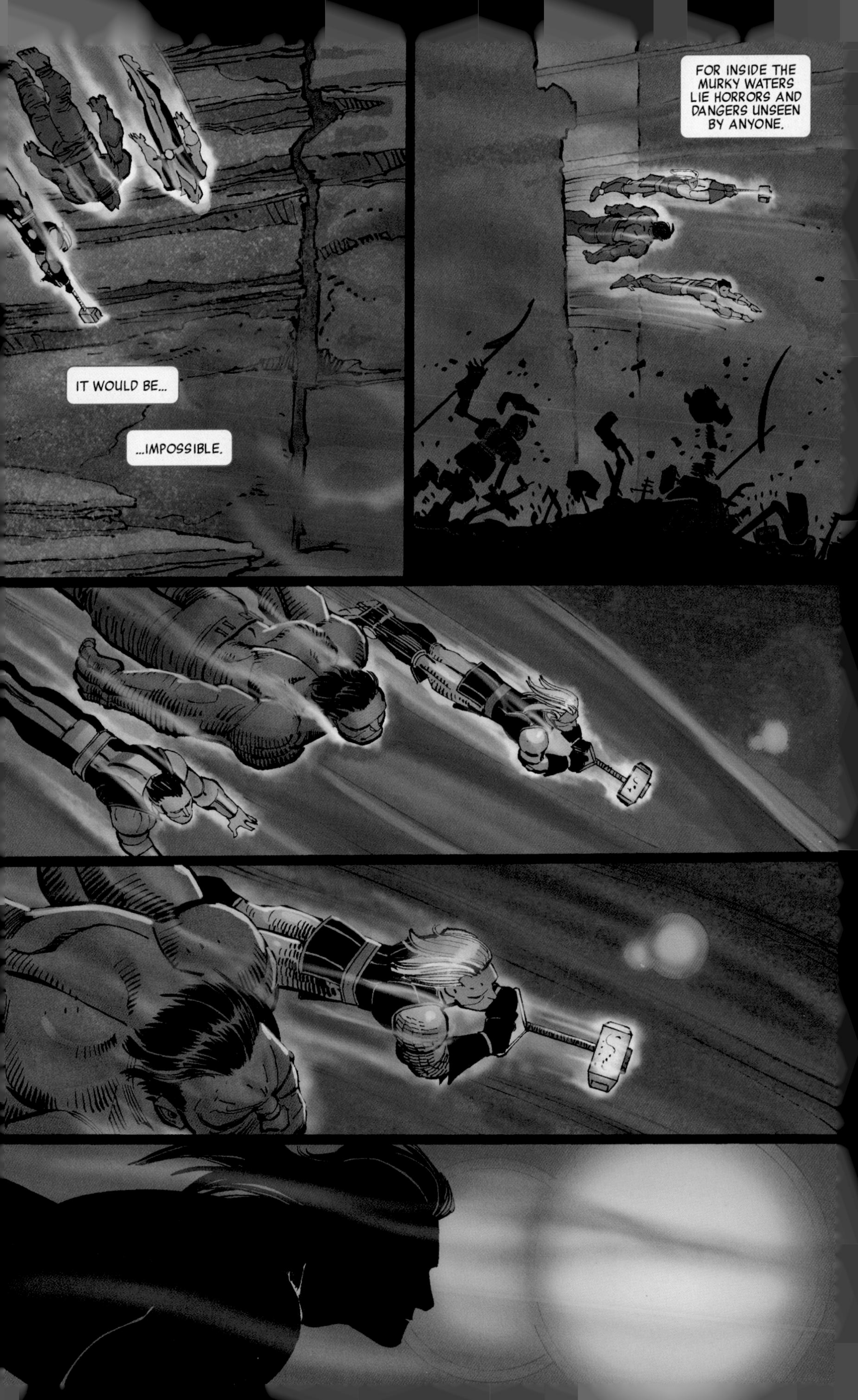
IT WOULD BE...
...IMPOSSIBLE.
FOR INSIDE THE MURKY WATERS LIE HORRORS AND DANGERS UNSEEN BY ANYONE.

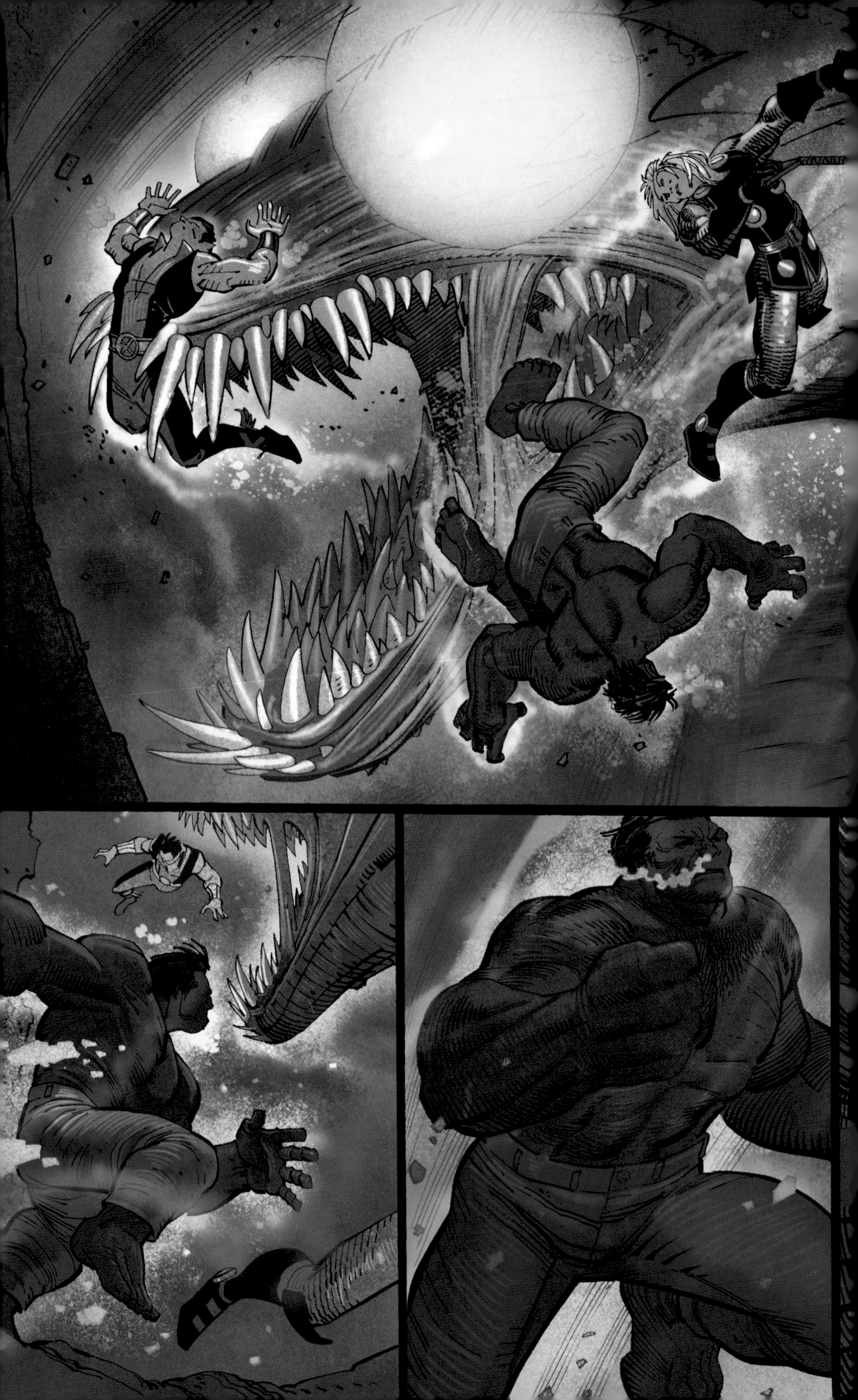

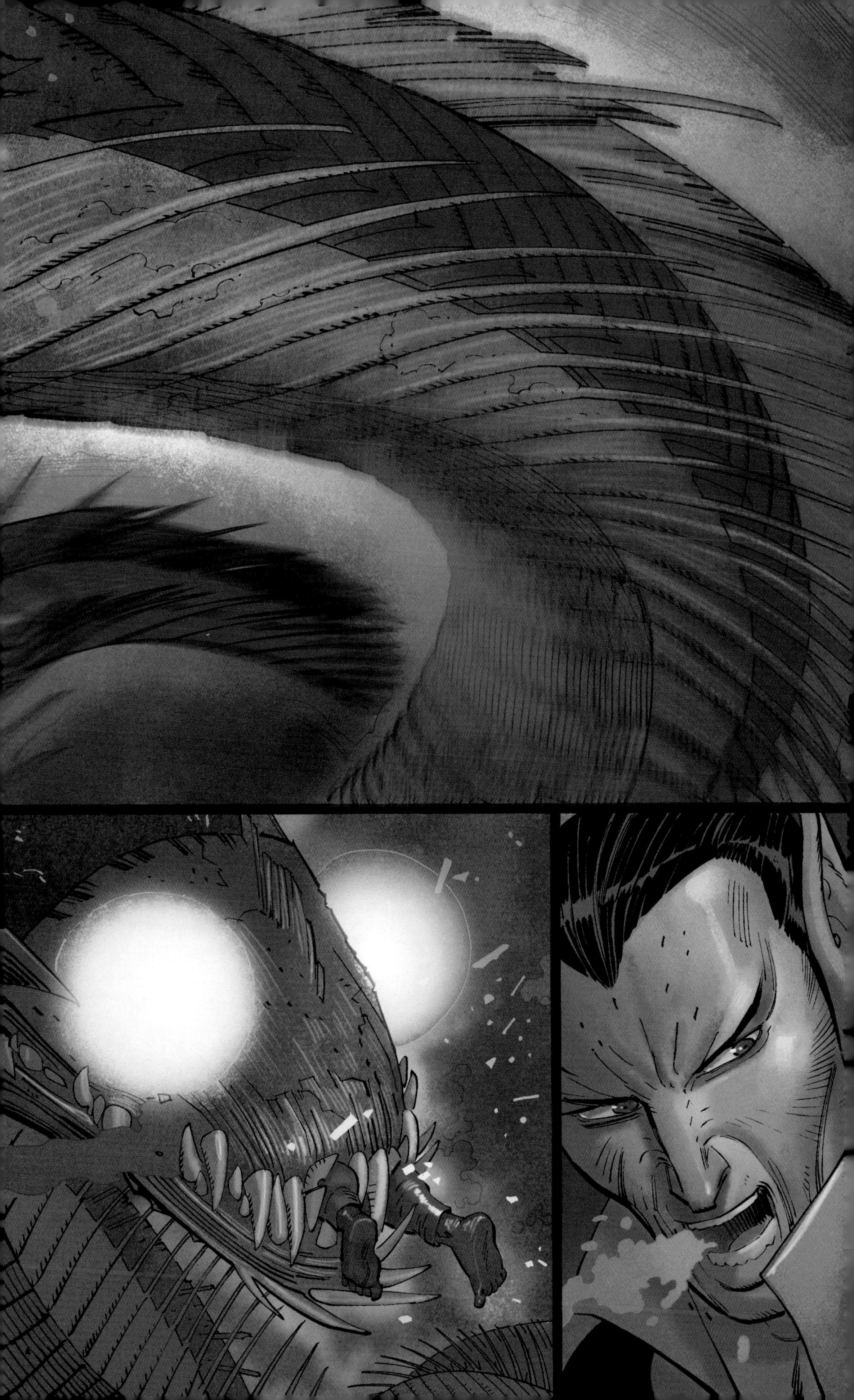

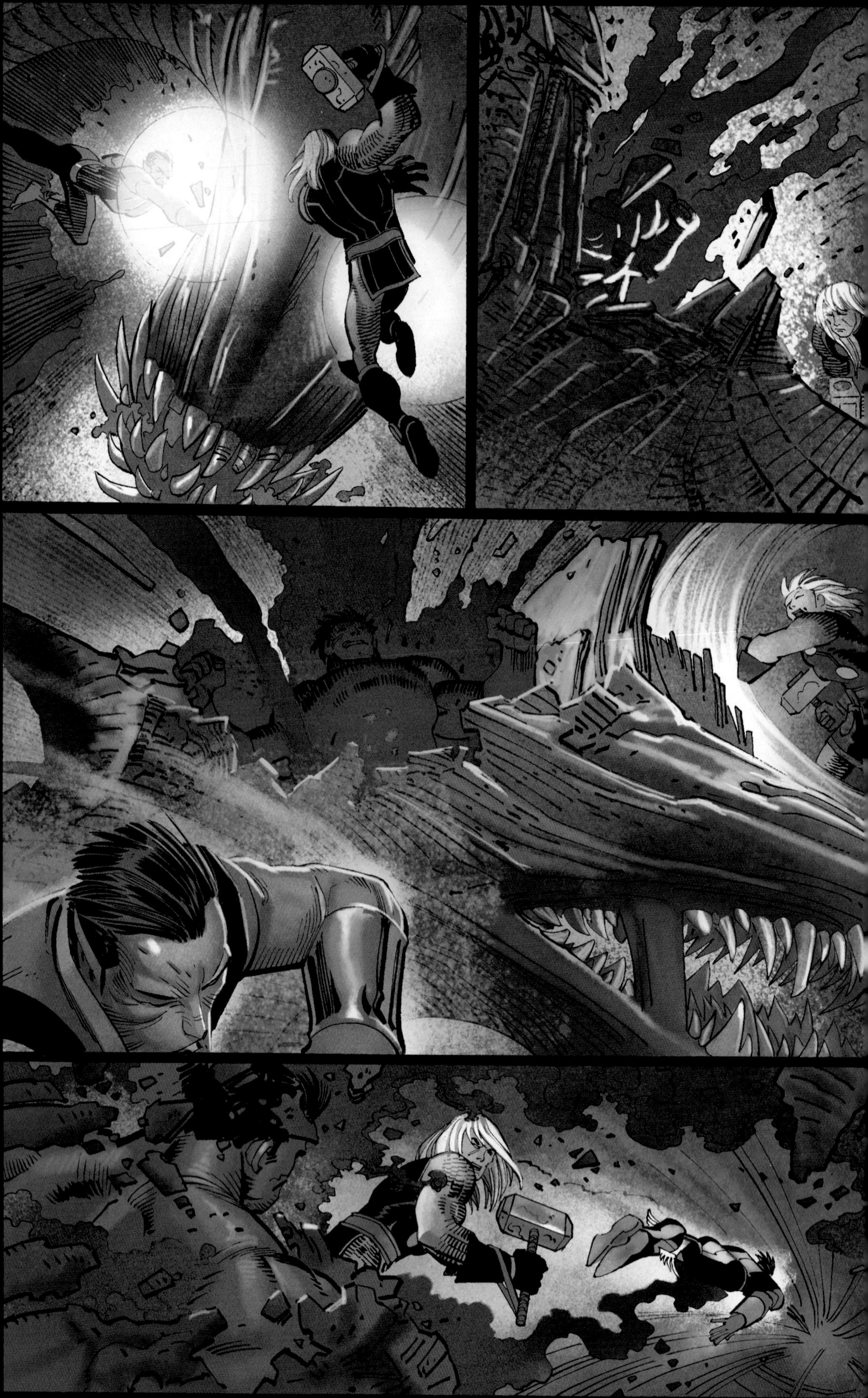

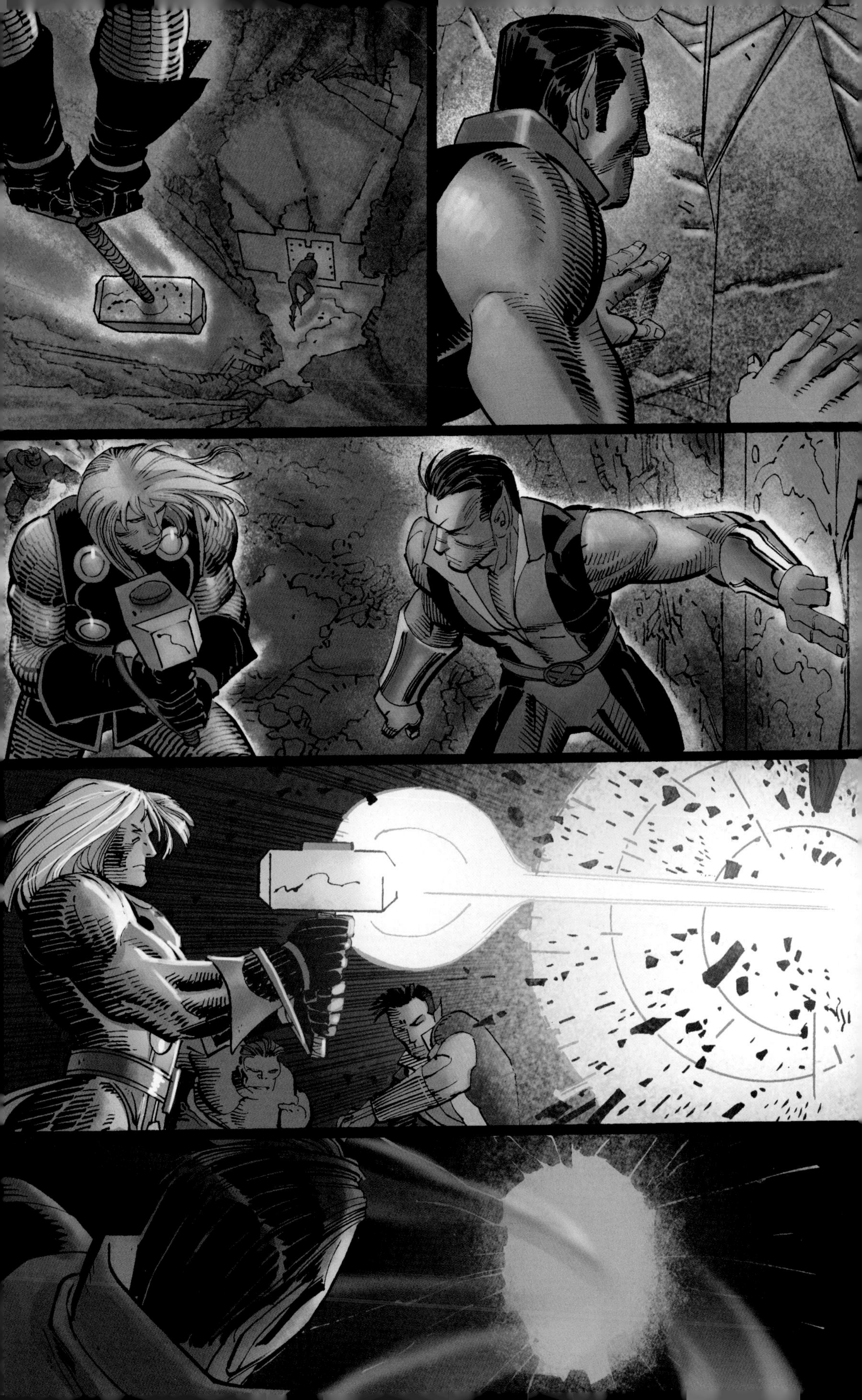

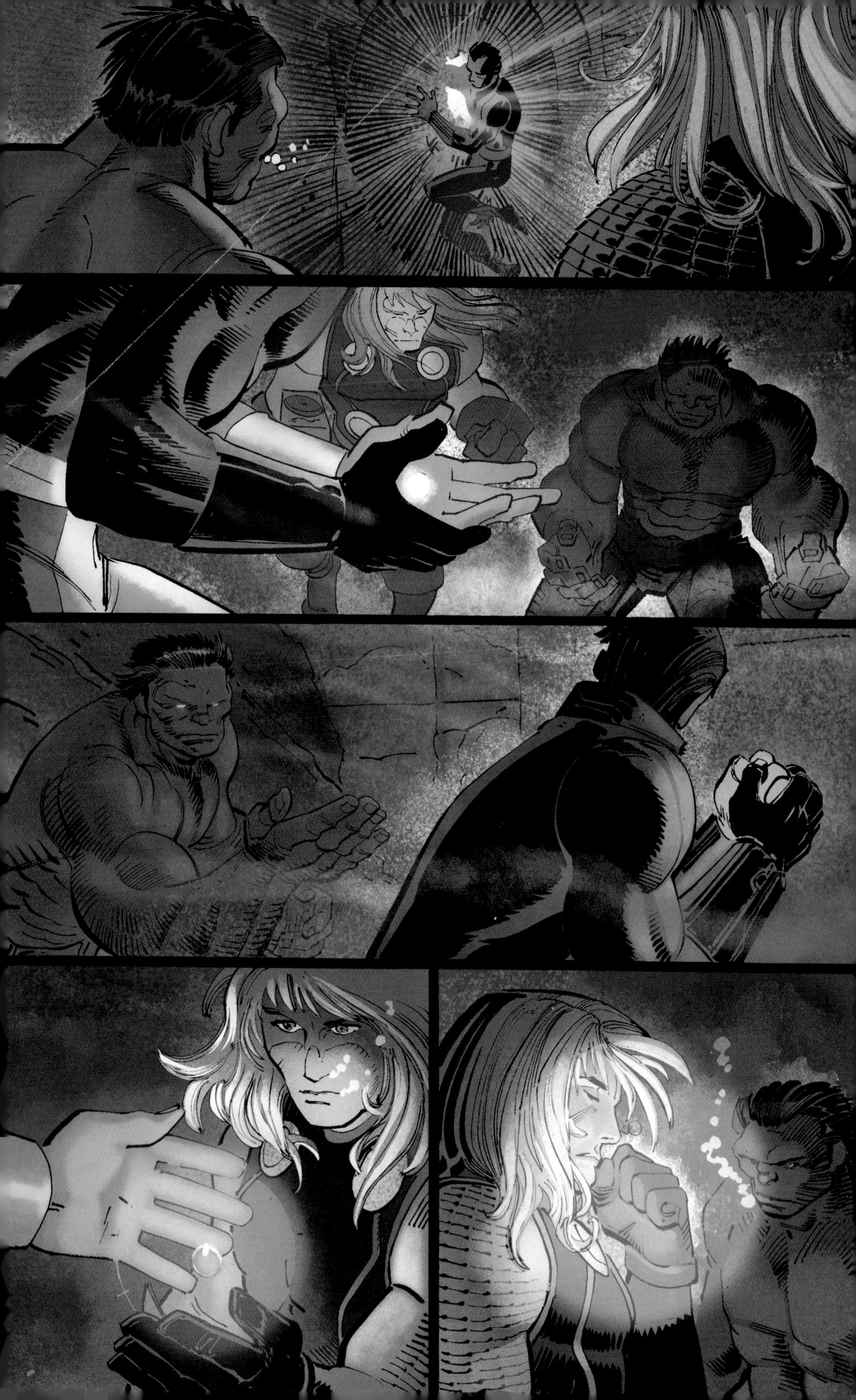

WESTCHESTER COUNTY, NEW YORK.

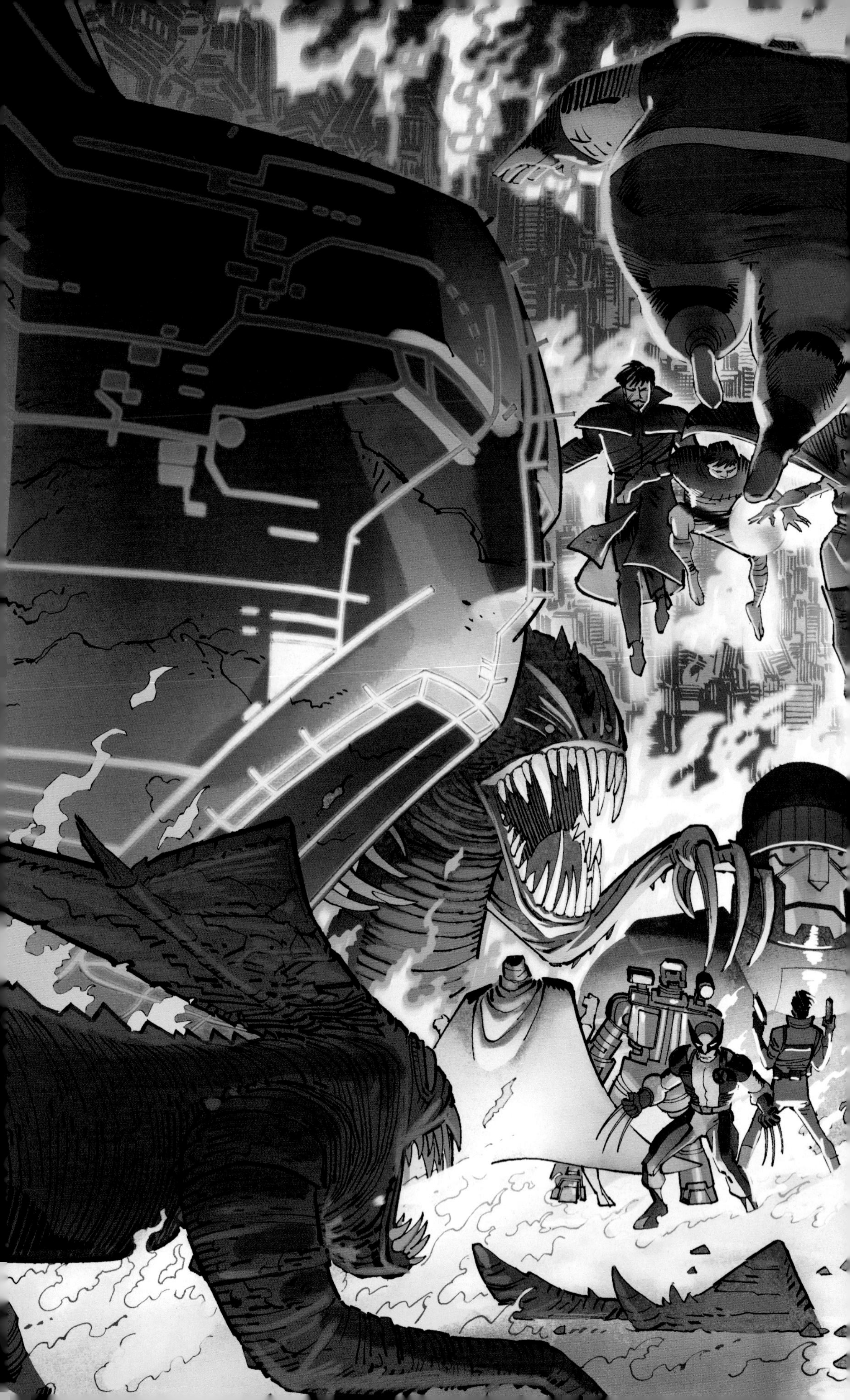

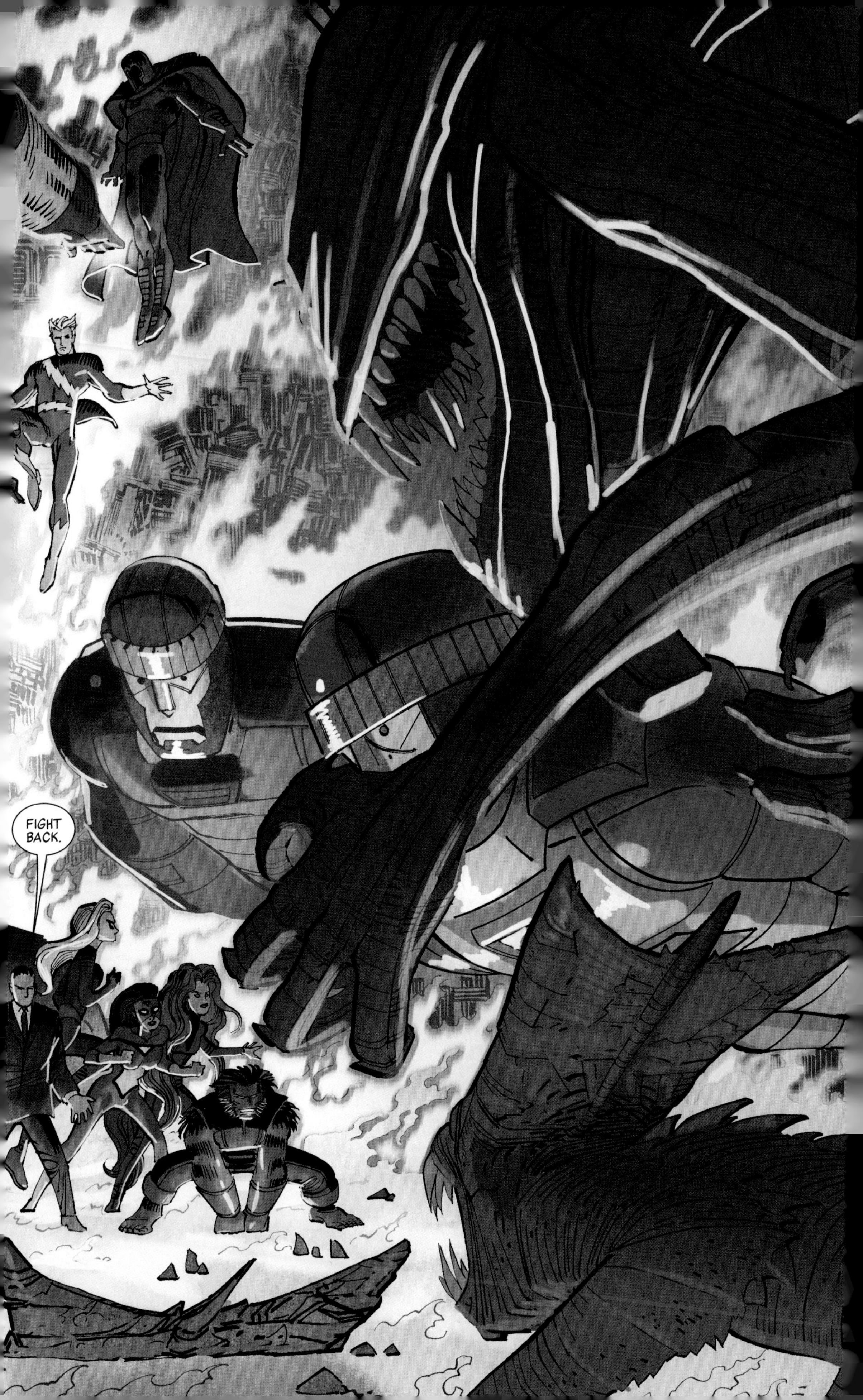
FIGHT BACK.

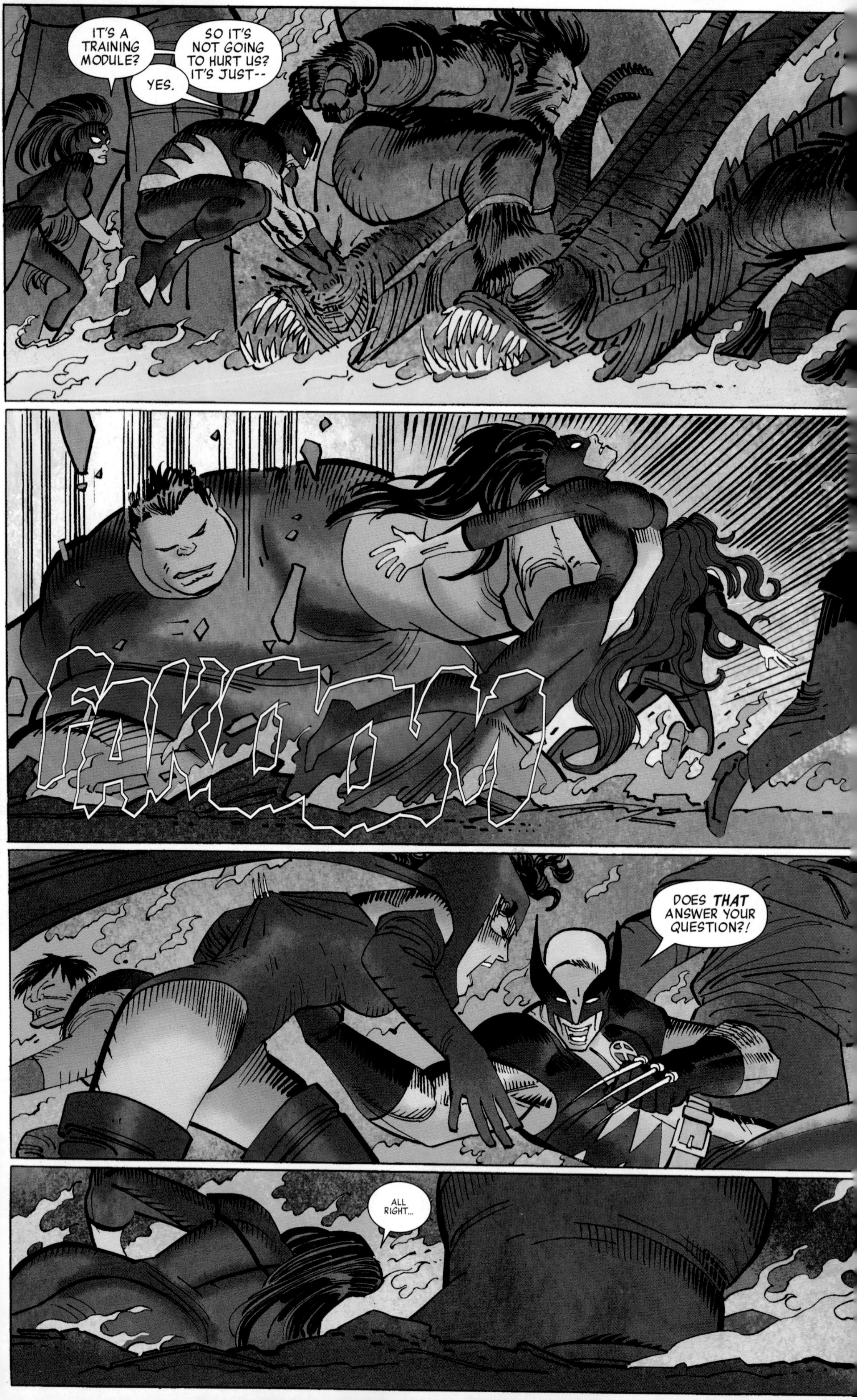
IT'S A TRAINING MODULE?
YES.
SO IT'S NOT GOING TO HURT US? IT'S JUST--
FAKOOOM
DOES THAT ANSWER YOUR QUESTION?!
ALL RIGHT...

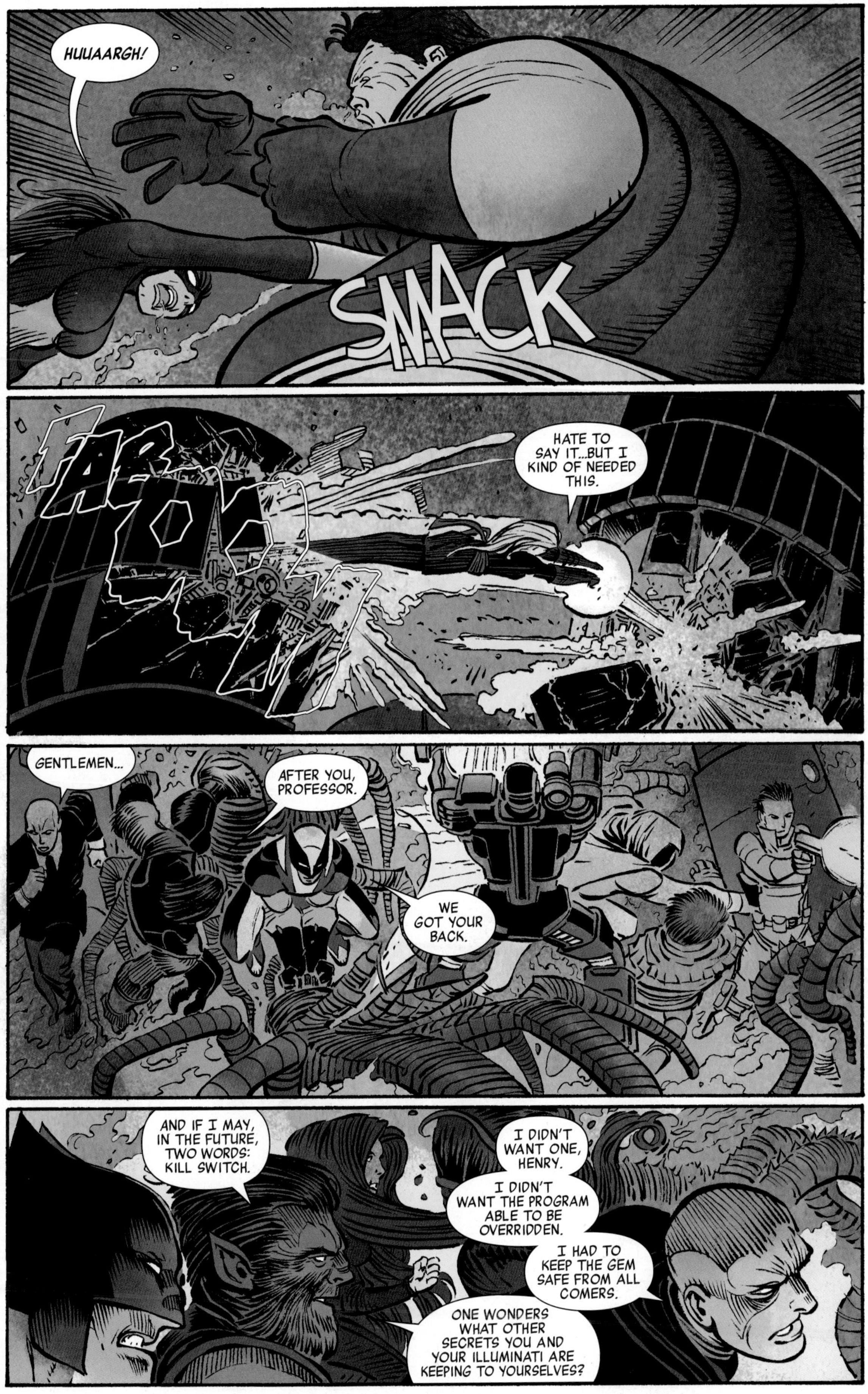
HUUAARGH!
SMACK
FAROOOM
HATE TO SAY IT...BUT I KIND OF NEEDED THIS.
GENTLEMEN...
AFTER YOU, PROFESSOR.
WE GOT YOUR BACK.
AND IF I MAY, IN THE FUTURE, TWO WORDS: KILL SWITCH.
I DIDN'T WANT ONE, HENRY.
I DIDN'T WANT THE PROGRAM ABLE TO BE OVERRIDDEN.
I HAD TO KEEP THE GEM SAFE FROM ALL COMERS.
ONE WONDERS WHAT OTHER SECRETS YOU AND YOUR ILLUMINATI ARE KEEPING TO YOURSELVES?

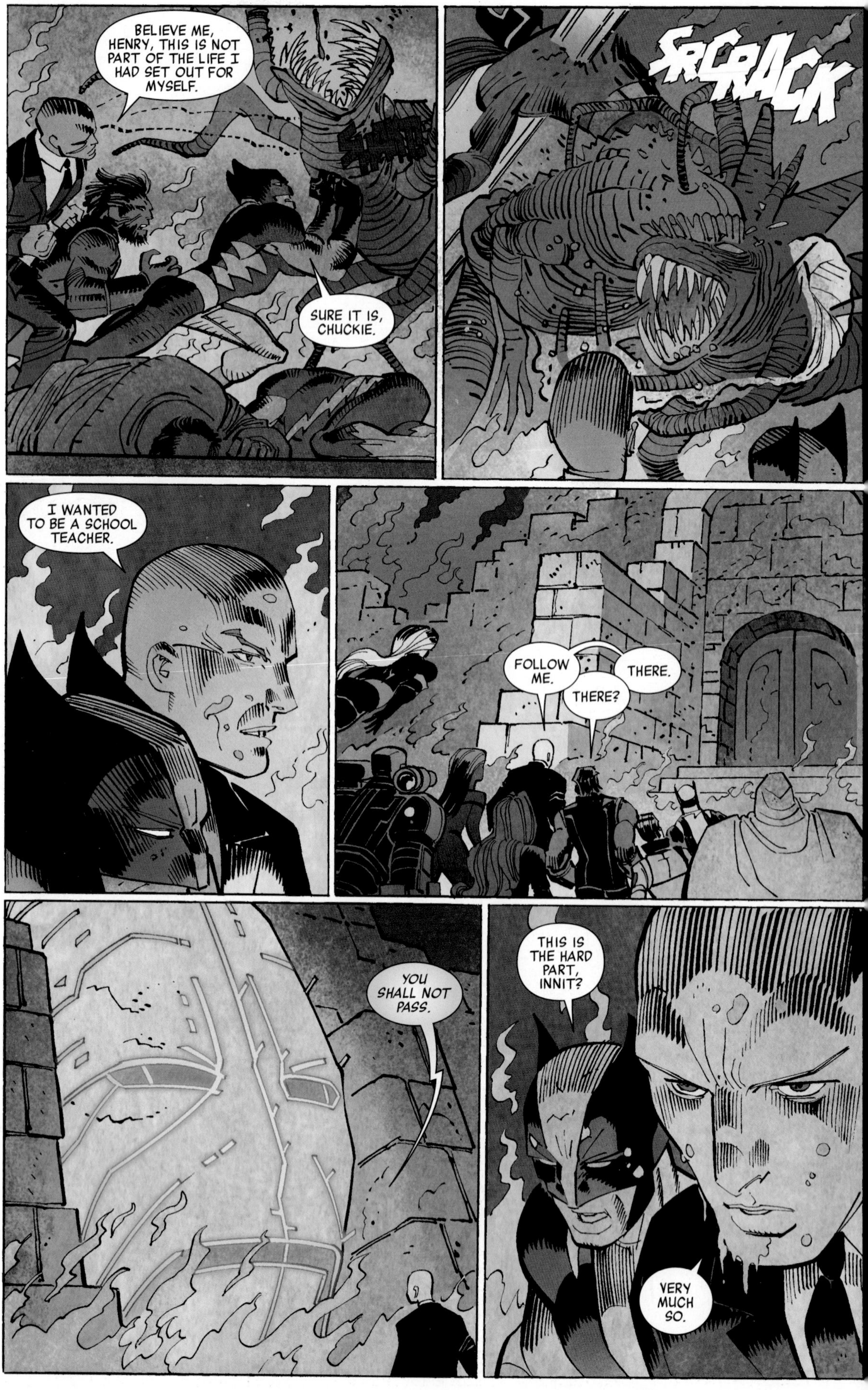
BELIEVE ME, HENRY, THIS IS NOT PART OF THE LIFE I HAD SET OUT FOR MYSELF.
SURE IT IS, CHUCKIE.
SRCRACK
I WANTED TO BE A SCHOOL TEACHER.
FOLLOW ME.
THERE?
THERE.
YOU SHALL NOT PASS.
THIS IS THE HARD PART, INNIT?
VERY MUCH SO.

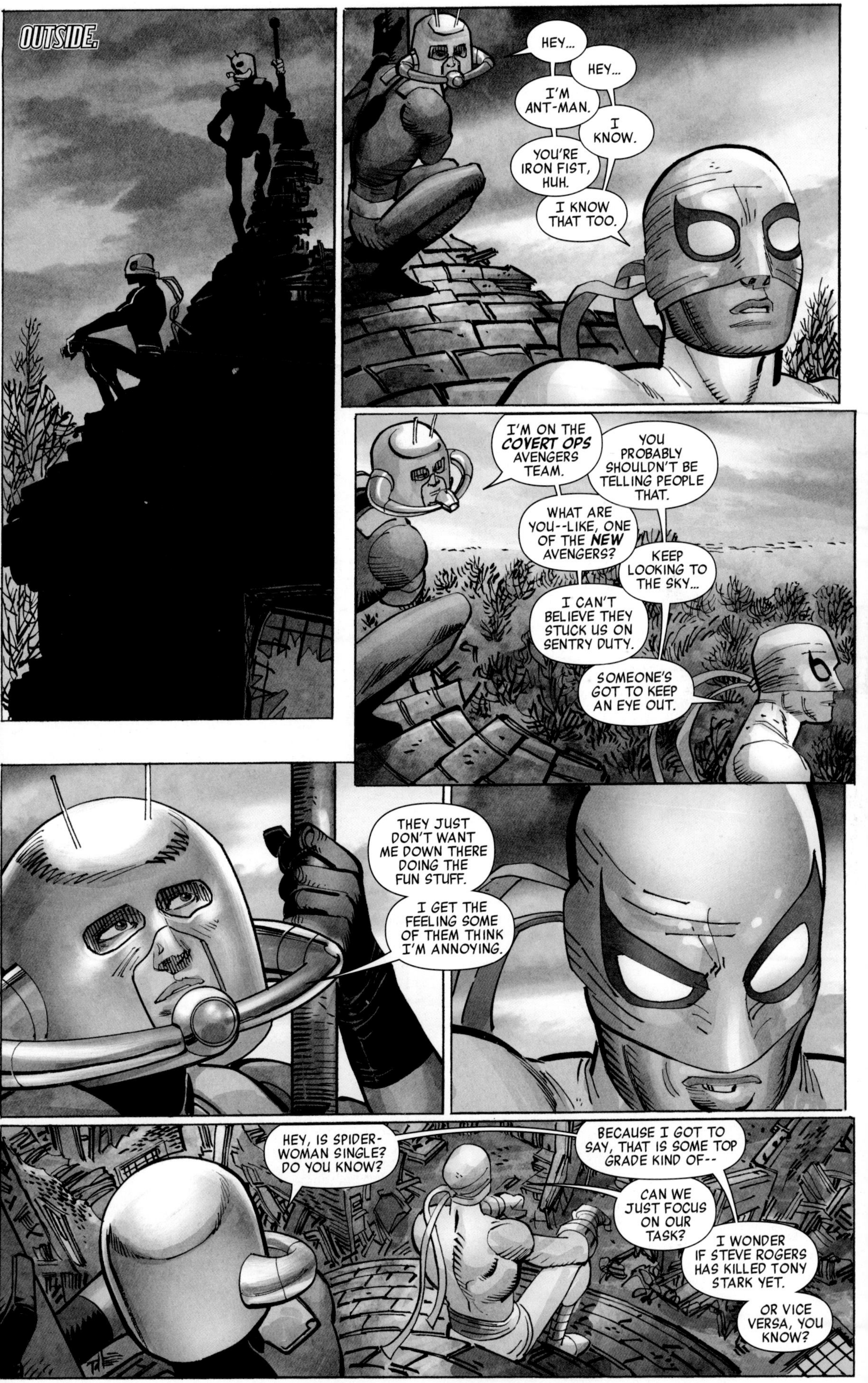
OUTSIDE.
HEY...
HEY...
I'M ANT-MAN.
I KNOW.
YOU'RE IRON FIST, HUH.
I KNOW THAT TOO.
I'M ON THE COVERT OPS AVENGERS TEAM.
YOU PROBABLY SHOULDN'T BE TELLING PEOPLE THAT.
WHAT ARE YOU--LIKE, ONE OF THE NEW AVENGERS?
KEEP LOOKING TO THE SKY...
I CAN'T BELIEVE THEY STUCK US ON SENTRY DUTY.
SOMEONE'S GOT TO KEEP AN EYE OUT.
THEY JUST DON'T WANT ME DOWN THERE DOING THE FUN STUFF.
I GET THE FEELING SOME OF THEM THINK I'M ANNOYING.
HEY, IS SPIDER-WOMAN SINGLE? DO YOU KNOW?
BECAUSE I GOT TO SAY, THAT IS SOME TOP GRADE KIND OF--
CAN WE JUST FOCUS ON OUR TASK?
I WONDER IF STEVE ROGERS HAS KILLED TONY STARK YET.
OR VICE VERSA, YOU KNOW?

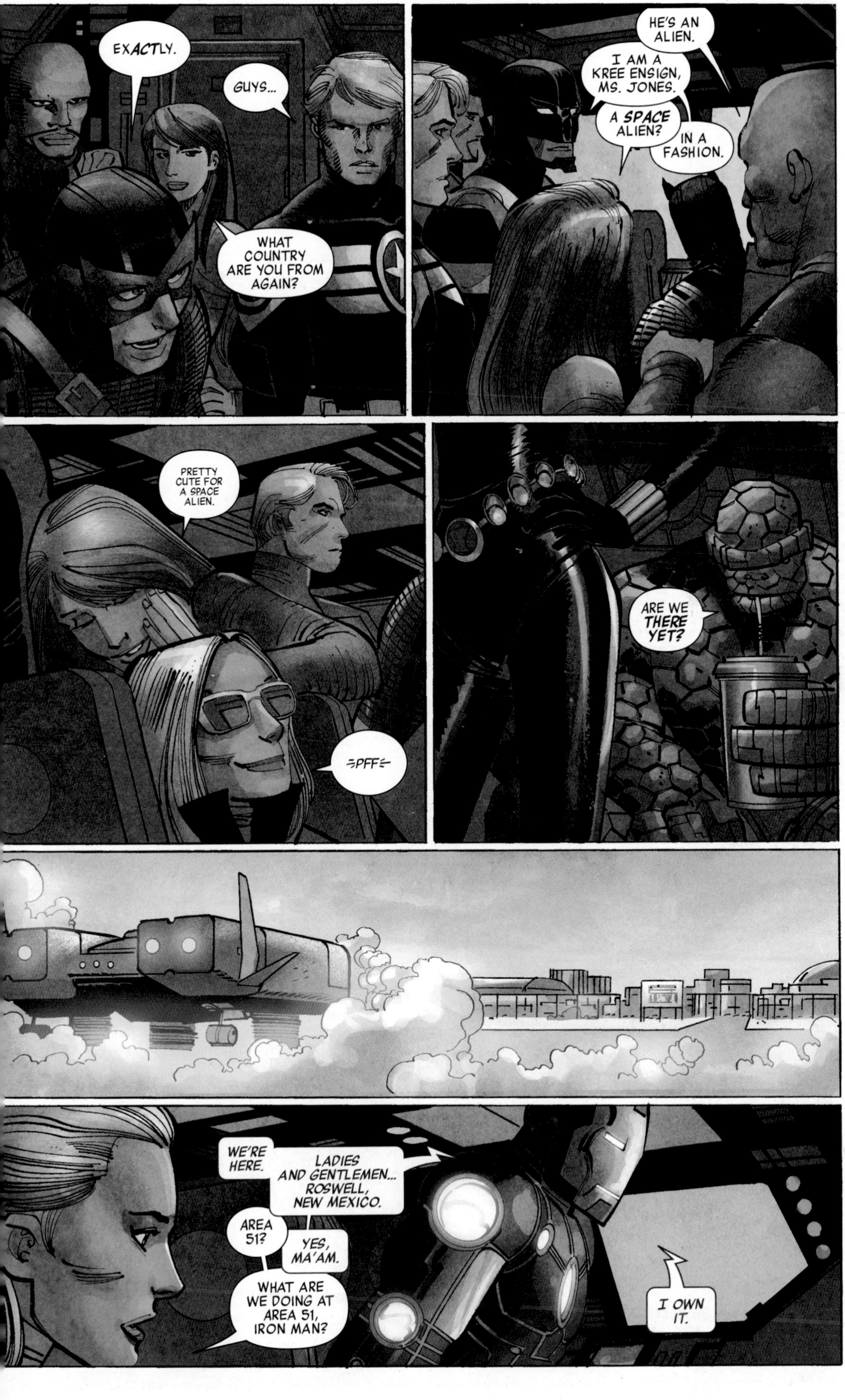
EXACTLY.
GUYS...
WHAT COUNTRY ARE YOU FROM AGAIN?
HE'S AN ALIEN.
I AM A KREE ENSIGN, MS. JONES.
A SPACE ALIEN?
IN A FASHION.
PRETTY CUTE FOR A SPACE ALIEN.
=PFF=
ARE WE THERE YET?
WE'RE HERE.
LADIES AND GENTLEMEN... ROSWELL, NEW MEXICO.
AREA 51?
YES, MA'AM.
WHAT ARE WE DOING AT AREA 51, IRON MAN?
I OWN IT.

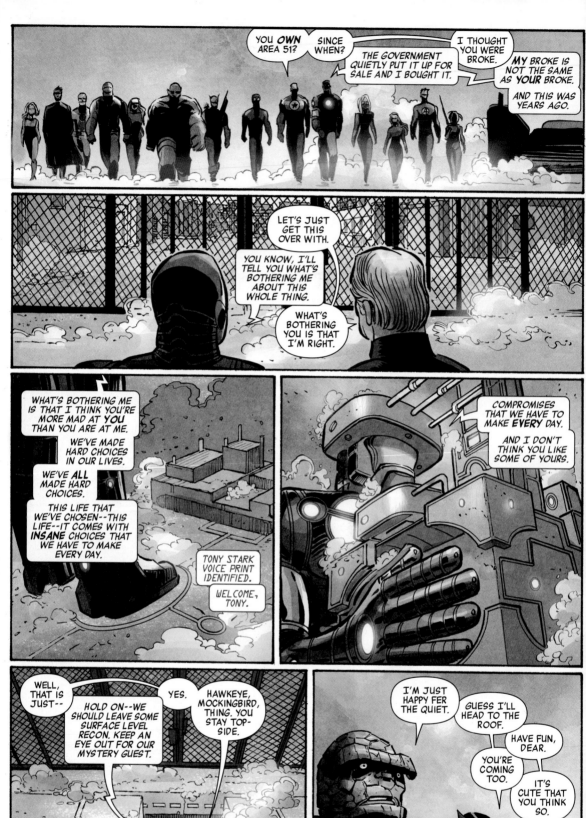

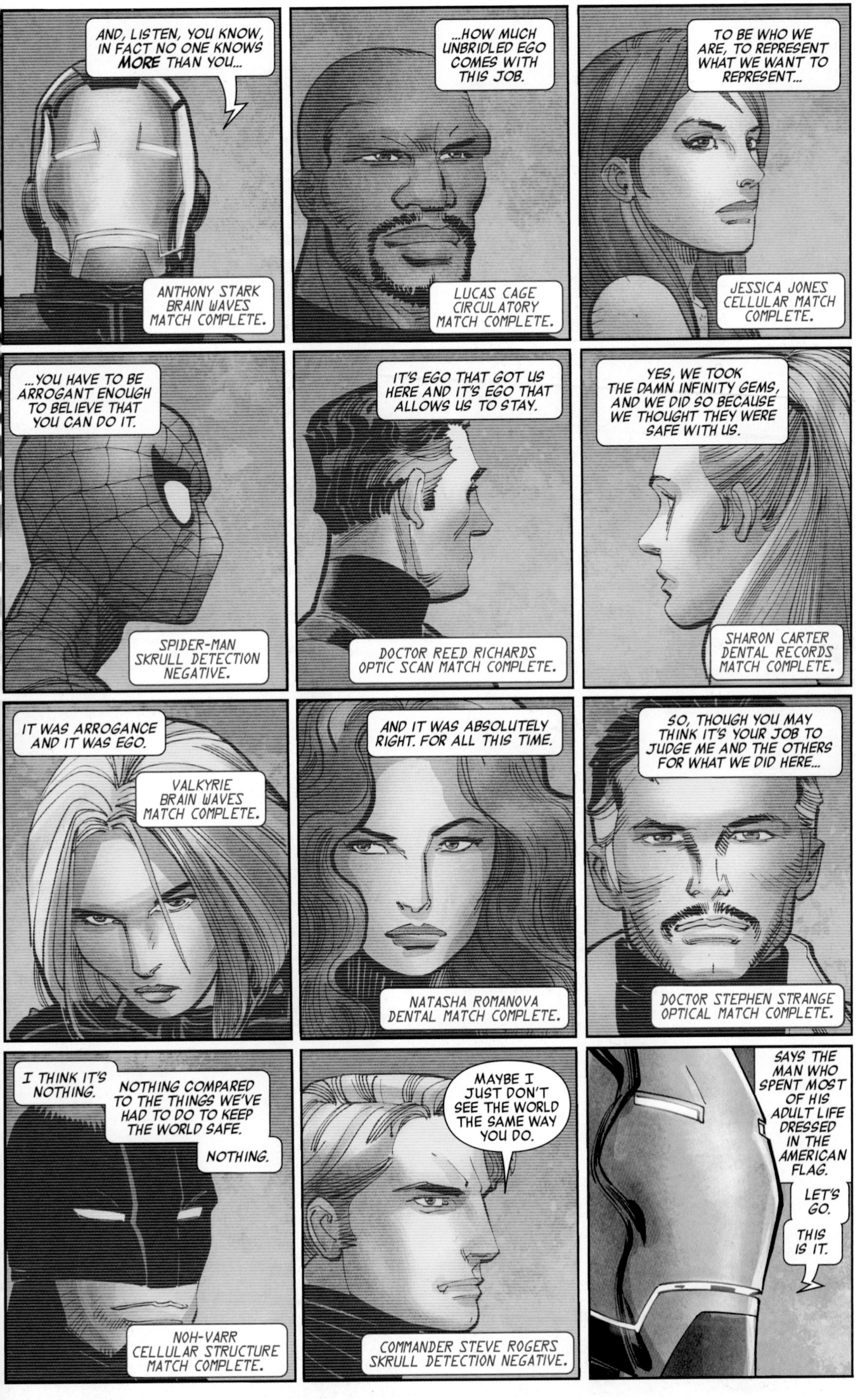
AND, LISTEN, YOU KNOW, IN FACT NO ONE KNOWS MORE THAN YOU...
ANTHONY STARK BRAIN WAVES MATCH COMPLETE.
...HOW MUCH UNBRIDLED EGO COMES WITH THIS JOB.
LUCAS CAGE CIRCULATORY MATCH COMPLETE.
TO BE WHO WE ARE, TO REPRESENT WHAT WE WANT TO REPRESENT...
JESSICA JONES CELLULAR MATCH COMPLETE.
...YOU HAVE TO BE ARROGANT ENOUGH TO BELIEVE THAT YOU CAN DO IT.
SPIDER-MAN SKRULL DETECTION NEGATIVE.
IT'S EGO THAT GOT US HERE AND IT'S EGO THAT ALLOWS US TO STAY.
DOCTOR REED RICHARDS OPTIC SCAN MATCH COMPLETE.
YES, WE TOOK THE DAMN INFINITY GEMS, AND WE DID SO BECAUSE WE THOUGHT THEY WERE SAFE WITH US.
SHARON CARTER DENTAL RECORDS MATCH COMPLETE.
IT WAS ARROGANCE AND IT WAS EGO.
VALKYRIE BRAIN WAVES MATCH COMPLETE.
AND IT WAS ABSOLUTELY RIGHT. FOR ALL THIS TIME.
NATASHA ROMANOVA DENTAL MATCH COMPLETE.
SO, THOUGH YOU MAY THINK IT'S YOUR JOB TO JUDGE ME AND THE OTHERS FOR WHAT WE DID HERE...
DOCTOR STEPHEN STRANGE OPTICAL MATCH COMPLETE.
I THINK IT'S NOTHING.
NOTHING COMPARED TO THE THINGS WE'VE HAD TO DO TO KEEP THE WORLD SAFE.
NOTHING.
NOH-VARR CELLULAR STRUCTURE MATCH COMPLETE.
MAYBE I JUST DON'T SEE THE WORLD THE SAME WAY YOU DO.
COMMANDER STEVE ROGERS SKRULL DETECTION NEGATIVE.
SAYS THE MAN WHO SPENT MOST OF HIS ADULT LIFE DRESSED IN THE AMERICAN FLAG.
LET'S GO.
THIS IS IT.

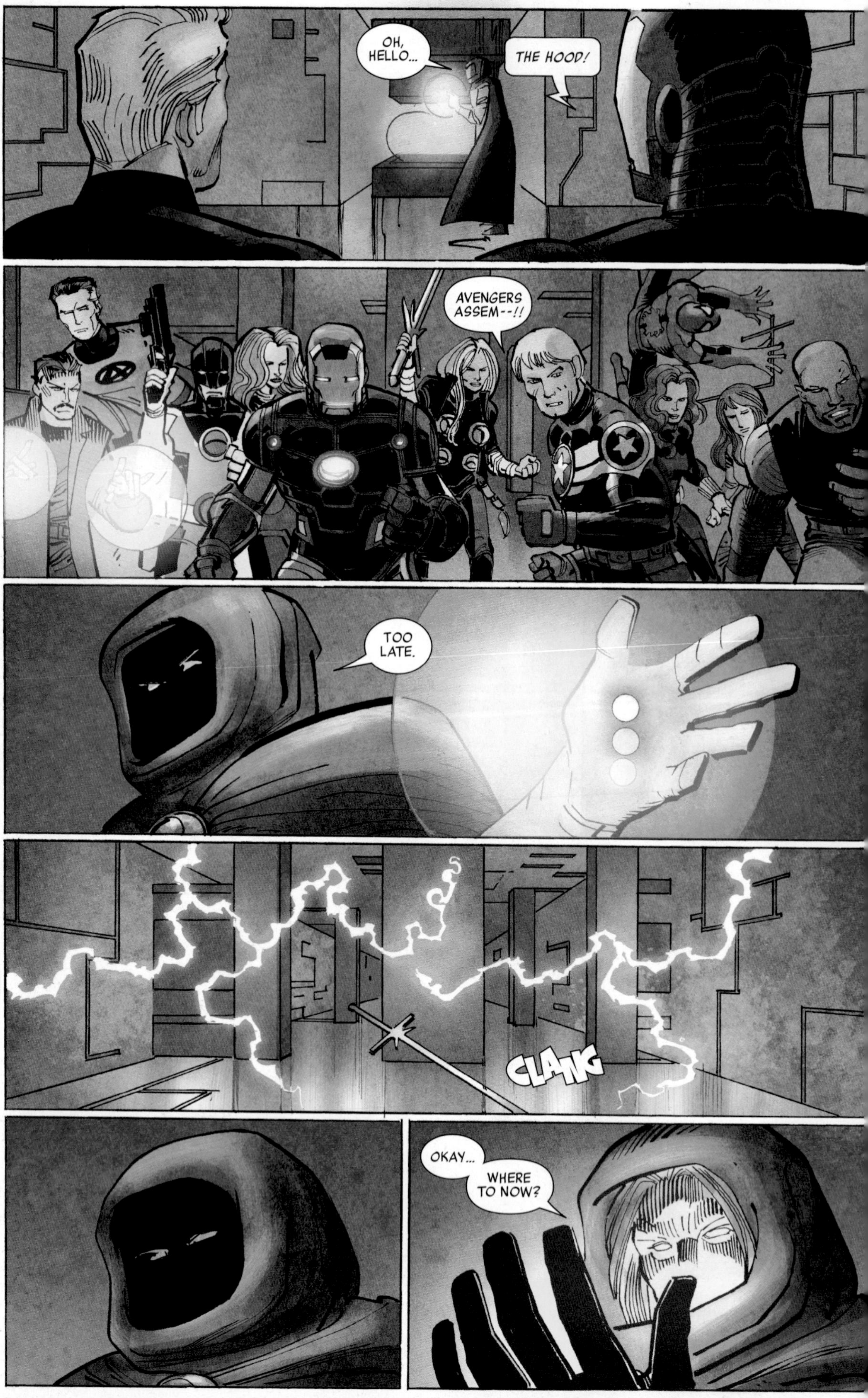
OH, HELLO...
THE HOOD!
AVENGERS ASSEM--!!
TOO LATE.
CLANG
OKAY...
WHERE TO NOW?

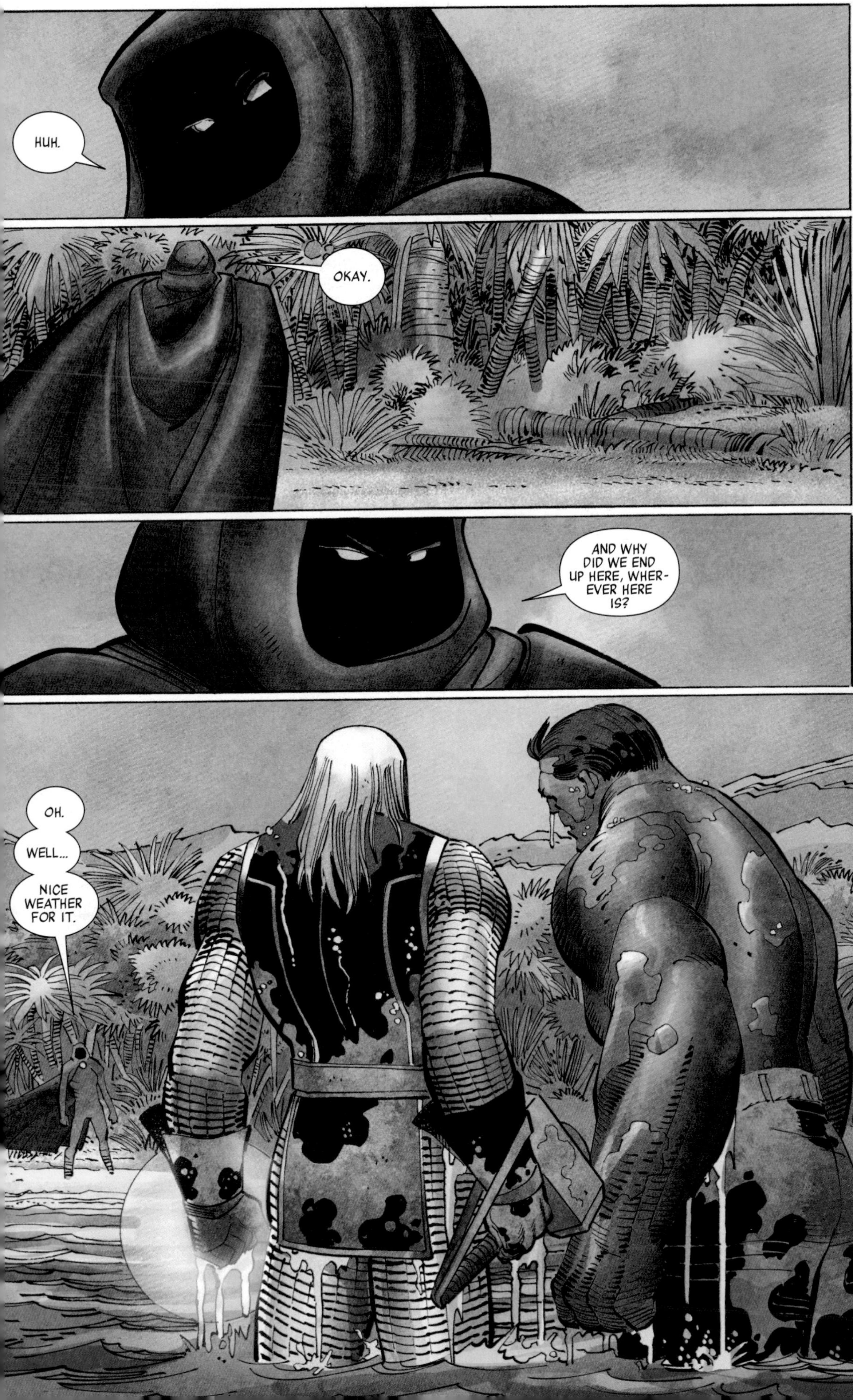
HUH.
OKAY.
AND WHY DID WE END UP HERE, WHER-EVER HERE IS?
OH.
WELL...
NICE WEATHER FOR IT.

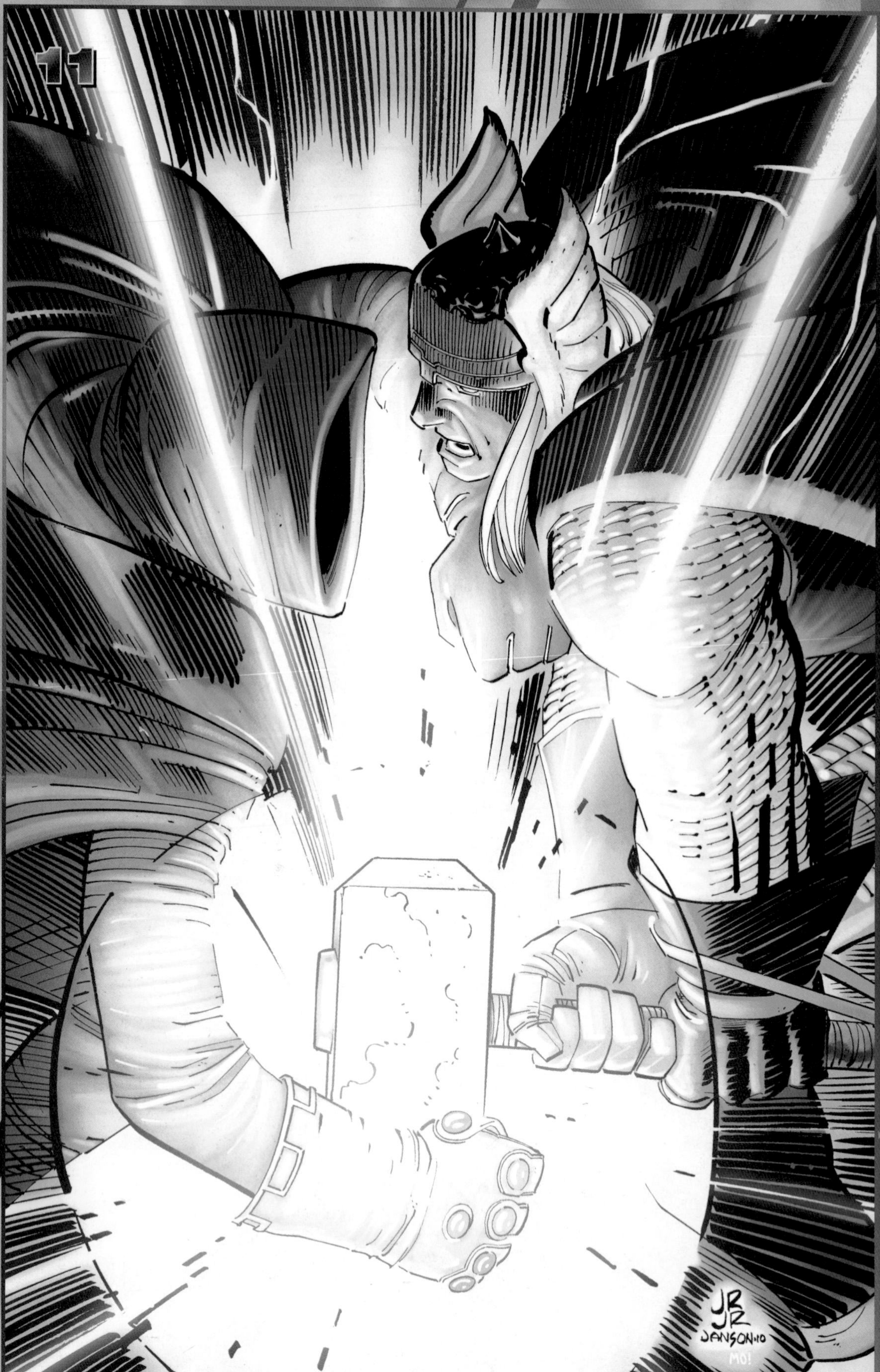
11
JR JR
JANSON.10
MO!

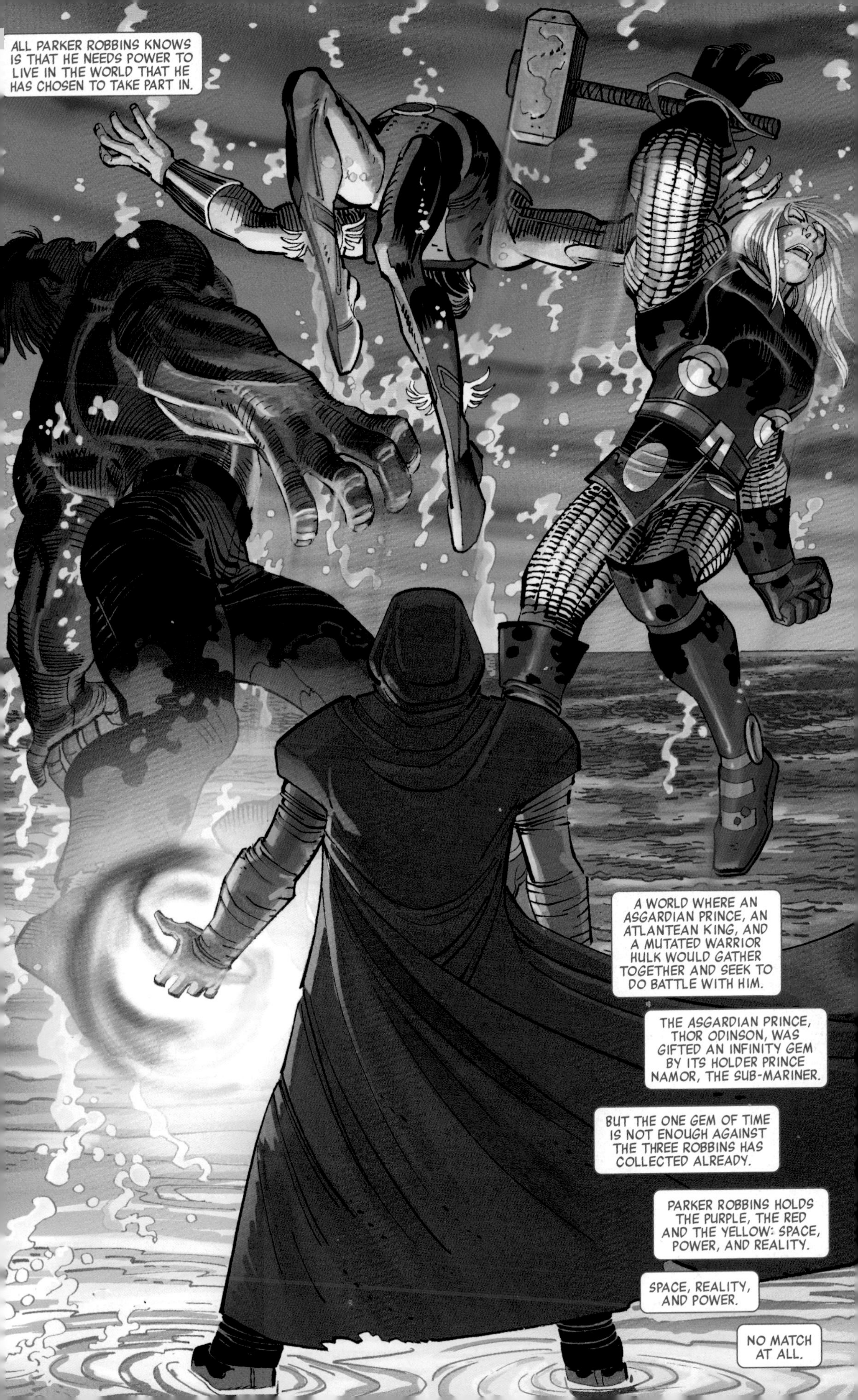
ALL PARKER ROBBINS KNOWS IS THAT HE NEEDS POWER TO LIVE IN THE WORLD THAT HE HAS CHOSEN TO TAKE PART IN.
A WORLD WHERE AN ASGARDIAN PRINCE, AN ATLANTEAN KING, AND A MUTATED WARRIOR HULK WOULD GATHER TOGETHER AND SEEK TO DO BATTLE WITH HIM.
THE ASGARDIAN PRINCE, THOR ODINSON, WAS GIFTED AN INFINITY GEM BY ITS HOLDER PRINCE NAMOR, THE SUB-MARINER.
BUT THE ONE GEM OF TIME IS NOT ENOUGH AGAINST THE THREE ROBBINS HAS COLLECTED ALREADY.
PARKER ROBBINS HOLDS THE PURPLE, THE RED AND THE YELLOW: SPACE, POWER, AND REALITY.
SPACE, REALITY, AND POWER.
NO MATCH AT ALL.

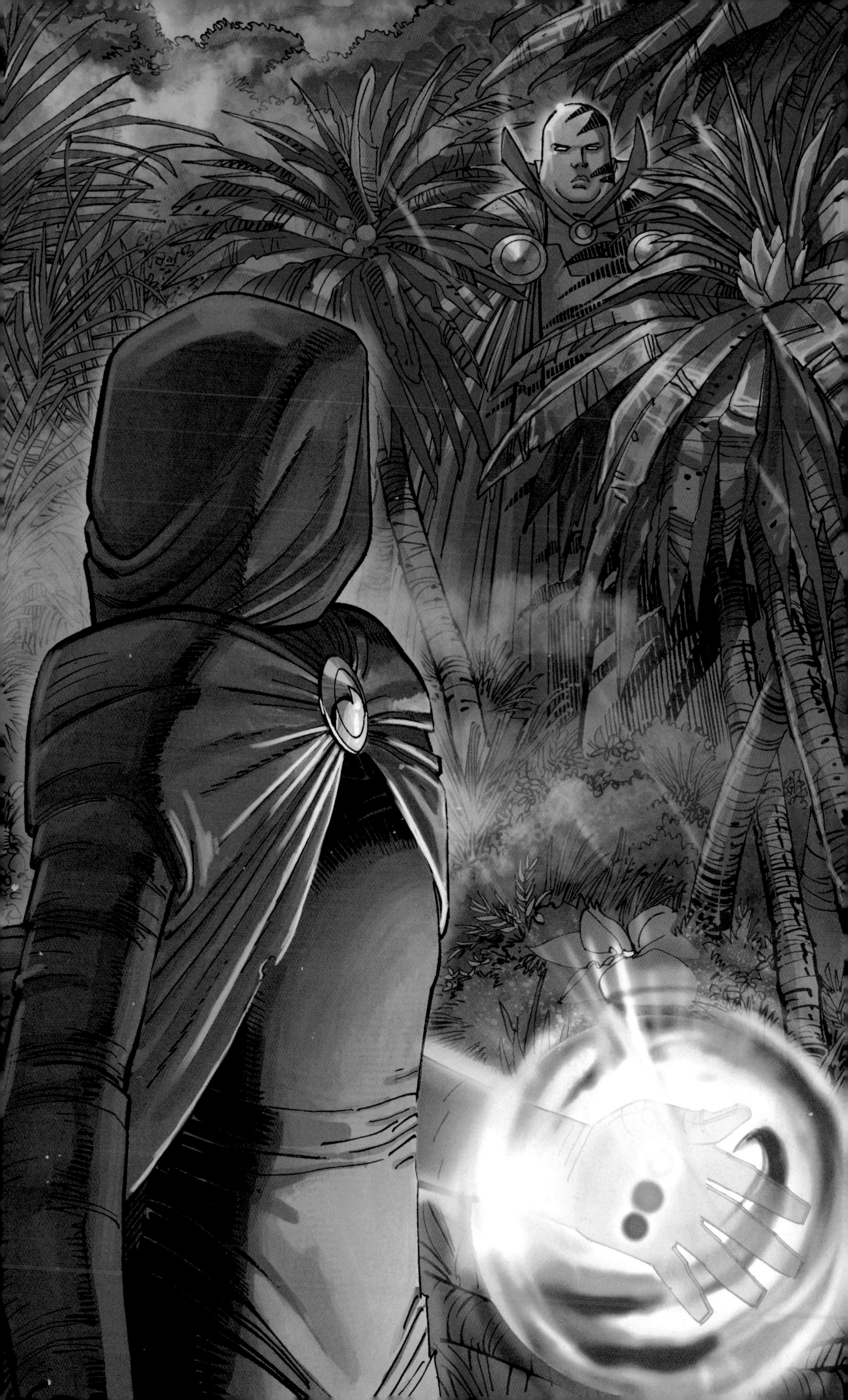

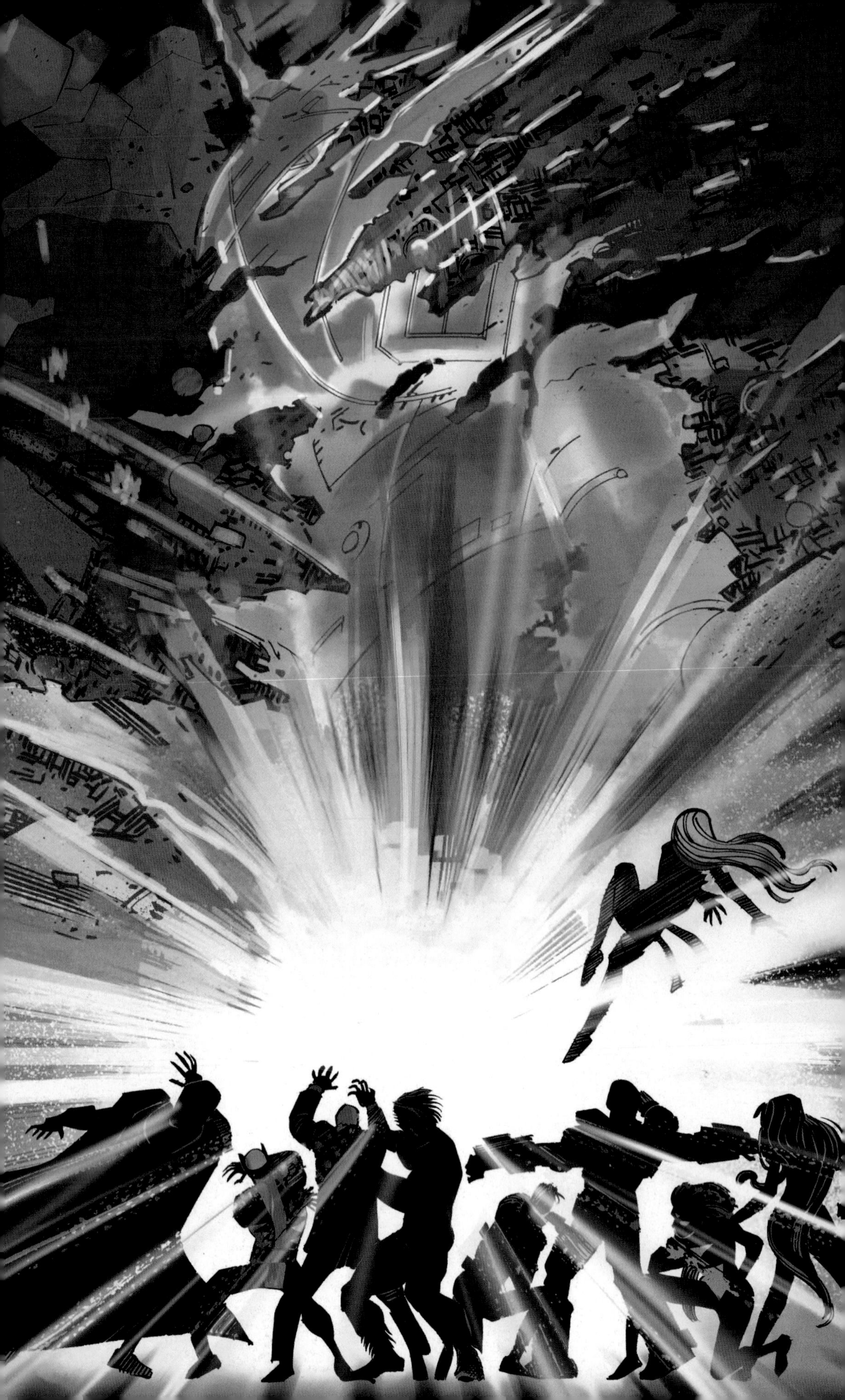

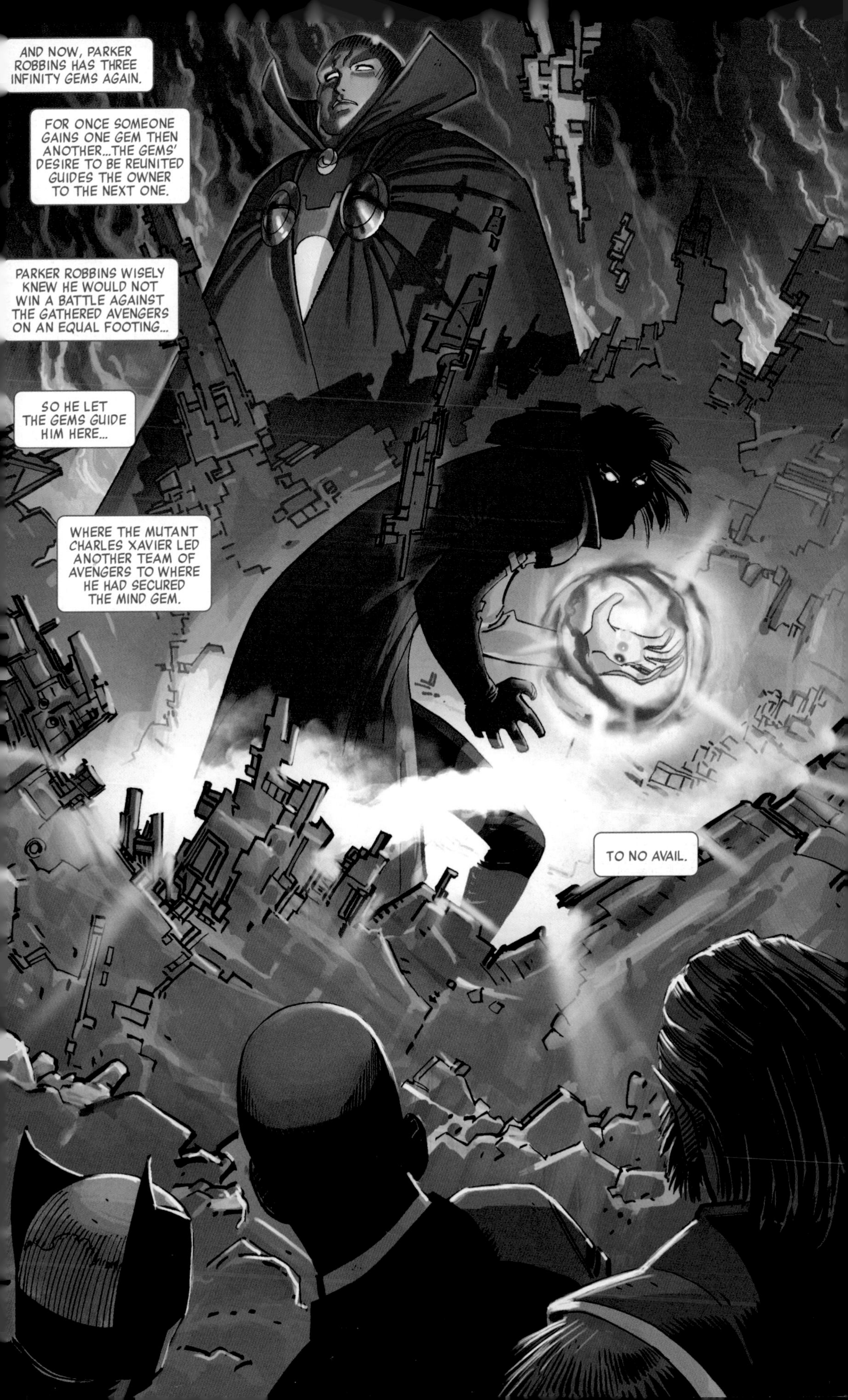
AND NOW, PARKER ROBBINS HAS THREE INFINITY GEMS AGAIN.
FOR ONCE SOMEONE GAINS ONE GEM THEN ANOTHER...THE GEMS' DESIRE TO BE REUNITED GUIDES THE OWNER TO THE NEXT ONE.
PARKER ROBBINS WISELY KNEW HE WOULD NOT WIN A BATTLE AGAINST THE GATHERED AVENGERS ON AN EQUAL FOOTING...
SO HE LET THE GEMS GUIDE HIM HERE...
WHERE THE MUTANT CHARLES XAVIER LED ANOTHER TEAM OF AVENGERS TO WHERE HE HAD SECURED THE MIND GEM.
TO NO AVAIL.

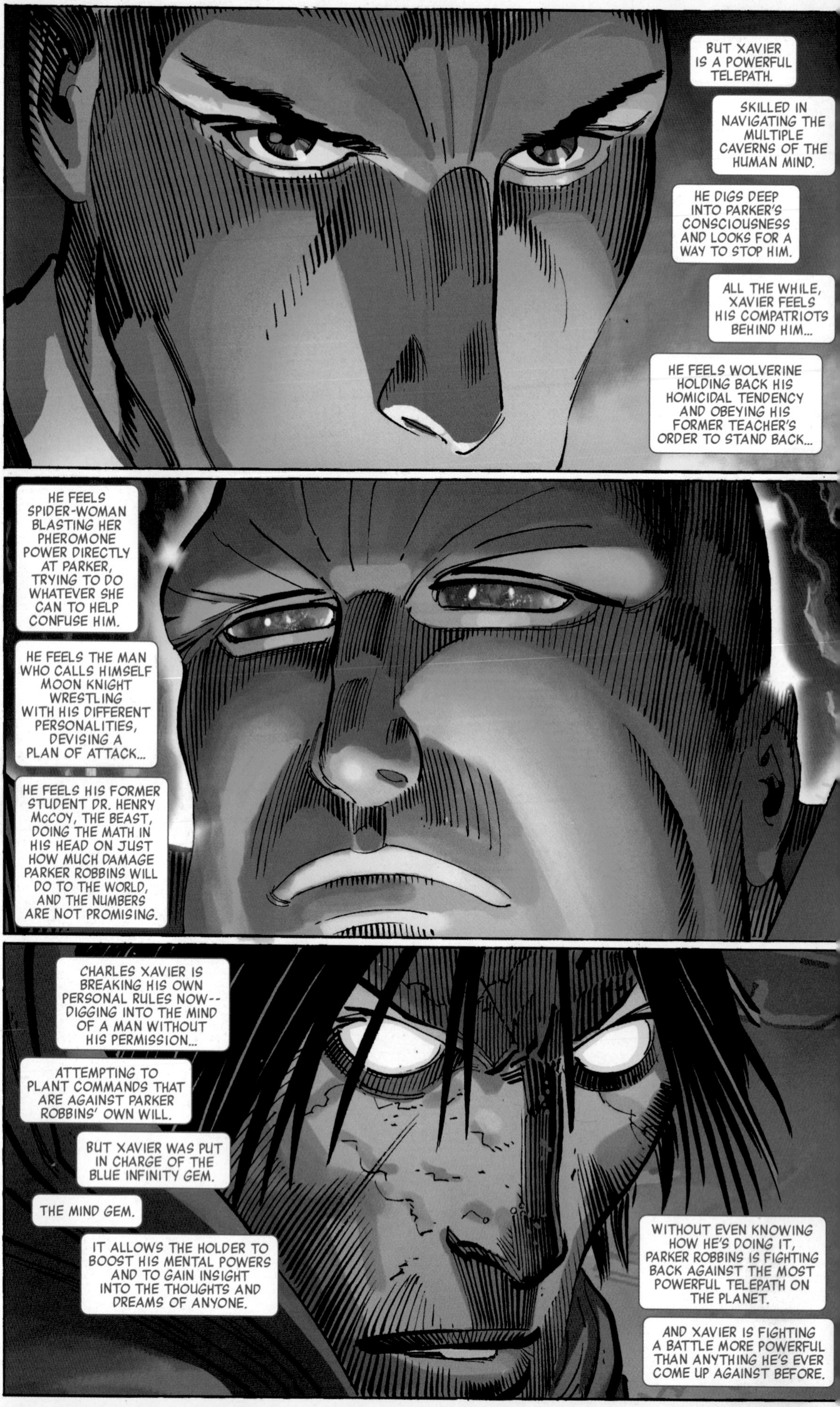
BUT XAVIER IS A POWERFUL TELEPATH.
SKILLED IN NAVIGATING THE MULTIPLE CAVERNS OF THE HUMAN MIND.
HE DIGS DEEP INTO PARKER'S CONSCIOUSNESS AND LOOKS FOR A WAY TO STOP HIM.
ALL THE WHILE, XAVIER FEELS HIS COMPATRIOTS BEHIND HIM...
HE FEELS WOLVERINE HOLDING BACK HIS HOMICIDAL TENDENCY AND OBEYING HIS FORMER TEACHER'S ORDER TO STAND BACK...
HE FEELS SPIDER-WOMAN BLASTING HER PHEROMONE POWER DIRECTLY AT PARKER, TRYING TO DO WHATEVER SHE CAN TO HELP CONFUSE HIM.
HE FEELS THE MAN WHO CALLS HIMSELF MOON KNIGHT WRESTLING WITH HIS DIFFERENT PERSONALITIES, DEVISING A PLAN OF ATTACK...
HE FEELS HIS FORMER STUDENT DR. HENRY McCOY, THE BEAST, DOING THE MATH IN HIS HEAD ON JUST HOW MUCH DAMAGE PARKER ROBBINS WILL DO TO THE WORLD, AND THE NUMBERS ARE NOT PROMISING.
CHARLES XAVIER IS BREAKING HIS OWN PERSONAL RULES NOW-- DIGGING INTO THE MIND OF A MAN WITHOUT HIS PERMISSION...
ATTEMPTING TO PLANT COMMANDS THAT ARE AGAINST PARKER ROBBINS' OWN WILL.
BUT XAVIER WAS PUT IN CHARGE OF THE BLUE INFINITY GEM.
THE MIND GEM.
IT ALLOWS THE HOLDER TO BOOST HIS MENTAL POWERS AND TO GAIN INSIGHT INTO THE THOUGHTS AND DREAMS OF ANYONE.
WITHOUT EVEN KNOWING HOW HE'S DOING IT, PARKER ROBBINS IS FIGHTING BACK AGAINST THE MOST POWERFUL TELEPATH ON THE PLANET.
AND XAVIER IS FIGHTING A BATTLE MORE POWERFUL THAN ANYTHING HE'S EVER COME UP AGAINST BEFORE.

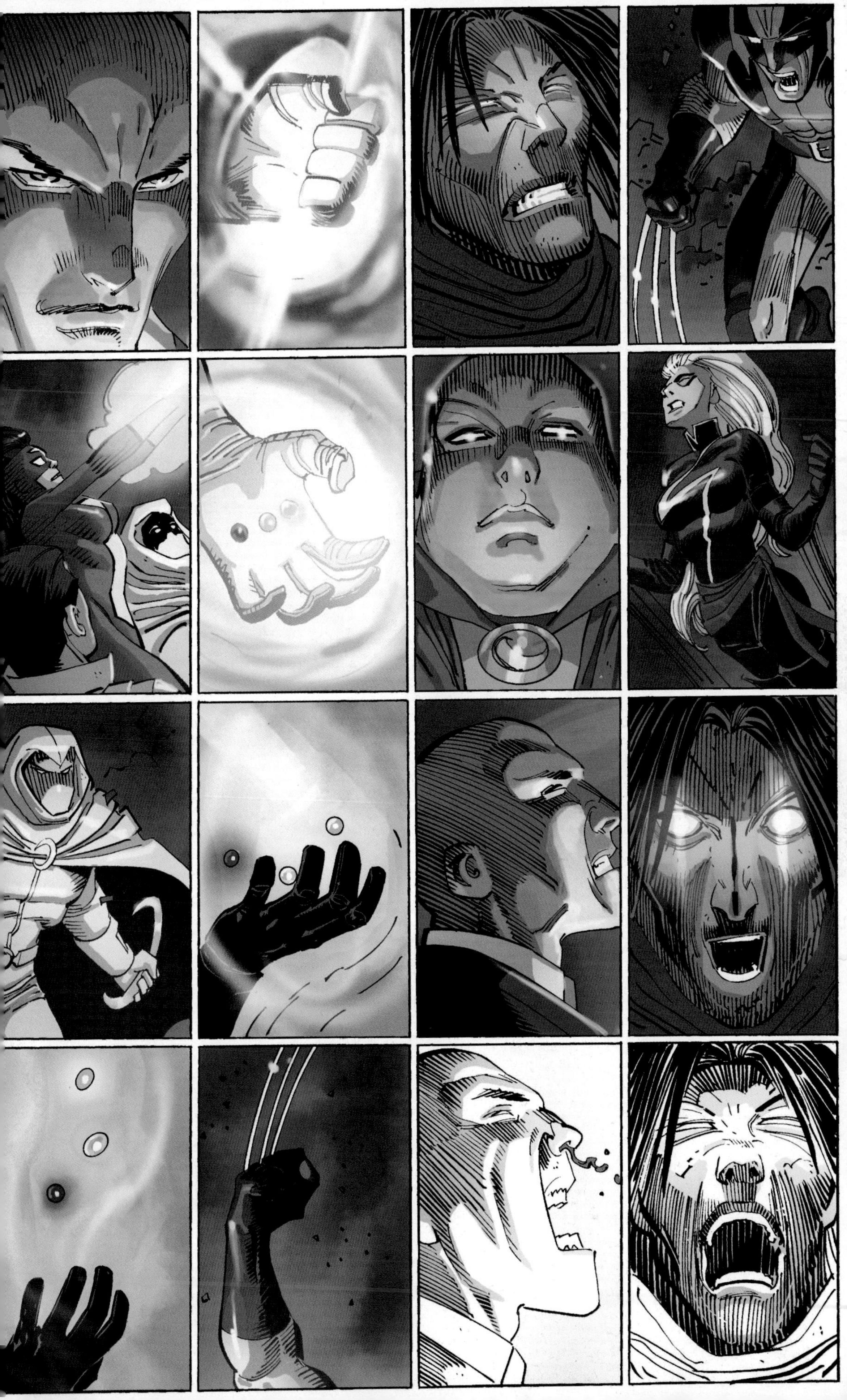

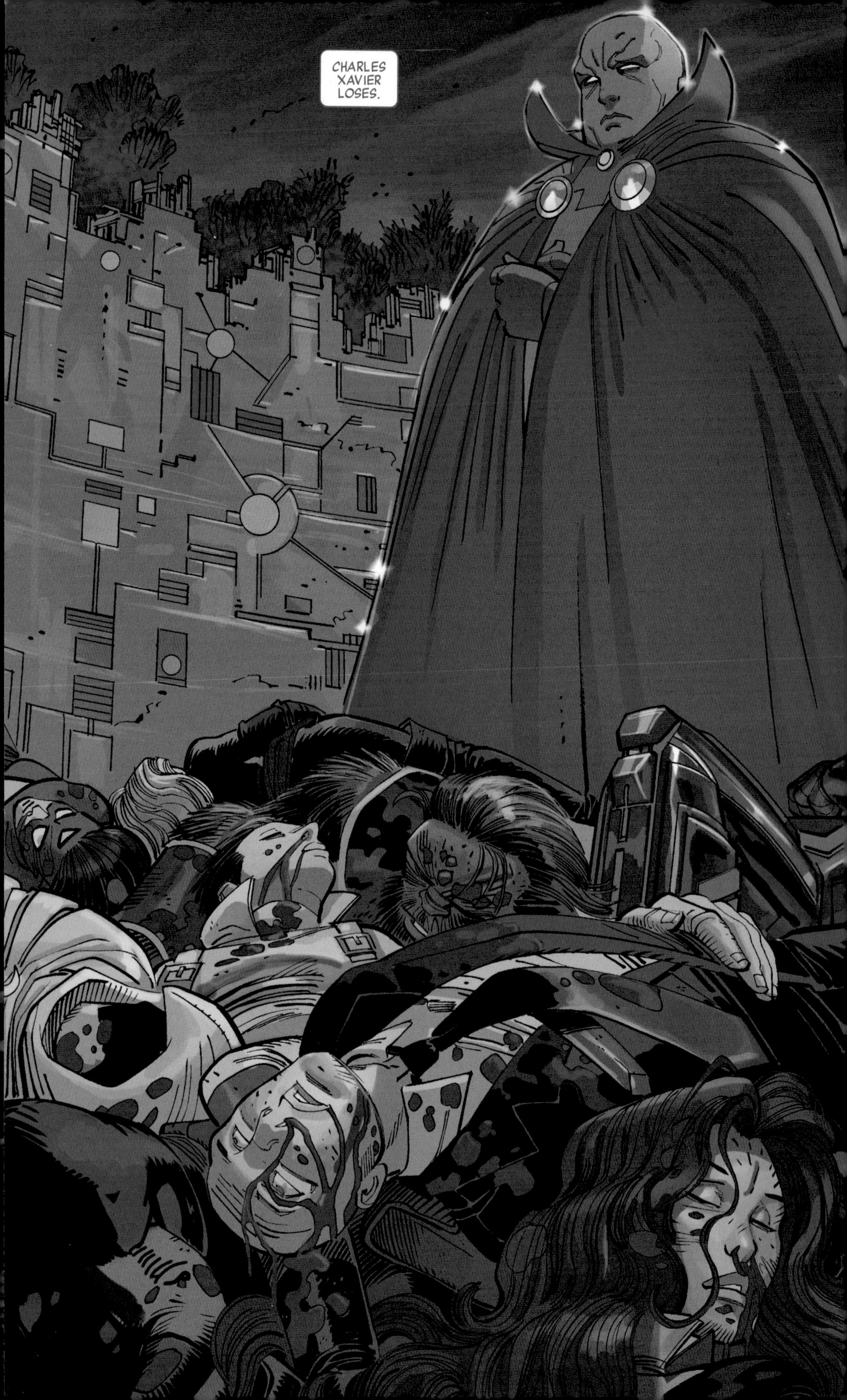
CHARLES XAVIER LOSES.

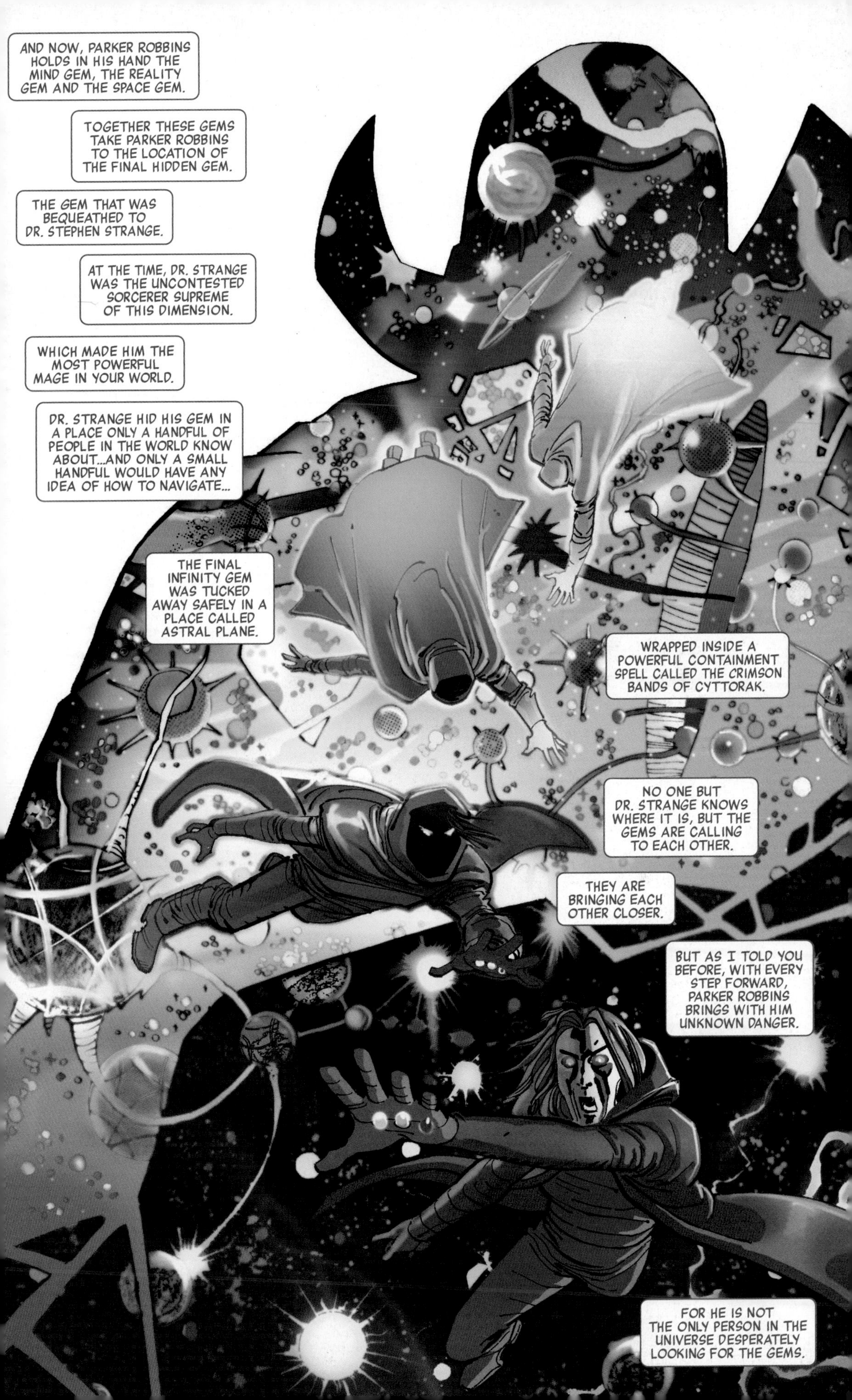
AND NOW, PARKER ROBBINS HOLDS IN HIS HAND THE MIND GEM, THE REALITY GEM AND THE SPACE GEM.
TOGETHER THESE GEMS TAKE PARKER ROBBINS TO THE LOCATION OF THE FINAL HIDDEN GEM.
THE GEM THAT WAS BEQUEATHED TO DR. STEPHEN STRANGE.
AT THE TIME, DR. STRANGE WAS THE UNCONTESTED SORCERER SUPREME OF THIS DIMENSION.
WHICH MADE HIM THE MOST POWERFUL MAGE IN YOUR WORLD.
DR. STRANGE HID HIS GEM IN A PLACE ONLY A HANDFUL OF PEOPLE IN THE WORLD KNOW ABOUT...AND ONLY A SMALL HANDFUL WOULD HAVE ANY IDEA OF HOW TO NAVIGATE...
THE FINAL INFINITY GEM WAS TUCKED AWAY SAFELY IN A PLACE CALLED ASTRAL PLANE.
WRAPPED INSIDE A POWERFUL CONTAINMENT SPELL CALLED THE CRIMSON BANDS OF CYTTORAK.
NO ONE BUT DR. STRANGE KNOWS WHERE IT IS, BUT THE GEMS ARE CALLING TO EACH OTHER.
THEY ARE BRINGING EACH OTHER CLOSER.
BUT AS I TOLD YOU BEFORE, WITH EVERY STEP FORWARD, PARKER ROBBINS BRINGS WITH HIM UNKNOWN DANGER.
FOR HE IS NOT THE ONLY PERSON IN THE UNIVERSE DESPERATELY LOOKING FOR THE GEMS.

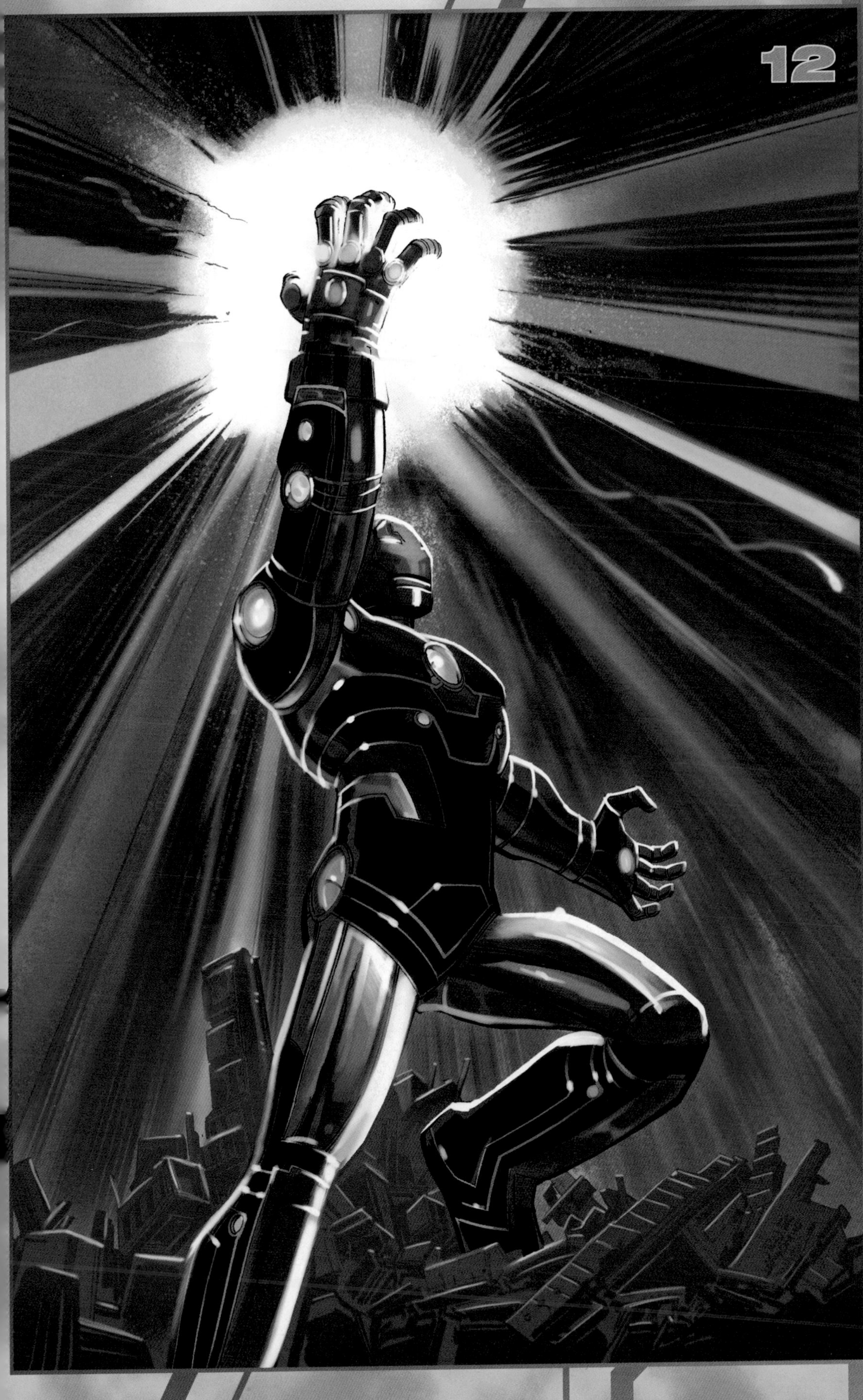
12

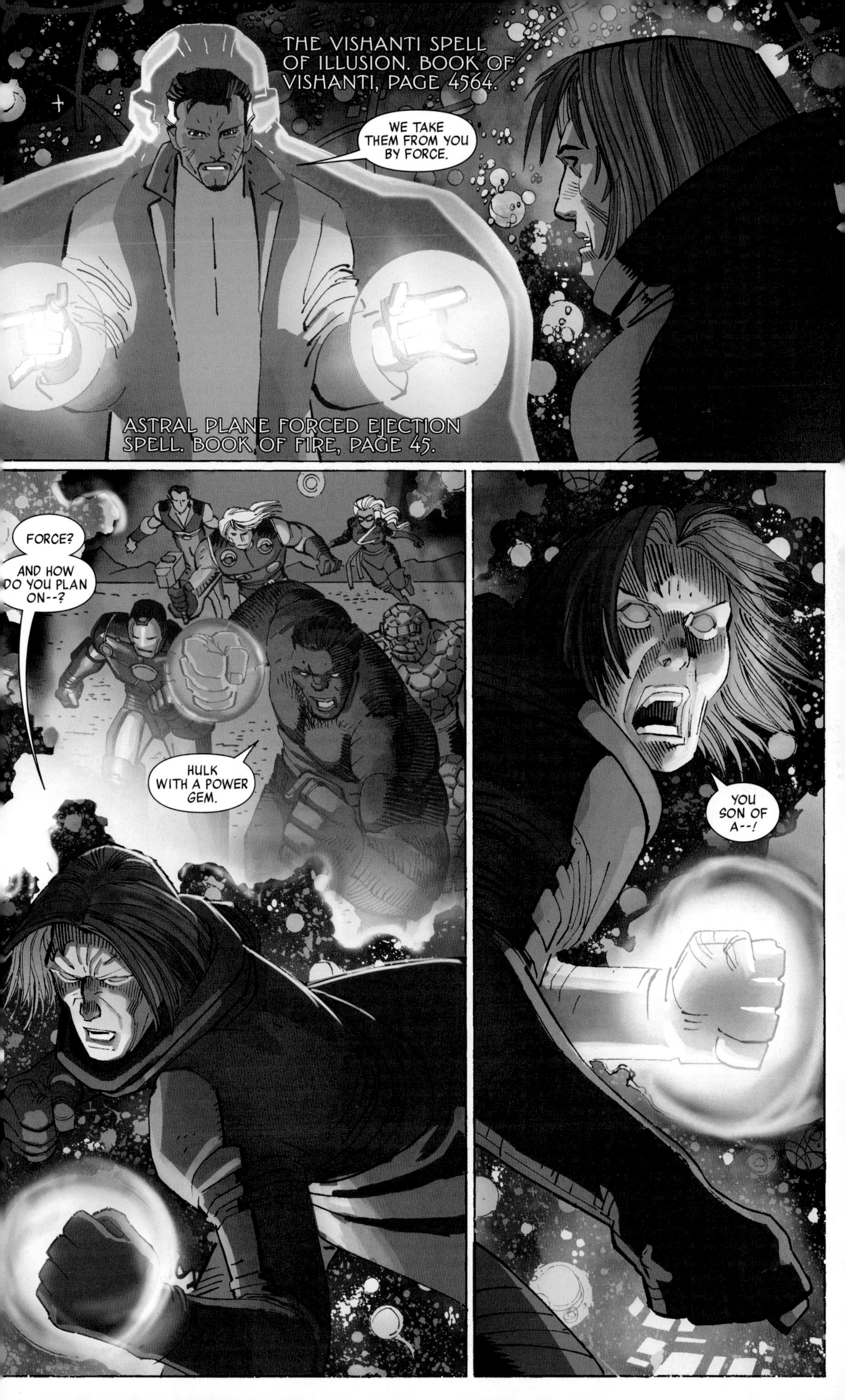
THE VISHANTI SPELL OF ILLUSION. BOOK OF VISHANTI, PAGE 4564.
WE TAKE THEM FROM YOU BY FORCE.
ASTRAL PLANE FORCED EJECTION SPELL. BOOK OF FIRE, PAGE 45.
FORCE?
AND HOW DO YOU PLAN ON--?
HULK WITH A POWER GEM.
YOU SON OF A--!

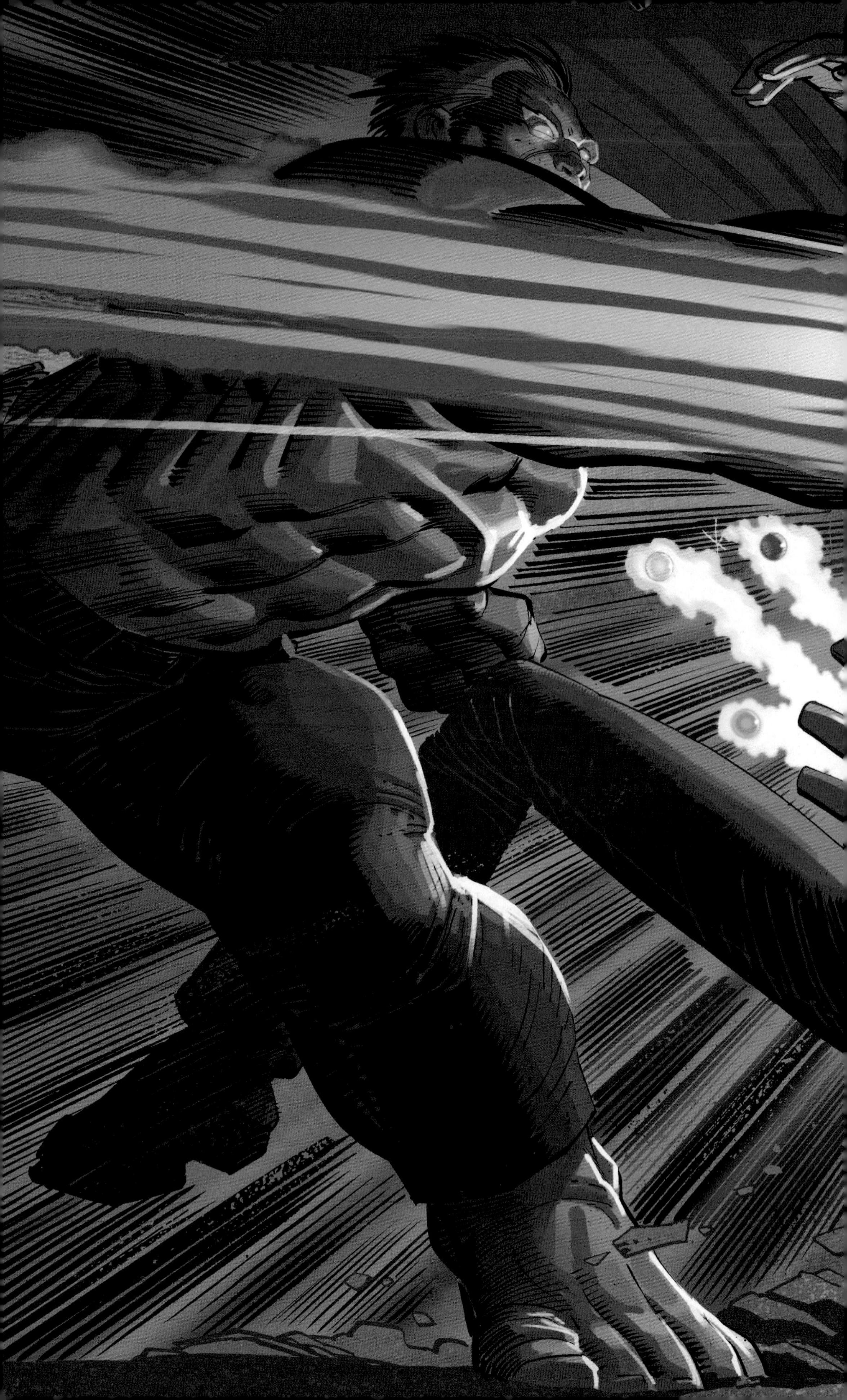

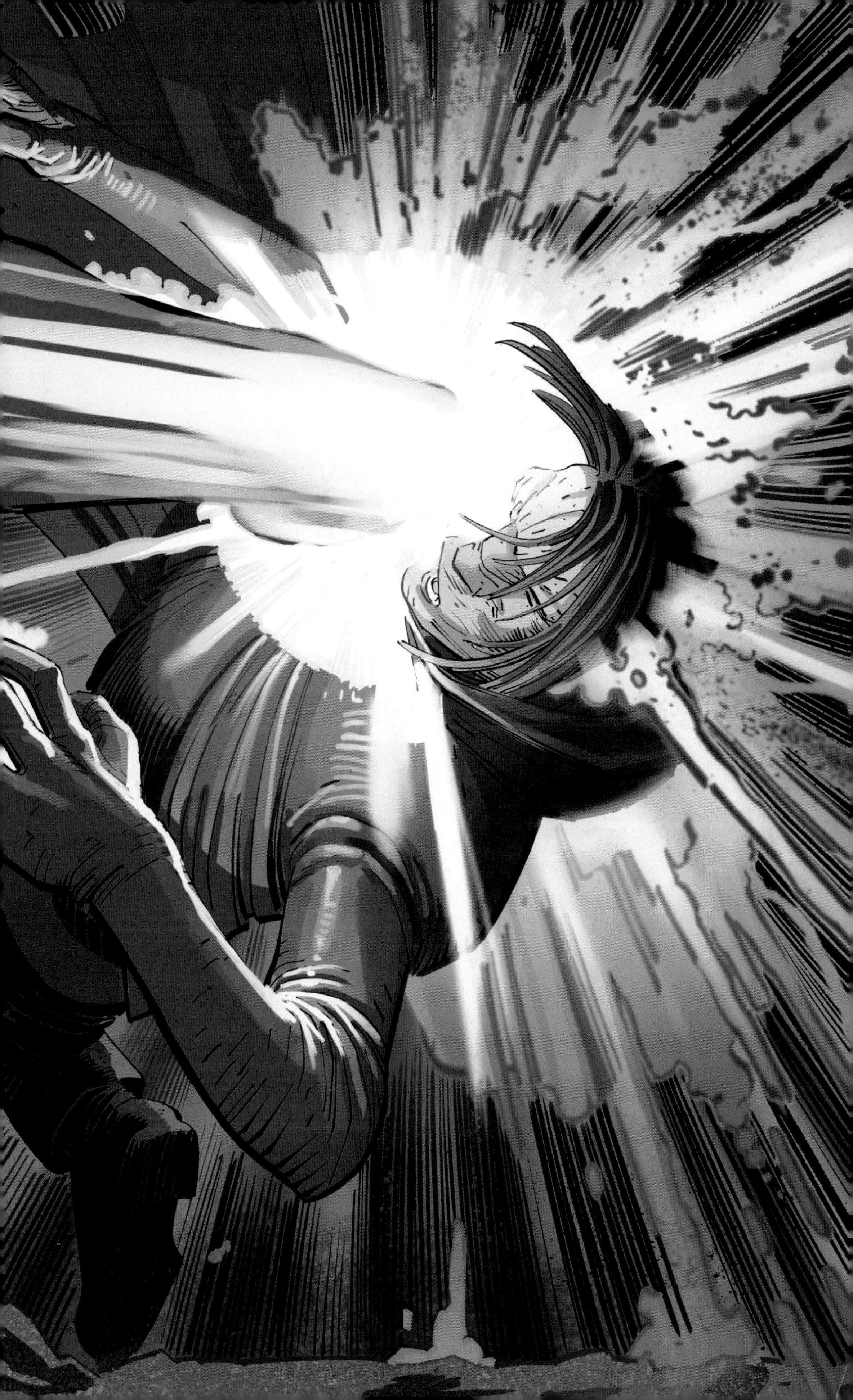

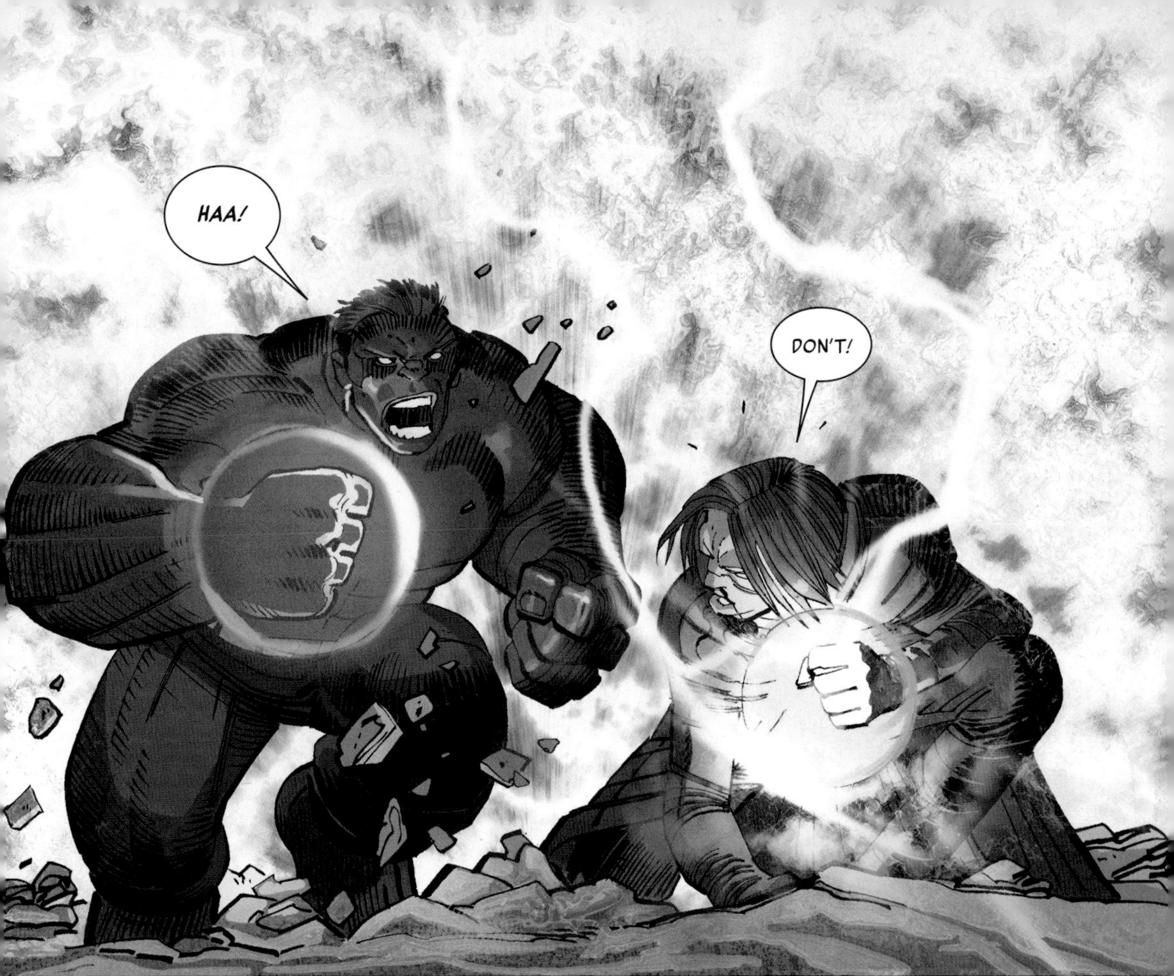
HAA!
DON'T!
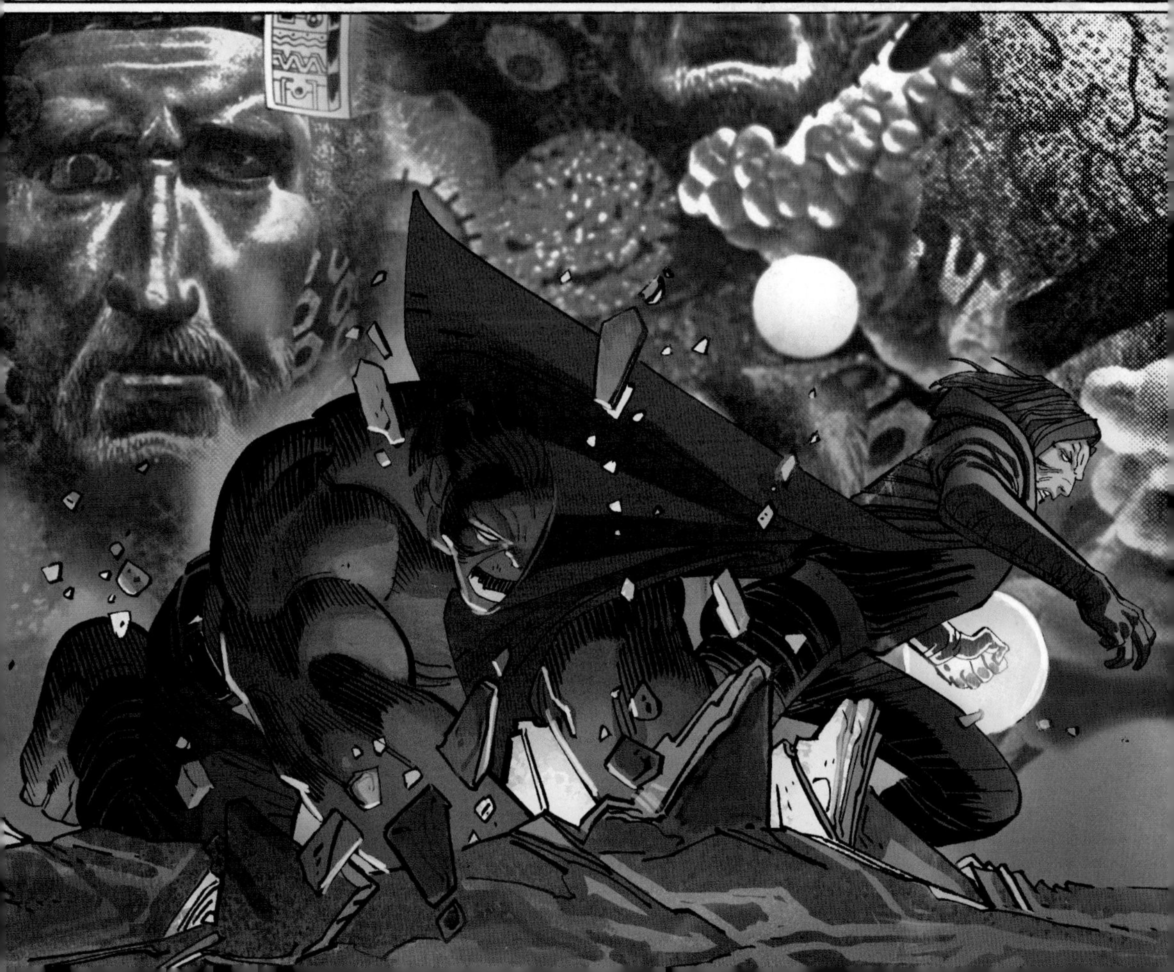

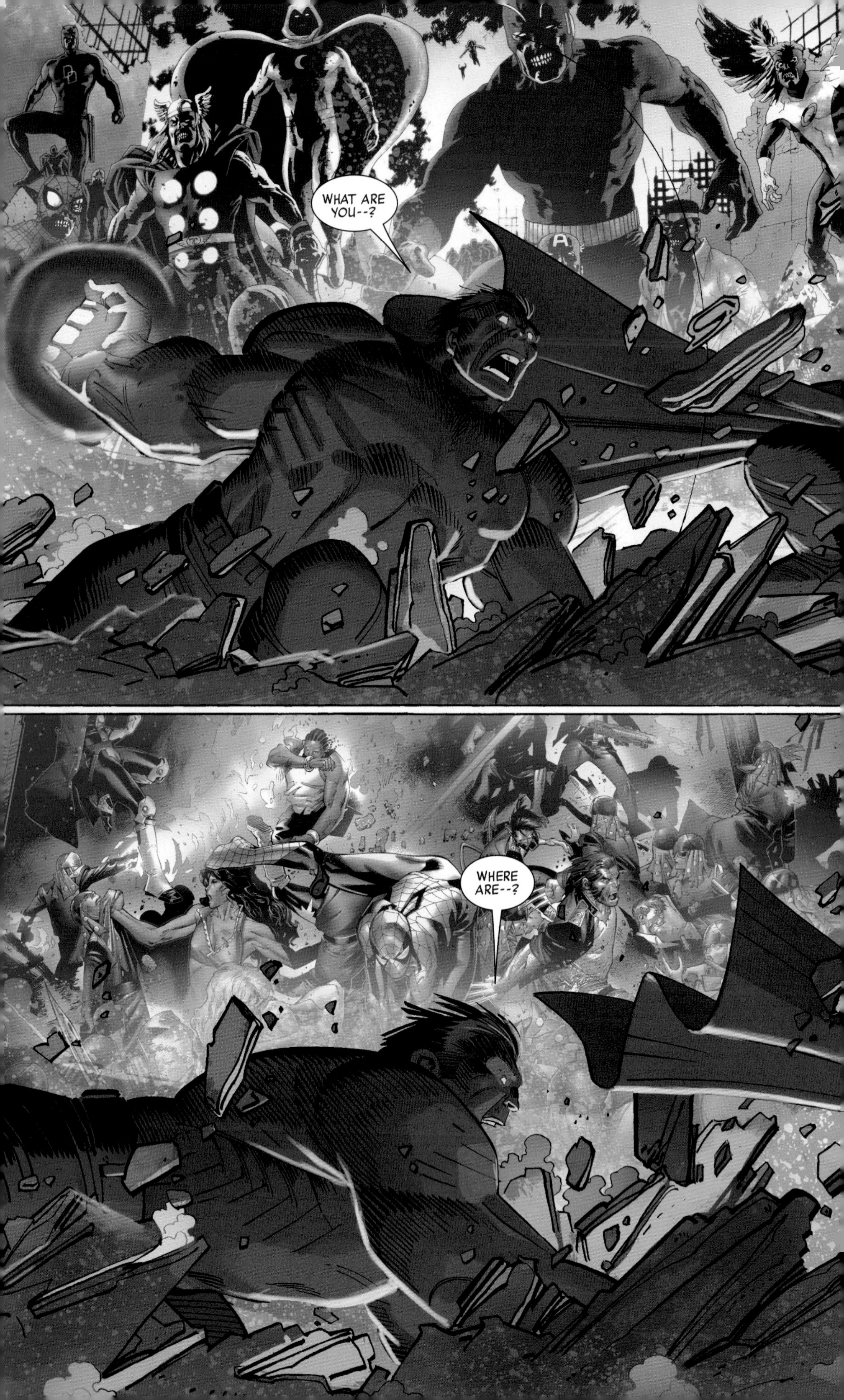
WHAT ARE YOU--?
WHERE ARE--?

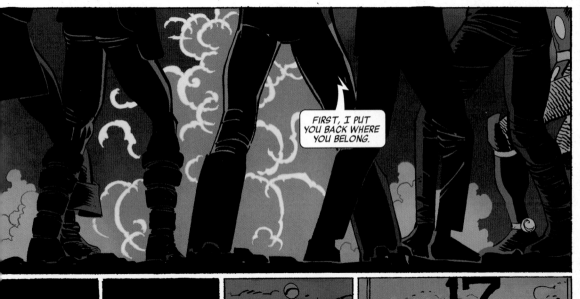

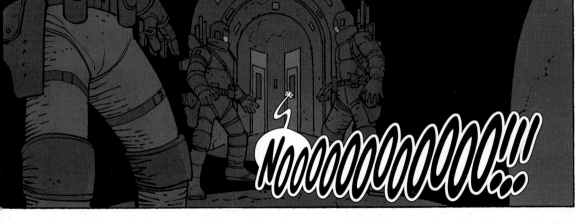

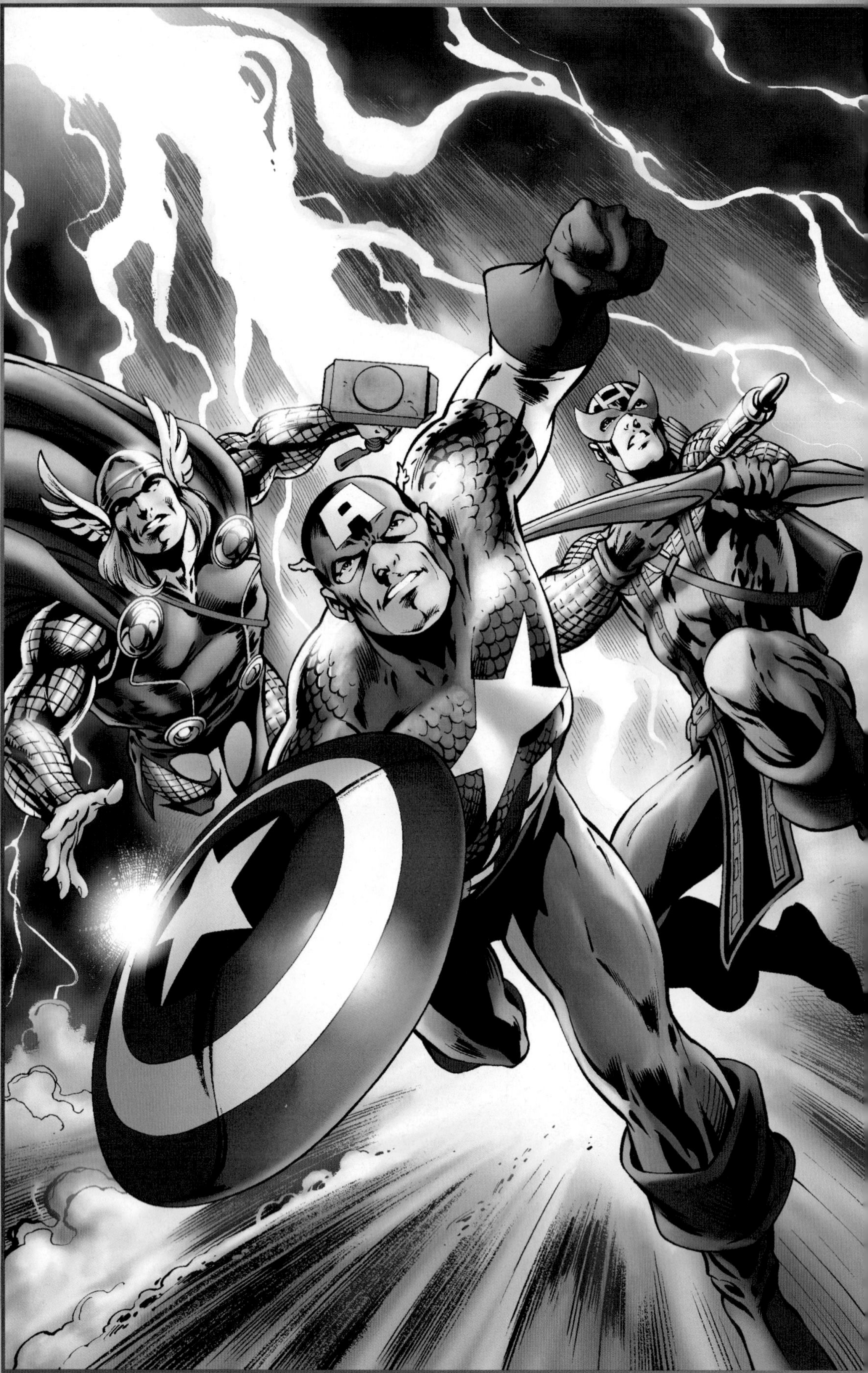

#11 VARIANT BY ALAN DAVIS, PAUL NEARY
& PAUL MOUNTS

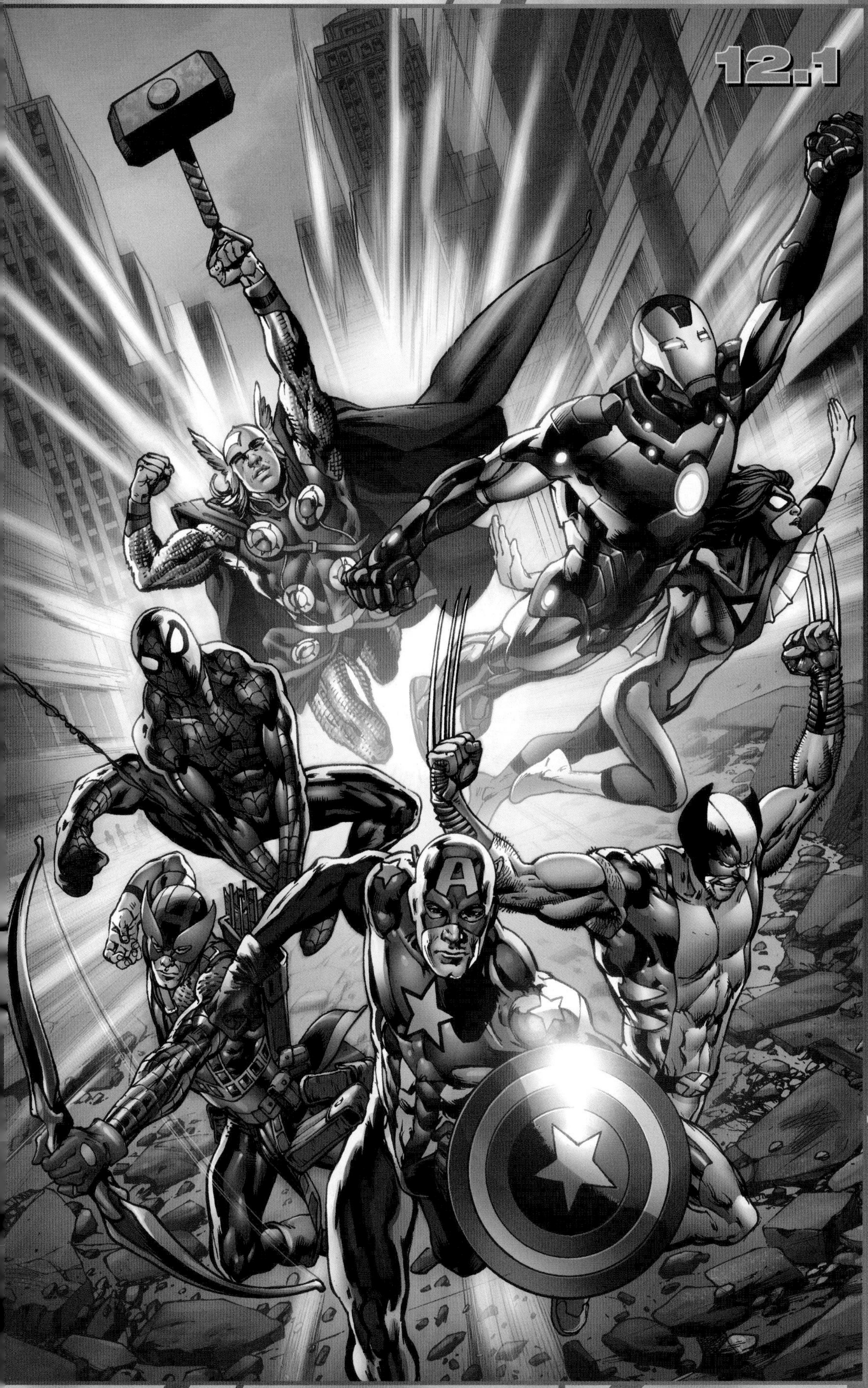
12.1

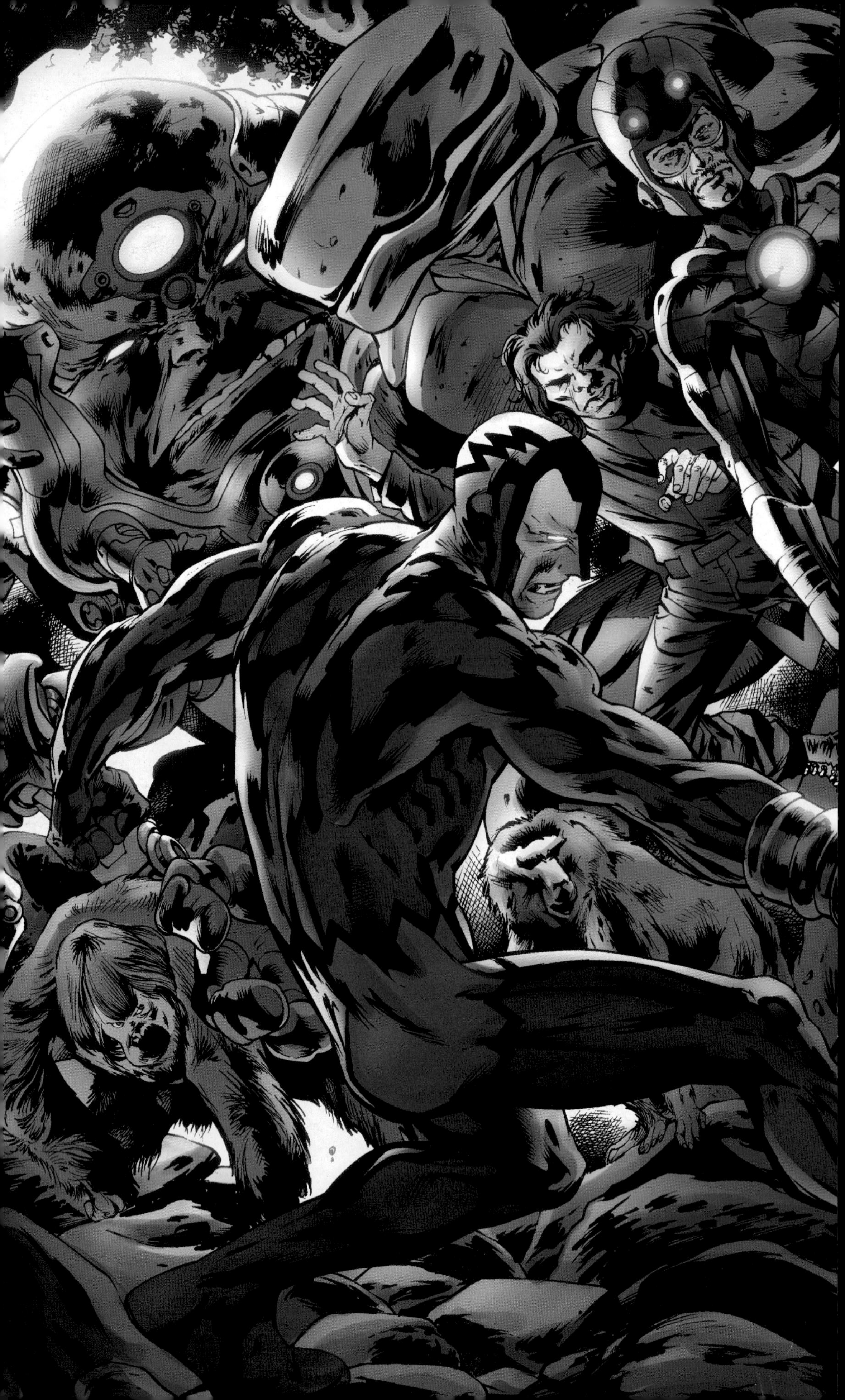

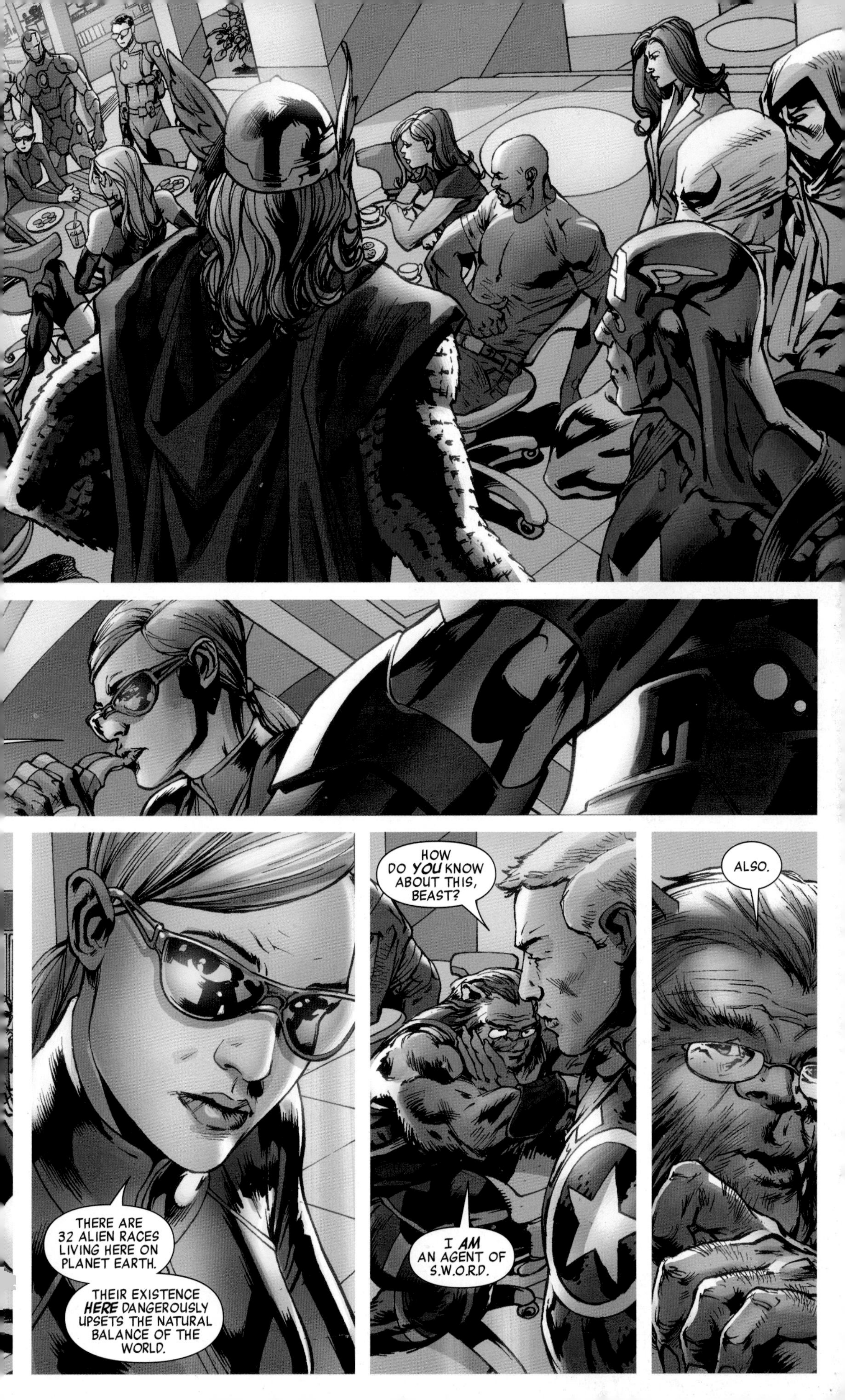
THERE ARE 32 ALIEN RACES LIVING HERE ON PLANET EARTH.
THEIR EXISTENCE HERE DANGEROUSLY UPSETS THE NATURAL BALANCE OF THE WORLD.
HOW DO YOU KNOW ABOUT THIS, BEAST?
I AM AN AGENT OF S.W.O.R.D.
ALSO.

WHAT ARE YOU DOING?

HE'S PICKING UP A SCENT.

LET HIM DO HIS THING.

I HAVE SOME READINGS.

SNFF

I HAVE SOMETHING TOO.

ENVIRONMENTAL SCAN UNDERWAY.

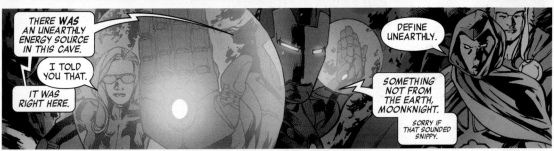

THERE *WAS* AN UNEARTHLY ENERGY SOURCE IN THIS CAVE.

I TOLD YOU THAT.

IT WAS RIGHT HERE.

DEFINE UNEARTHLY.

SOMETHING NOT FROM THE EARTH, MOONKNIGHT.

SORRY IF THAT SOUNDED SNIPPY.

SHE WAS RIGHT HERE.

CROUCHED DOWN.

SHE TURNED ON HER FOOT.

SEE THE MARKINGS IN THE DIRT?

NO.

SHE TURNED RIGHT HERE.

SOMEONE CAME UP BEHIND HER.

THERE...

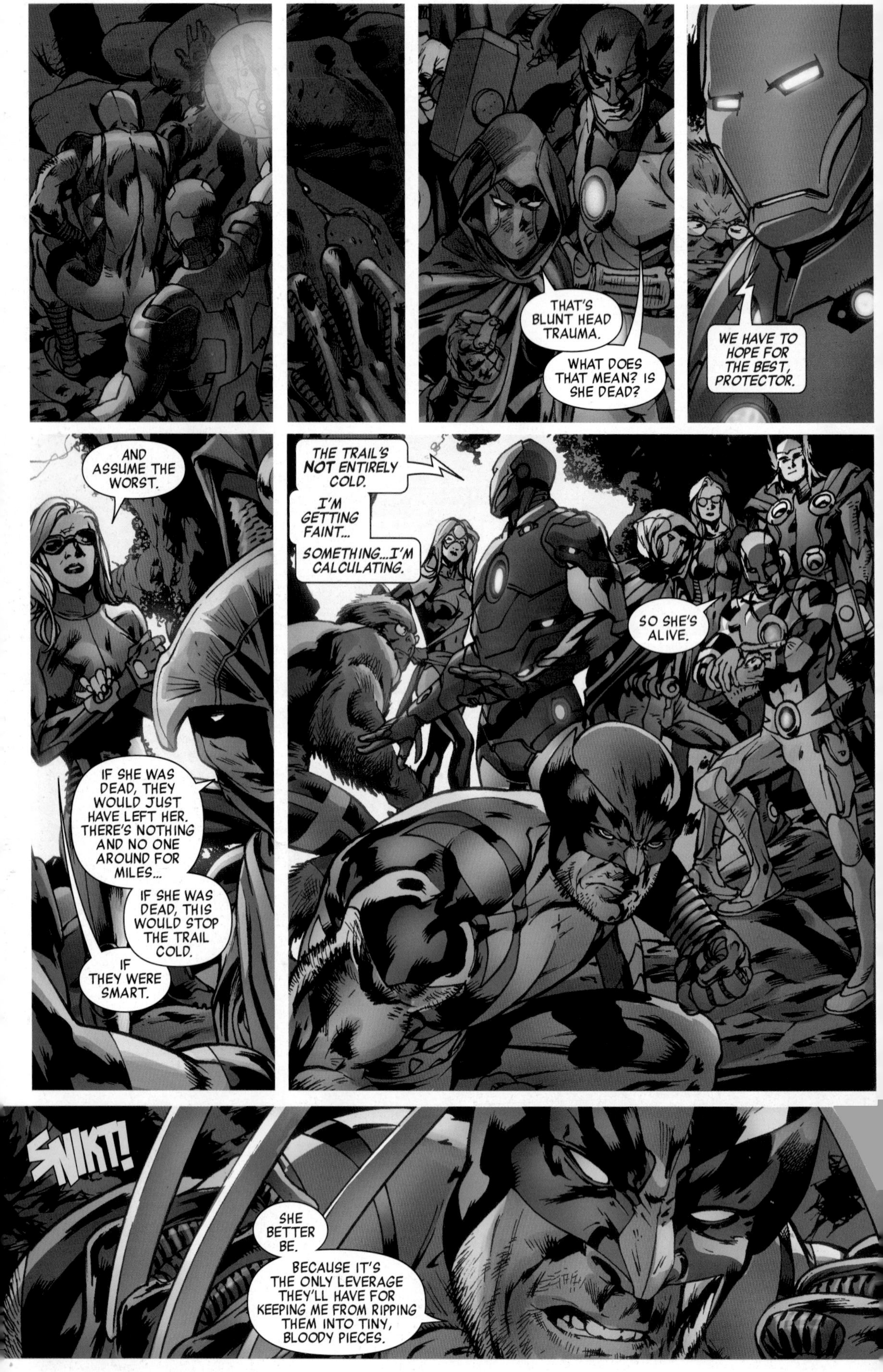
THAT'S BLUNT HEAD TRAUMA.
WHAT DOES THAT MEAN? IS SHE DEAD?
WE HAVE TO HOPE FOR THE BEST, PROTECTOR.
AND ASSUME THE WORST.
IF SHE WAS DEAD, THEY WOULD JUST HAVE LEFT HER. THERE'S NOTHING AND NO ONE AROUND FOR MILES...
IF SHE WAS DEAD, THIS WOULD STOP THE TRAIL COLD.
IF THEY WERE SMART.
THE TRAIL'S NOT ENTIRELY COLD.
I'M GETTING FAINT...
SOMETHING...I'M CALCULATING.
SO SHE'S ALIVE.
SNIKT!
SHE BETTER BE.
BECAUSE IT'S THE ONLY LEVERAGE THEY'LL HAVE FOR KEEPING ME FROM RIPPING THEM INTO TINY, BLOODY PIECES.

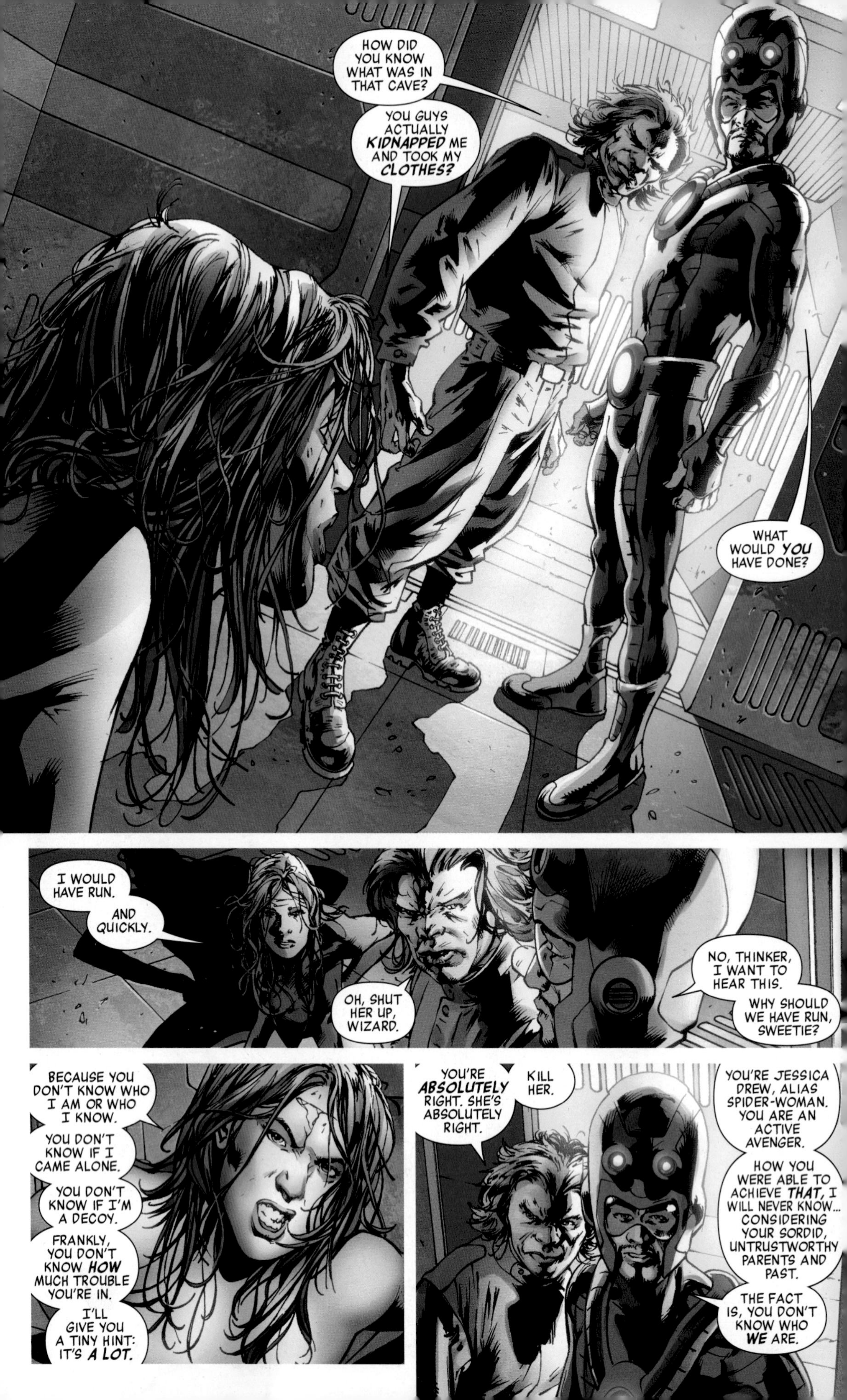
HOW DID YOU KNOW WHAT WAS IN THAT CAVE?
YOU GUYS ACTUALLY KIDNAPPED ME AND TOOK MY CLOTHES?
WHAT WOULD YOU HAVE DONE?
I WOULD HAVE RUN.
AND QUICKLY.
OH, SHUT HER UP, WIZARD.
NO, THINKER, I WANT TO HEAR THIS.
WHY SHOULD WE HAVE RUN, SWEETIE?
BECAUSE YOU DON'T KNOW WHO I AM OR WHO I KNOW.
YOU DON'T KNOW IF I CAME ALONE.
YOU DON'T KNOW IF I'M A DECOY.
FRANKLY, YOU DON'T KNOW HOW MUCH TROUBLE YOU'RE IN.
I'LL GIVE YOU A TINY HINT: IT'S A LOT.
YOU'RE ABSOLUTELY RIGHT. SHE'S ABSOLUTELY RIGHT.
KILL HER.
YOU'RE JESSICA DREW, ALIAS SPIDER-WOMAN. YOU ARE AN ACTIVE AVENGER.
HOW YOU WERE ABLE TO ACHIEVE THAT, I WILL NEVER KNOW... CONSIDERING YOUR SORDID, UNTRUSTWORTHY PARENTS AND PAST.
THE FACT IS, YOU DON'T KNOW WHO WE ARE.

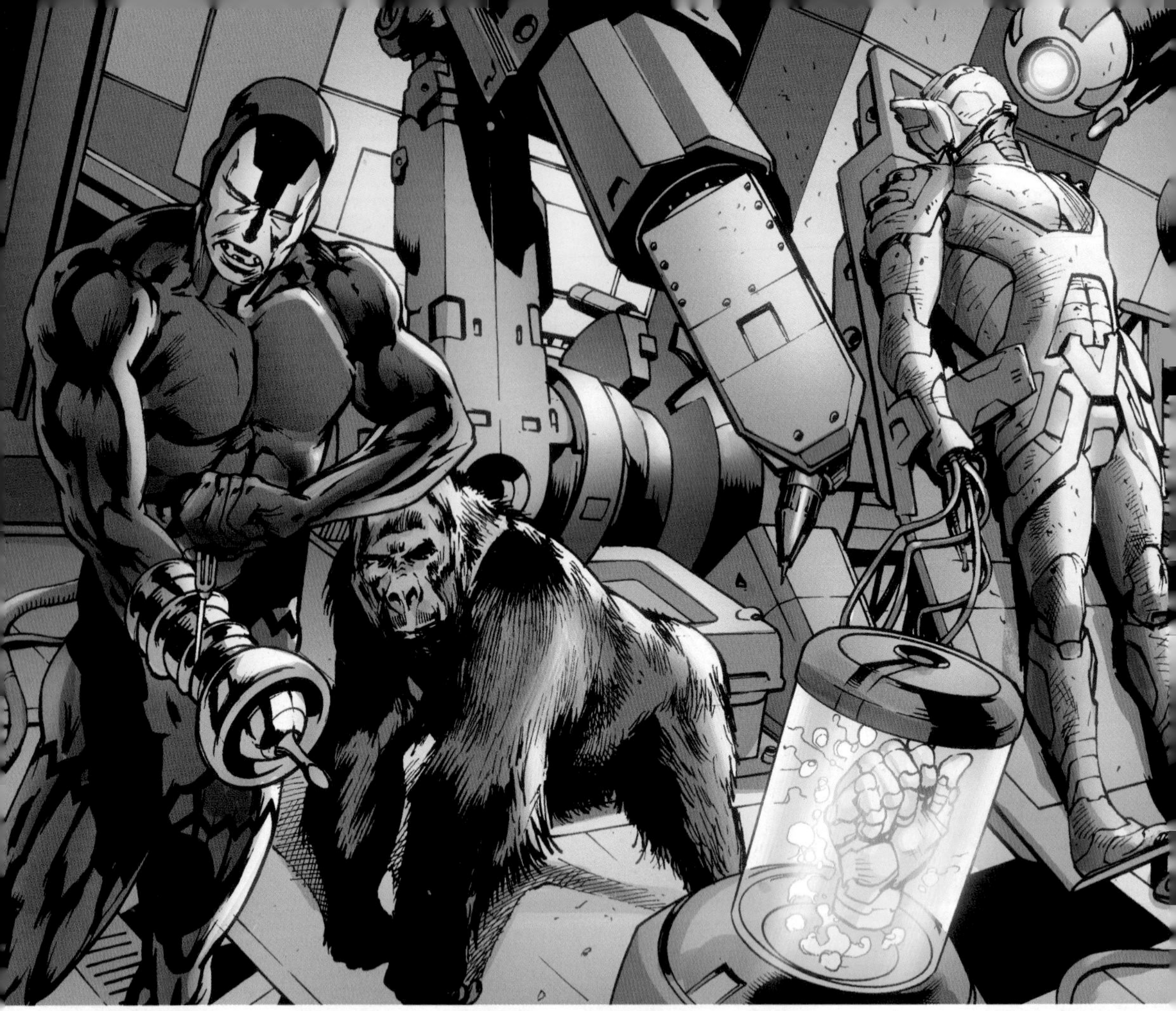

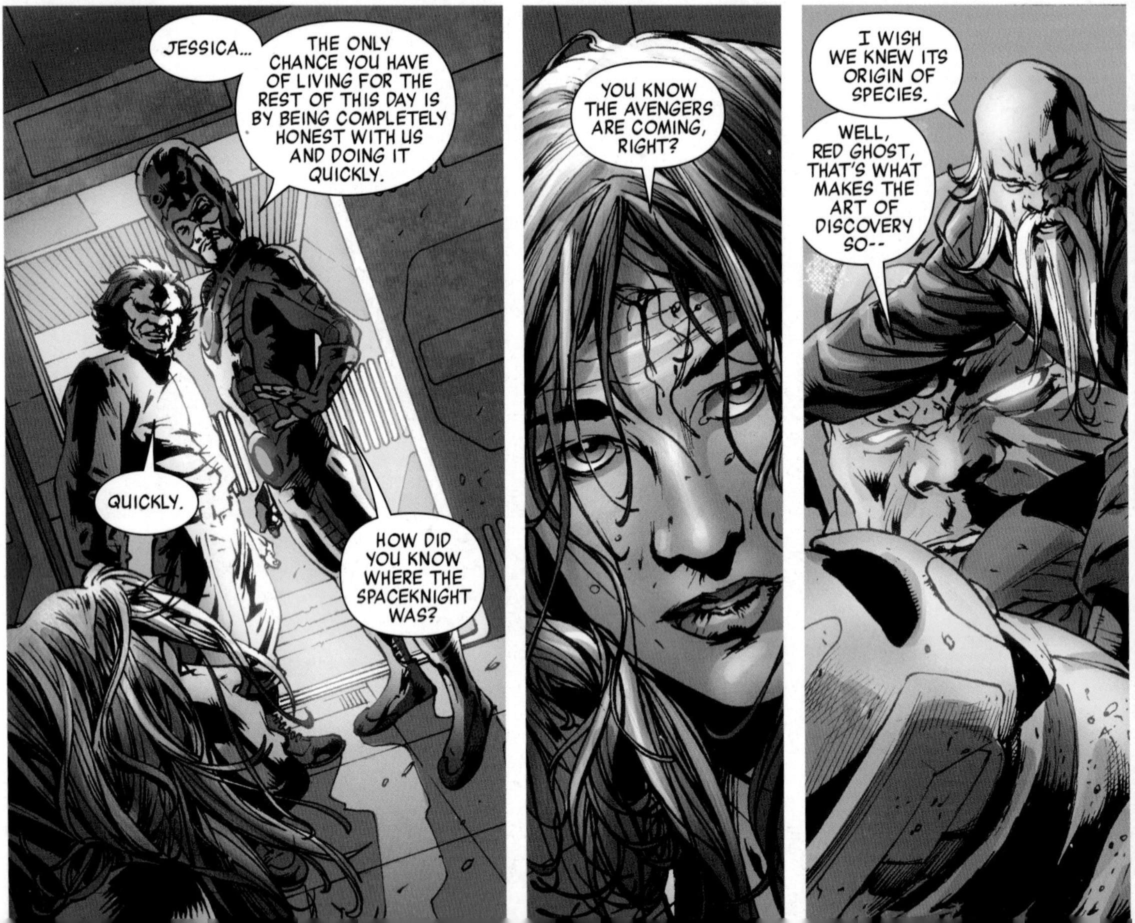
JESSICA...
THE ONLY CHANCE YOU HAVE OF LIVING FOR THE REST OF THIS DAY IS BY BEING COMPLETELY HONEST WITH US AND DOING IT QUICKLY.
QUICKLY.
HOW DID YOU KNOW WHERE THE SPACEKNIGHT WAS?
YOU KNOW THE AVENGERS ARE COMING, RIGHT?
I WISH WE KNEW ITS ORIGIN OF SPECIES.
WELL, RED GHOST, THAT'S WHAT MAKES THE ART OF DISCOVERY SO--

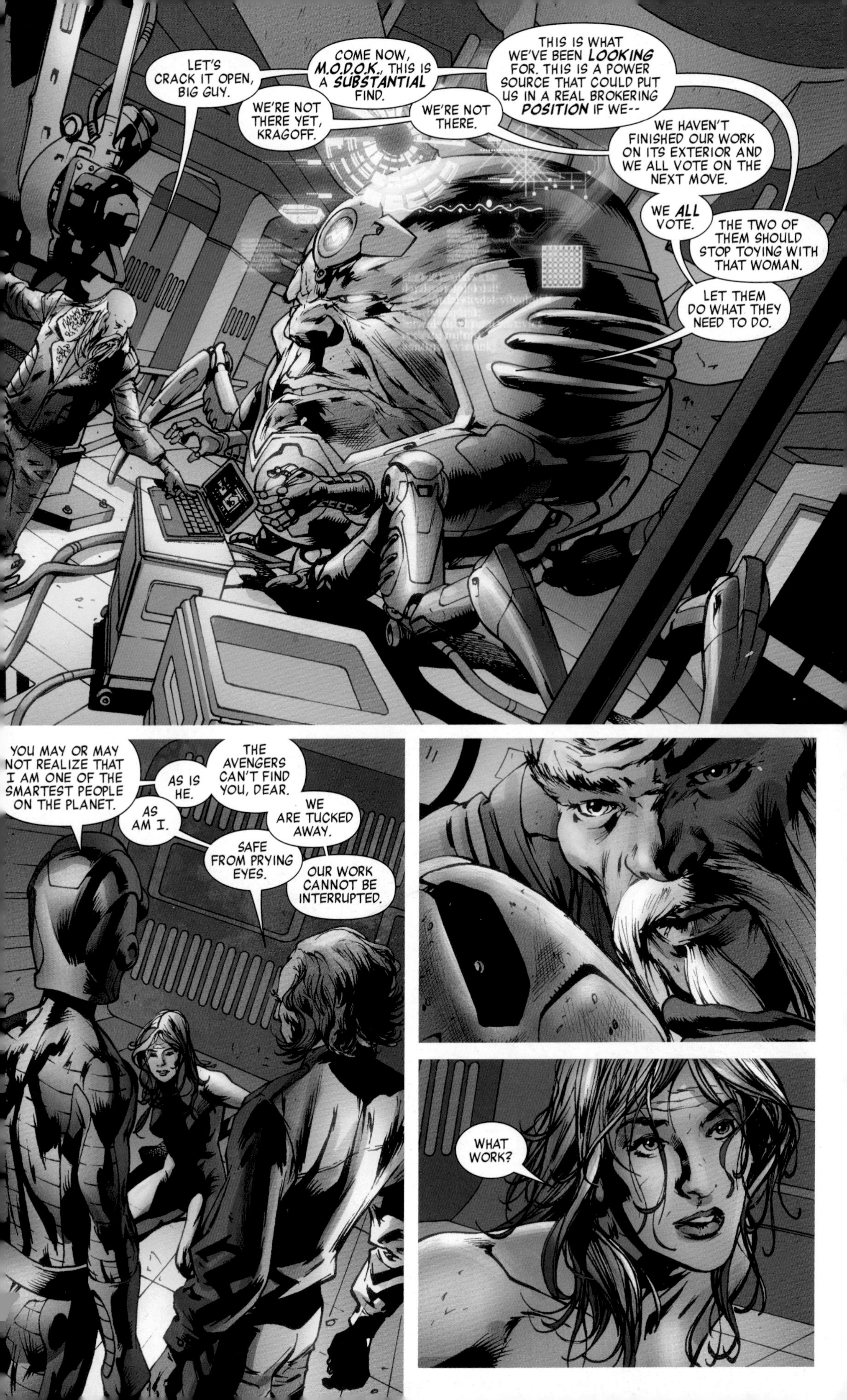
LET'S CRACK IT OPEN, BIG GUY.
COME NOW, M.O.D.O.K., THIS IS A SUBSTANTIAL FIND.
WE'RE NOT THERE YET, KRAGOFF.
THIS IS WHAT WE'VE BEEN LOOKING FOR. THIS IS A POWER SOURCE THAT COULD PUT US IN A REAL BROKERING POSITION IF WE--
WE'RE NOT THERE.
WE HAVEN'T FINISHED OUR WORK ON ITS EXTERIOR AND WE ALL VOTE ON THE NEXT MOVE.
WE ALL VOTE.
THE TWO OF THEM SHOULD STOP TOYING WITH THAT WOMAN.
LET THEM DO WHAT THEY NEED TO DO.
YOU MAY OR MAY NOT REALIZE THAT I AM ONE OF THE SMARTEST PEOPLE ON THE PLANET.
AS IS HE.
AS AM I.
THE AVENGERS CAN'T FIND YOU, DEAR.
WE ARE TUCKED AWAY.
SAFE FROM PRYING EYES.
OUR WORK CANNOT BE INTERRUPTED.
WHAT WORK?

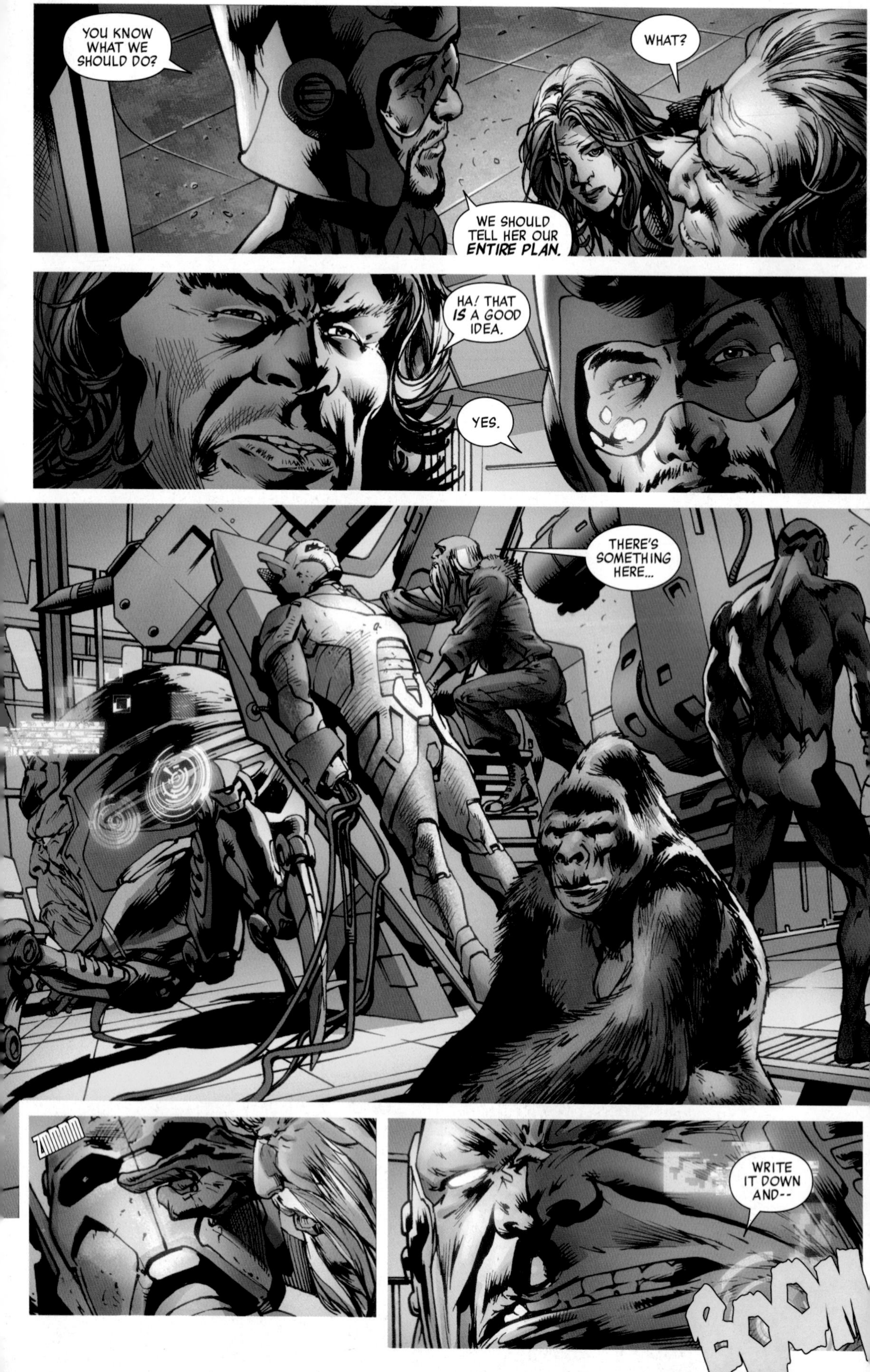

YOU KNOW WHAT WE SHOULD DO?
WHAT?
WE SHOULD TELL HER OUR ENTIRE PLAN.
HA! THAT IS A GOOD IDEA.
YES.
THERE'S SOMETHING HERE...
ZMMM
WRITE IT DOWN AND--
BOOM

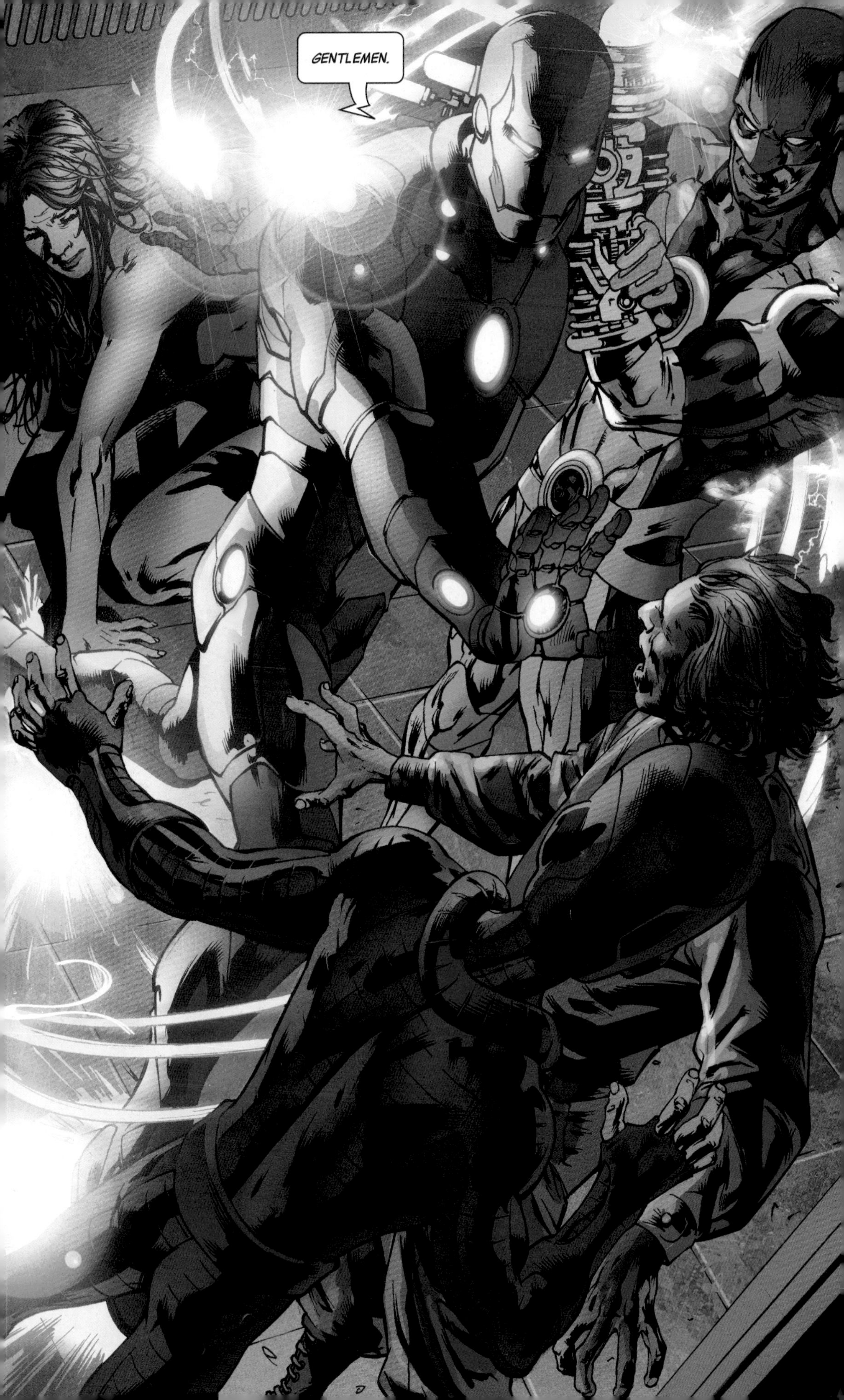
GENTLEMEN.

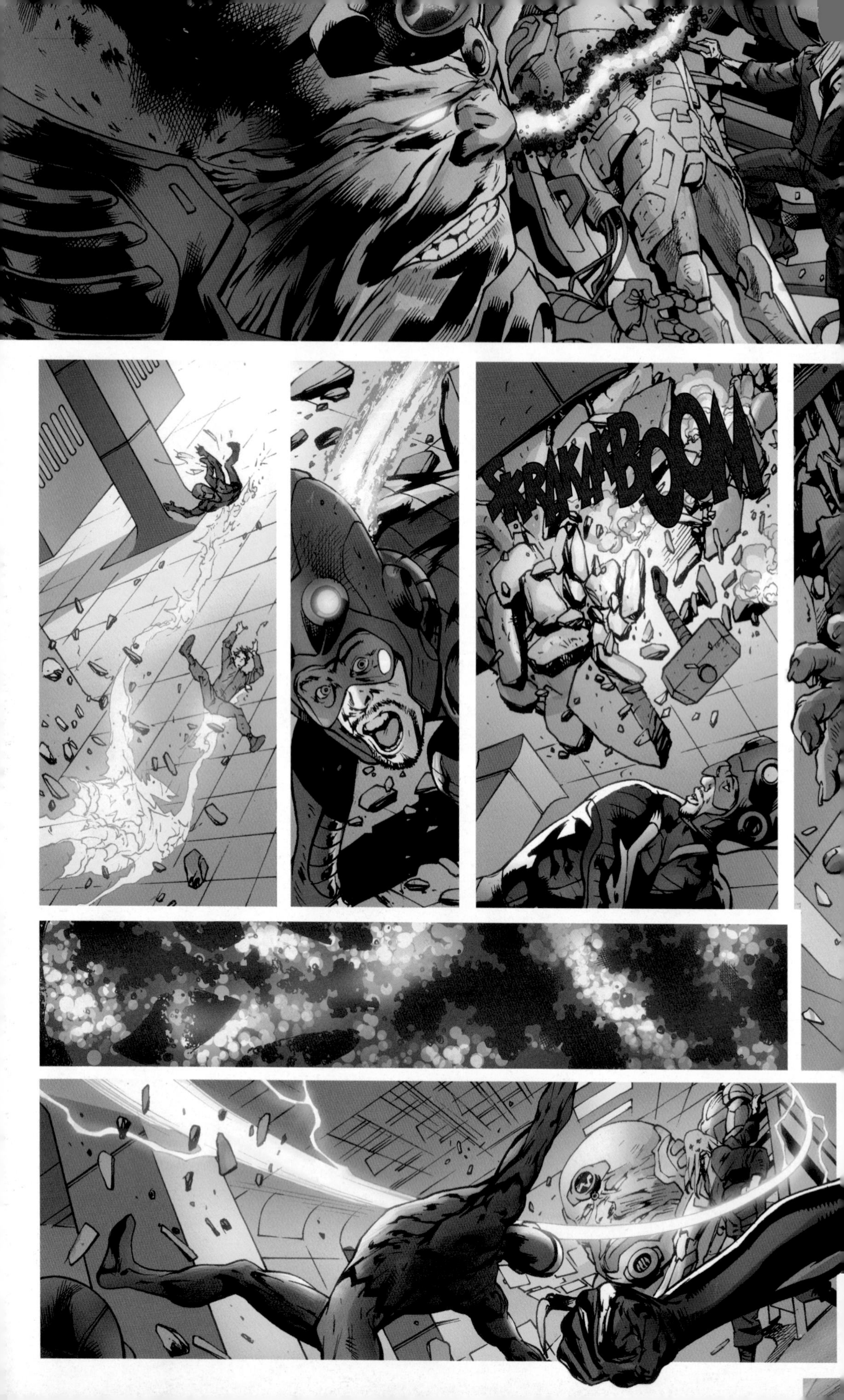
KRAKAKBOOM

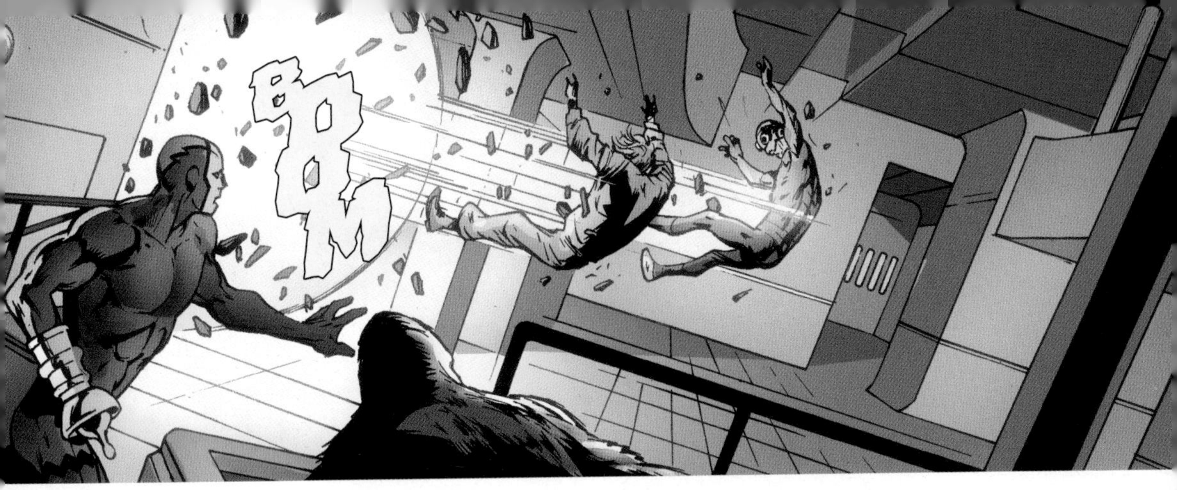
BOOM

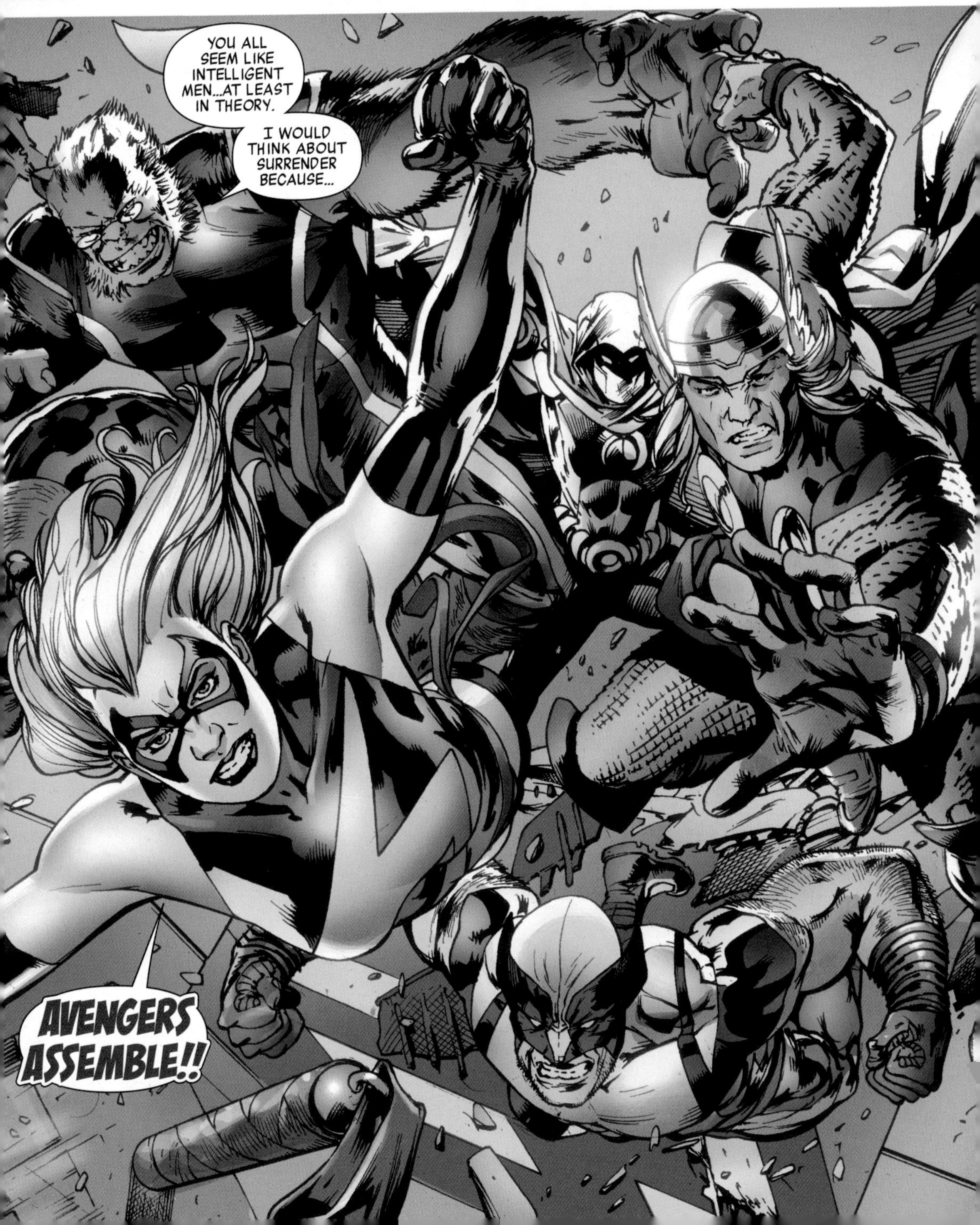
YOU ALL SEEM LIKE INTELLIGENT MEN...AT LEAST IN THEORY.
I WOULD THINK ABOUT SURRENDER BECAUSE...
AVENGERS ASSEMBLE!!

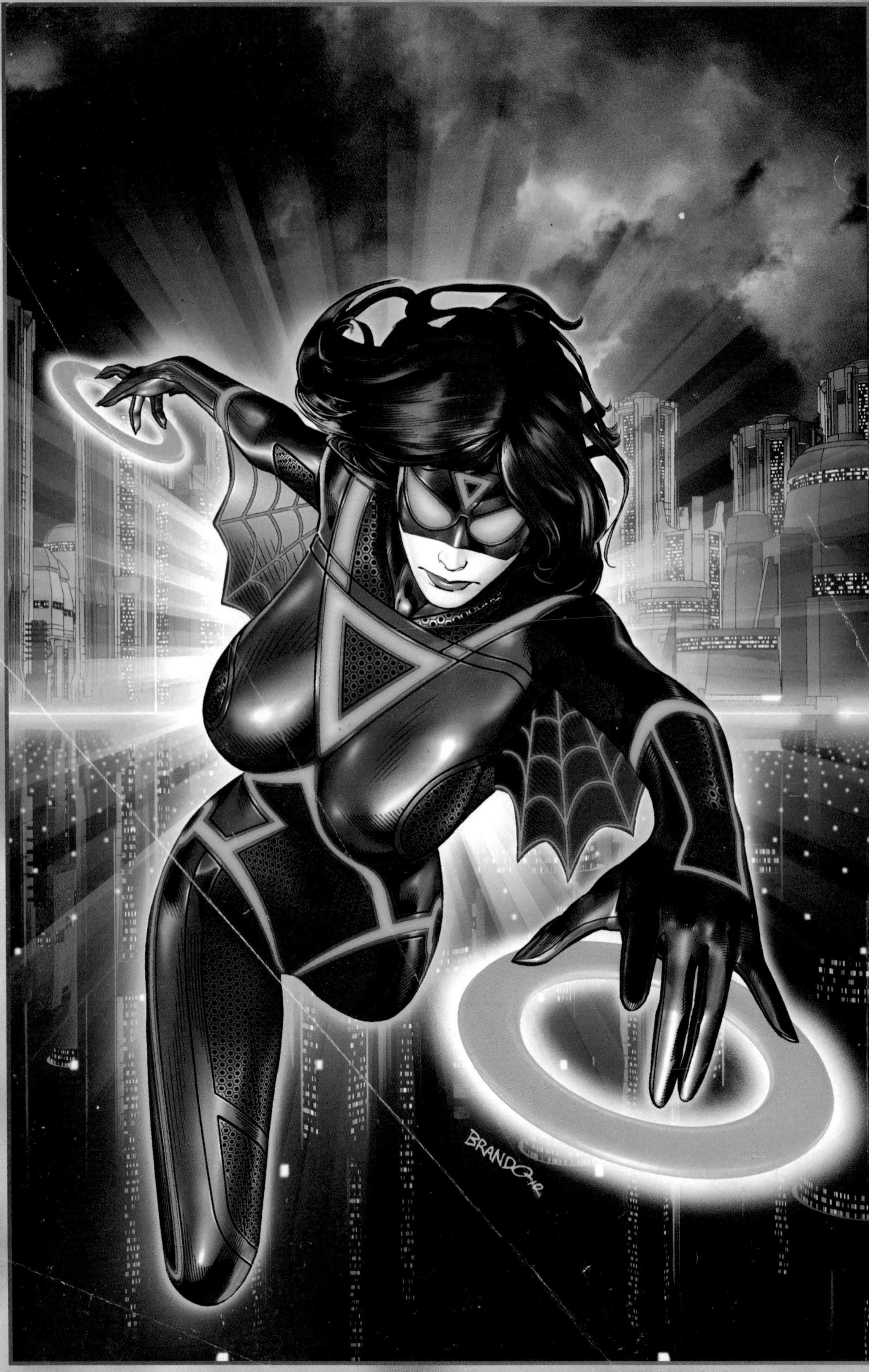
BRANDO

#9 TRON VARIANT BY BRANDON PETERSON